D1604215

The WAY *of the*
88 TEMPLES

The WAY *of the*
88 TEMPLES

JOURNEYS
ON THE
SHIKOKU
PILGRIMAGE

Robert C. Sibley

UNIVERSITY OF VIRGINIA PRESS
CHARLOTTESVILLE & LONDON

University of Virginia Press
© 2013 by Robert C. Sibley
All rights reserved
Printed in the United States of America on acid-free paper

First published 2013

9 8 7 6 5 4 3 2 1

LIBRARY OF CONGRESS CATALOGING-IN-PUBLICATION DATA
Sibley, Robert C. (Robert Cameron), 1951–
  The way of the 88 temples : journeys on the Shikoku pilgrimage /
Robert C. Sibley.
      pages   cm
  Includes bibliographical references and index.
    ISBN 978-0-8139-3472-3 (cloth : alk. paper) — ISBN 978-0-8139-3473-0 (e-book)
    1. Sibley, Robert C. (Robert Cameron), 1951—Travel—Japan—Shikoku Region.
2. Buddhist pilgrims and pilgrimages—Japan—Shikoku Region. 3. Buddhist
temples—Japan—Shikoku Region. 4. Shikoku Region (Japan)—Description and
travel. 5. Spiritual biography. I. Title. II. Title: Way of the eighty-eight temples.
  BQ6450.J32S486724 2013
  294.3′43509523—dc23

                                                    2013008668

This book is dedicated to Yukuo Tanaka.
Dōgyō ninin.

Contents

Acknowledgments

I want to thank the editors, past and present, at the *Ottawa Citizen*—in particular, Gerry Nott, Neil Reynolds, Scott Anderson, Lynn McAuley, Christina Spencer, Derek Shelly, Rob Warner, Julius Majerczyk, Kurt Johnson, Sue Allen, Peter Robb, and Mike Gillespie—who, in their various capacities, contributed to this work, which first appeared in a shorter and different form in the *Citizen*. Gerry Nott, the current *Citizen* Publisher and Editor-in-Chief, has been generous in giving permission to turn that series into this book. I am also grateful to Postmedia Network (formerly Canwest Publications) for supporting my pilgrimages.

I would also like to thank Ikuko Niwano and Kazuko Tanaka for their gracious hospitality in inviting me into their homes. I am grateful to Emiko Miyashita and Michael Dylan Welch for translating Shūji Niwano's haiku so I could read some of them at the Haiku Society of America's annual convention where I was a keynote speaker in 2009. I must also thank Fumiyo Fuji for her Japanese lessons and Yumiko Tsunakawa and Sam Toma for their friendship and translation services. I am also indebted to David Moreton and David Turkington for their generous help and advice. My greatest gratitude is, as always, to my wife and fellow writer, Margret Kopala, for making my pilgrimages possible.

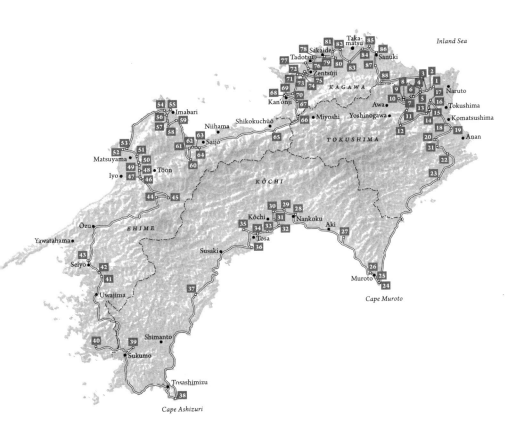

The WAY of the
88 TEMPLES

Inland Sea

Taka-
matsu
81 82 85
78 Sakaide 86 Sanuki
77 Tadotsu 79 80 84
72   83
71 76 73 Zentsūji 87 88
75 74   3   1
68 69   KAGAWA   8   2
70   9   4 Naruto
Kan'onji 67   6 17
54 55   66   10 5 16 Tokushima
56 Imabari   Shikokuchūo 7 13 Komatsushima
57 59 58   Miyoshi 11 14 15
53 63 62 Niihama Awa 12 18 19
52 51 61   Yoshinogawa 20 Anan
Matsuyama 50 64 65 TOKUSHIMA 21
49 48 60   22
Iyo 47 46 Tōon   23
     44 45

        KŌCHI
Ozu   30 29 28
EHIME   Kōchi 31 Nankoku
Yawatahama 35   33 Aki 27
        34 32
        Tosa 36
Seiyo 43   Susaki   26
42   37   25
41 Uwajima   Muroto 24
                        Cape Muroto
40 39 Shimanto
Sukumo
        Tosashimizu
        38
Cape Ashizuri

1

Bells

A holy person
met so soon
on this pilgrimage.
—SHŪJI NIWANO

I stumbled up the bell tower steps, grasped the rope, and hauled the long wooden pole back as far as possible in its cradle. Then I swung the rope forward and slammed the pole against the bronze bell. A loud *bong* echoed through the courtyard of Shōsanji temple and across the mountain valley. It was, I thought, a satisfying way to announce my presence to the presiding deities and, presumably, scare away any evil spirits lurking in the surrounding forest. As it was, I flushed a flock of pigeons from the temple roof, sending them flapping into the drizzling sky. The bell's echoes faded and the birds returned to their roost, but I lingered in the shelter of the tower's gabled roof.

Across the gravel expanse of the courtyard, a flagstone walkway cut between two rows of tall cedars to the main hall of the temple. The gray-tile roof shone in the rain. Tendrils of incense smoke curled from the urn in front of the hall. Even at this distance the sweet odor permeated the damp air. Nearby, half a dozen bus pilgrims, dressed in traditional white robes and wide-brimmed straw hats, prayed in the small hall dedicated to the Buddhist saint Kōbō Daishi, their heads bowed as they chanted.

I caught snatches of the Hannya Shingyō, or Heart Sutra—the short prayer that is said to articulate the essence of Buddhism: "Gyate, gyate, hara gyate, hara so gyate, boji sowaka." I didn't understand the language, but I'd heard the prayer so often during the past three days that the words were beginning to stick in my head. And so they should. As a *henro*, or pilgrim, I wore the *hakui*, a white robe or vest, carried the *kongō-tsue*, a walking staff, and possessed the *nōkyōchō*, the book in which every *henro* has a temple seal stamped as a testament to their visit. I even had my pack of *osamefuda*, or name slips, on which to write my name and address before depositing them in special bins at the temples. And I, too, intended to complete the Henro Michi, the oldest and most famous Buddhist pilgrimage route in Japan.

What set me apart from most other *henro* was that, unlike the majority who take buses or drive cars, I was going to walk 1,400 kilometers, visiting each of the eighty-eight temples that are strung out like beads on a rosary around the perimeter of Shikoku, the smallest of Japan's four main islands. The route supposedly follows the footsteps of Kōbō Daishi, the ninth-century ascetic who founded the Shingon Buddhist sect. The saint, according to tradition, accompanies all pilgrims as a spiritual companion.

The Shikoku pilgrimage is probably the best known of Japan's many hundreds of pilgrimage routes. It's certainly popular among the Japanese. An estimated 15,000 *henro* a year performed the pilgrimage in the 1960s, whether on foot or by car or bus. By the late 1980s that number had increased to 80,000. These days, however, an estimated 150,000 engage in the pilgrimage—on foot, by bicycle, or by vehicle—thanks in part to three huge bridges built in recent decades linking Shikoku to the larger island of Honshu across the Inland Sea. The Shikoku pilgrimage, with its white-robed *henro* and picturesque temples, has also become popular with the Japanese media. Television reports, newspaper articles, and magazine features, as well as documentaries and plays, have embedded the pilgrimage in Japan's popular culture.[1]

Arguably, though, this popularity reflects something deeper. Ian Reader, a British scholar of Japanese religion, writes that for many Shikoku pilgrims, the pilgrimage provides "a reaffirmation of their social and cultural identity and a way of consolidating the religious outlooks that underpin their existence."[2] In researching the pilgrimage, I'd read that religion no longer plays a significant role in the lives of most Japanese. Yet they still turn to the local Buddhist temple to bury the dead, and most homes—as I would discover—have a *butsudan*, a family altar that contains memorials to ancestors and on which family members set flowers, burn incense, or place food and drink. Millions of Japanese also pray each day at the neighborhood Buddhist temple or Shinto shrine before going to work or school.[3] That said, some of the major temples in, say, Nara and Kyoto no longer seem to reflect or sustain a living religion. While they remain beautiful, they have become tourist sites or, at most, nostalgic reminders of Japan's past. I had visited some of Kyoto's famous temples before my pilgrimage. Shuffling along with the other tourists, I felt I was seeing beautiful shells, forms without substance.

It was different on Shikoku. The temples have a decidedly lived-in look, perhaps because, as one of my guidebooks put it, "the 88 temples are still alive for the pilgrims themselves."[4] I had decided that if I was to undertake a two-month religious pilgrimage, I would at least participate in the formalities even if I didn't understand their meaning or significance or, for that matter, wasn't very good at being religious. Perhaps not surprisingly, I found that by going through the motions— visiting the sacred sites, trying to recite the Heart Sutra, following in the steps that thousands of others have taken for hundreds of years—I was absorbed by the pilgrimage. The spirit of Kōbō Daishi, it seemed, laid a claim on my psyche.

During the two months of my pilgrimage I heard many reasons for enduring the route's hardships. Some regarded the trek, in its evocation of ancient traditions, as a means to affirm their sense of being Japanese. Still others saw the route as a zone of meditation, a spiritual space that allowed them the time and place for reflection, a chance to slow down and enjoy nature's beauty, a means of escape from the madhouse of modernity. These motives were familiar to me from my research on the Henro Michi. Reader, who has studied the Shikoku pilgrimage for years, observes that it often serves as "a means of escape from society," a way to step aside from the ordinary and "the often restrictive patterns of everyday life in Japan."[5]

I tended to put myself in the escapist category, at first anyway. I was only too happy to abandon the confines of everyday life. But then I also hesitated to ascribe spiritual motives to myself. I wasn't a Buddhist. I was a Westerner with all the psychological and cultural overlay of the West's Judeo-Christian heritage, along with the resulting confusions of a modern secularist education that denied much veracity to spiritual sentiments. But by the end of my walk, I found that I'd become so emotionally and psychologically attached to the pilgrimage that I was doubting my own skepticism. The Henro Michi opened me to a hitherto unsuspected spiritual sensibility.

It takes between forty-five and sixty days to perform the Shikoku pilgrimage. It took me fifty-four days, from the last week of March to late May, most of the time walking. Japan is heavily urbanized, and trekking through Shikoku's four prefectures, or provinces—Tokushima, Kōchi, Ehime, and Kagawa—I tromped along too many traffic-heavy highways and through too many long dark tunnels, which, as I discovered, are the main complaints that pilgrims have about the temple route.[6] I hiked six to eight hours a day with an always too heavy pack and endured blistered feet that hobbled me and leg muscles so sore that I would be whimpering by day's end. There were also times as I crawled up some rock-strewn slope that I thought I was going to have a heart attack.

But I also had a wonderful, enchanted time. I wandered deep into Shikoku's verdant valleys, stood on mountain ridges that offered timeless panoramas of sea and sky and landscape, and strolled through thatch-roofed villages that hadn't changed in their essentials for centuries. I fell in love with things Japanese—the traditional inns, with their tatami-covered floors and sliding wood-and-paper *shōji* panels that opened onto gardens of sculptured trees and burbling ponds; temples with their gracefully terraced, spire-topped roofs and peaceful atmosphere; the bathing rituals of *o-furo* where I soaked away the day's aches and pains. I met friendly, helpful people—from hairdressers to postal clerks—who, surprised at the sight of a foreign *henro*, treated me with great generosity and tolerated my fractured Japanese phrases and ignorance of their customs. Best of all, I acquired friends who shared my journey and made it much more enlightening.

I started out thinking of my pilgrimage trek as little more than an adventure—a "secular journey to sacred places," as a Japanese sociologist puts it.[7] But walking twenty to thirty kilometers a day for two months has both physical and psychological consequences. By the end of my trek, I was no longer able to dismiss the spiritual dimensions of the Henro Michi, including the presence of Kōbō Daishi, as mere folk superstitions. There were too many serendipitous situations and synchronistic circumstances for me not to wonder if someone, or something, was watching over me. I set out on one kind of journey but ended up on a very different one. This, of course, was not unusual. Pilgrims are often subject to "psychosomatic sensations," and these sensations "are often the most significant aspects of pilgrimage in the view of the participants themselves."[8]

***

I knew none of this as I sheltered from the rain beneath the *shōrō*, or bell tower, at Shōsanji temple. I was just grateful to have reached the twelfth of Shikoku's eighty-eight temples. I'd visited the first eleven temples during my first two days of walking. It had seemed easy. But this day, my third, was a killer. I walked—staggered—for nearly nine hours, covering fourteen kilometers along a trail that climbs and descends three mountain ranges. By late afternoon, when I reached the final steep staircase that climbs to Shōsanji, I was trembling with exhaustion. My leg muscles burned and my back ached from the load of my pack. I was seeing spots in front of my eyes. Worse, the worm of uncertainty had crawled into my mind: the prospect of two months on the road was suddenly daunting. Rational or not, ringing the temple bell was a gesture of defiance against the demons of doubt as well as an expression of thanks to whatever deities might exist for having delivered me from my inadequacy. It was also an appeal, superstitious though it might have been, for the gods' help in the weeks to come. Standing beneath the *shōrō*, looking across the temple courtyard to the distant mountains, with my thigh muscles twitching in relief, I thought I would need it.

The pilgrim group was breaking up, its recitations complete. I watched as one by one each *henro* climbed the steps to ring the acorn-shaped brass bell, or *waniguchi*, hanging from the eaves above the entrance to the small hall, the *daishidō*, where, as in every temple, a statue of Kōbō Daishi was enshrined. Several paused to bow and roll the string of *nenju* beads between the palms of their hands as they recited prayers or offered homage to the saint. When they finished, they tossed a few coins in the offertory bin and dropped their *osamefuda* into another bin. They then hustled to the temple office to have their *nōkyōchō* and temple scrolls signed and stamped.

Most of the pilgrims were older women, some barely taller than their walking sticks. Several glanced at me as they shuffled past the bell tower, their eyes widening in surprise at the sight of a mud-spattered, red-faced gaijin, or foreigner. I would get used to that look. During my two months on the pilgrimage trail, I didn't see another non-Japanese *henro*. The Japanese were surprised, even flattered, that a Westerner would walk the temple route.

I bowed to the women and smiled. "Konnichi wa. Yoku omairi-deshita. Gokurō-sama," I said. "Good afternoon. Nice of you to offer a prayer. Bless you." I had memorized this and several other phrases in preparing for my trip. By their reaction I assumed I hadn't butchered the language too badly. My fractured phrases garnered a burst of giggles and smiles and even a few instinctive bows. One woman hauled out a camera and snapped my picture.

When the women were gone, I stumbled down the belfry's stairs, grabbed my backpack that I'd dumped inside the temple gate, and made my way to the temple halls. I intended to carry out the temple rituals as best I could. Perhaps, after a month, the rituals and mantras, words of spiritual power, would become meaningful. Substance would follow style. Form would acquire content.

I performed the required ablutions at the stone cistern in front of the main temple, filling a long-handled bamboo ladle with water from the spouting mouth of a bronze dragon. I splashed the icy water over one hand, switched the ladle and washed the other, then poured some in my cupped hand and rinsed my mouth, spitting into a drainage moat at the base of the cistern. Walking to the main hall, or *hondō*, to say my prayers, I realized I should have performed the ritual cleansing before ringing the bell. Next time, I told myself, I would do it right.[9]

The day had taken its toll. My legs started to cramp as I stood on the veranda of the main hall. Thin needles of pain jabbed at my heels. A wave of fatigue washed over me. I curtailed my prayers, such as they were, and sat on the temple steps. I pulled two name slips from my pouch and wrote my name and address.

Japanese pilgrims say they *utsu*, or hit, a temple once they've visited it. A temple is a *fudasho*, a card place. The label harkens to a time when pilgrims nailed wooden cards inscribed with their names to temple walls. Today pilgrims scrawl their names or those of their families on the *osamefuda* and deposit them in the bins at the temple. These paper slips contain written prayers for happiness, health, prosperity, or peace, along with a sketch of Kōbō Daishi. They are eventually burned in a special ceremony, whereupon the temple's presiding deities become aware of the pilgrim's desires as the smoke rises to the celestial plane. Presumably the deities do what they can to help.

Most of the name slips I saw in the temple bins were white, indicating a pilgrim who had made between one and four visits to the temple. A green slip means that a pilgrim has made five to six circuits of the entire route, while red designates seven to twenty-four. A silver card signifies twenty-five to forty-nine circuits, while gold implies fifty or more. I saw several green and even a few red slips. Only once did I see a silver one. I never saw a gold *osamefuda*, although I heard of pilgrims who'd performed the pilgrimage three hundred or more times, albeit by vehicle. Considering the way I felt that third day, I thought I'd be lucky to complete one circuit.

The only thing motivating me at that moment was the desire for a bath, some food, and a place to sleep. I deposited my name slip in the bin and found the temple office to have my *nōkyōchō* signed and stamped. Then I stumbled along to the *shukubō*, the temple lodge, where I had a reservation for the night.[10]

Many of the Shikoku temples offer accommodations, but I quickly formed a preference for *ryokan* and *minshuku*, the traditional inns and guesthouses, or even business hotels. Not only was it easier to obtain lodgings—the temples are often booked by bus tours—but the temple regimen, with its set times for eating, bathing, and lights out, was often inconvenient. At Shōsanji, for instance, I arrived close to 6 p.m., just before the supper service. I had to hustle after my arrival to get anything to eat.

A gray-haired woman in a jogging suit greeted me at the *shukubō* entrance. I assumed she was the lodge hostess. "Irasshaimase." "Welcome, please come in," she said, smiling and bowing.

"Konban wa," I replied, returning the bow. "Watakushi no namae wa Robert Sibley desu. Konya yoyaku wo shitan desu kedo." "Good evening. My name is Robert Sibley. I believe I have a reservation for tonight." At least I thought that's what I was saying; it had taken me a long time to memorize those phrases.

She responded, but I recognized only the word *henro*. Still, her gestures were plain enough: she showed me the basin in which to wash my walking stick and a rack for storing my wet boots. After I pulled off my boots she handed me a pair of slippers and led me down a hallway to my room. She stopped to slide open a *shōji* panel, gesturing for me to enter and giving me a querulous look as if to say, "Does the foreigner know how to behave properly?"

I took off my slippers before stepping on the tatami mats that covered the floor. I made sure to set my pack against a wall and not in the decorative alcove known as a *tokonoma*, with its long scroll and simple flower arrangement in a thin elegant white vase. Presumably I did everything properly because my hostess was smiling and chattering as she followed me into the room. I couldn't understand her, so I just nodded and grinned and said "hai" or "dōmo" repeatedly as she laid out the futon and prepared a pot of tea. Finally, before she bowed herself out, she handed me a folded and freshly laundered *yukata*, a cotton robe.

Along with the end-of-day *o-furo*, or bath, the donning of a *yukata* would become my reward after a hard day's walk. I stripped off my wet clothes and wrapped myself in the fresh-smelling garment. But as much as I came to appreciate the *yukata*, there was always one small problem I never resolved. I was taller and bigger-boned than most Japanese men, around whom the *yukata* wrapped easily and was at least calf-length. None of the *yukata* I received were wide or long enough to fit me without threatening to expose more than was socially acceptable even in Japan. They were both too short and too tight. So were the slippers. I became adept at keeping a strategic grip on my robe while walking or, even trickier, sitting down. It didn't always work, which provided a source of amusement for my pilgrimage companions.

I got the heater going, strung up my clothes to dry, rearranged the futon so I could sit and lean against the wall, and took my leisure with a steaming cup of green tea. It was sheer pleasure to be warm and dry and at rest. I would have fallen asleep, but the supper bell rang. I struggled to my feet and hobbled down the hallway, trying not to lose my slippers and gripping my embarrassingly small *yukata*.

The dining room was packed. Some thirty or forty guests sat cross-legged on tatami between long rows of low tables. The room went quiet as I paused at the entrance to remove my slippers. Every eye was on me, or so it seemed, as I bowed to the room. I spotted an empty cushion between two older women and headed in their direction. They looked slightly panicked at the prospect of my company. Keeping a tight grip on my *yukata*, I started to shuffle my way down the narrow aisle between two rows of back-to-back pilgrims when I heard my name.

"Sibley-san, sumimasen."

I looked up to see two pilgrims, a father and son duo from Tokyo, with whom I'd walked the previous day after they'd introduced themselves. I remembered that the father, Shūji Niwano, was a sixty-three-year-old retired telecommunications salesman; his son Jun was in his early twenties. They were sitting with two men I'd seen on the trail earlier that afternoon. Niwano-san gestured for me to join the group. He introduced the others at the table as Goki Sayama, a retired banker from Sendai, north of Tokyo, and Takashi Murakoshi, a vacationing businessman from Hokkaido, Japan's northernmost island.[11]

"Ikaga desu ka?" "How are you doing?" Niwano-san asked.

"Hai." "Okay," I said.

"Would you like bīru?"

"Dōmo arigatō." "Thanks very much."

Niwano-san waved to one of the women servers and ordered beer. She returned with two large bottles of Kirin, three glasses, and a bottle opener. Niwano-san filled my glass and poured some for Jun and then for himself. He raised his glass in the traditional Japanese toast, gesturing at the two men and me: "Kampai."

We clinked glasses. The beer was icy cold. We finished one bottle before our food arrived. We drained the other as we ate, with Niwano-san topping up my glass. In Japan, it is bad form to fill your own glass. To do so is to admit to others that you drink too much. Instead, you fill the glass of the person next to you and wait for them to fill yours. The idea, as I understand it, is that everybody is obligated to look out for others in the group.

We managed to converse, sort of. Niwano-san knew some basic English, while I had the benefit of a couple of courses in basic Japanese. Jun spoke better English than I spoke Japanese. When we ran into difficulty, Niwano-san or Jun used a Casio electronic dictionary to translate Japanese words into English. It was slow and cumbersome, but between my minimalist Japanese, their modest English, and the electronic dictionary, we worked out that Niwano-san and his son had been ahead of me all day. The father explained that, like me, he planned to walk the entire Shikoku route, visiting every temple—at least as long as his son kept walking. He was happy to be on the pilgrimage trail. But Jun, he said, had a "condition" that made it difficult for him to walk for a long time.

Jun certainly didn't seem interested in the pilgrimage. He was more interested in what I knew about Hollywood movie stars and pop singers and animal life in Canada. "Do you like Madonna?" "Do you have bears in Ottawa?" "Have you seen a moose?" "Do you know the French movie star Jean Reno? You look like him." His questions seemed immature for a young man his age. I looked at his father.

"Jun is noisy," he said with a shrug.

Perhaps, but Jun was also an enthusiastic teacher. When the food came, we began what would become a mealtime habit of identifying food in our respective languages. I recognized some items: a bowl of steaming rice, miso soup with mushrooms, and a block of tofu. There were vegetables pickled in vinegar. Pointing with his chopsticks, Jun identified slices of a crunchy, yellowish vegetable as *takenoko*, or bamboo shoots. The sour pickled plums were *umeboshi*. The soy sauce was, well, *shōyu*. Two quarter sections of apple were *ringo*. I pointed to a spongy gray triangle of what looked like compressed mush and a bowl of greenery that reminded me of kelp washed up on a beach. The gray mush, Jun told me, was *yōkan*, a sweet bean-paste cake. The greenery was what it looked like—kelp, or, as Jun identified it, *konbu*. Politeness required that I try everything. To my surprise, all of it was edible. I even enjoyed the bean paste.

Sayama-san spoke reasonable English, having traveled to Europe and the United States. He asked why I was walking the Shikoku pilgrimage. I had stock phrases ready: I was a journalist and was traveling in Japan to walk the pilgrimage route. They seemed impressed, both at my intentions and my effort to speak Japanese.[12]

Murakoshi-san filled my glass. I lifted it slightly off the table as he poured, as Japanese custom requires. I would eventually learn to place my hand over the glass to indicate I'd had enough.

It was my first pilgrim meal *en famille*. Listening to my companions, conscious of the unintelligible chatter around me, I was suddenly struck by the wonderful strangeness of being several thousand miles

from home, sitting cross-legged on a tatami mat at a low lacquered
table in a Buddhist temple, and knocking back Japanese beer. Tired as I
was, I still enjoyed myself.

But it wasn't long before the day's stresses caught up with me. After
the second beer, fatigue finally set in. I asked Niwano-san to check if
I could still get a bath and another *biru*. He spoke to one of the serving women who went away and came back a few minutes later to say
the bath was still available. I excused myself and, with another beer
in hand, said good night. "Oyasuminasai," I said, bowing to my dinner companions. At the dining room door, after I'd put on my slippers
and taken care to hold my *yukata* closed, I bowed to the others in the
room. The two older women with whom I'd intended to sit were smiling, probably in relief that the gaijin had gone elsewhere.

***

I'd been in Japan for about a week and had already concluded that the
o-furo had to be the country's greatest contribution to civilization. The
bath is where you relieve aching muscles and soothe jangled nerves.
Naturally, this being Japan, there is a proper way to have a bath: you
soap and rinse your body outside the tub, squatting on a low stool in
front of a basin-and-tap and using the water from a bowl to rinse away
soap, sweat, and the day's grime. Only when you're squeaky clean do
you step into the deep tub, submerging yourself into the hundred-
degree water to soak as long as you can. Half an hour in an *o-furo* and
you begin to think the world is a pretty good place.

I gratefully lowered myself into the hot water and popped the beer.
I took a long swallow, relishing the cold liquid, stretching out my legs,
and letting the hot water lap at my chest as the events of the past few
days floated across my memory. Unlike this particular day, the first two
days—and the first eleven temples—had been easy. Like most *henro*,
I'd started at Ryōzenji temple in the village of Bando, just outside the
city of Tokushima. While the pilgrim route is roughly circular and a
pilgrim can begin anywhere, Ryōzenji is traditionally regarded as the
first pilgrimage temple, the place where pilgrims buy those items—the
white robe, walking stick, name slips, straw hat, and stamp book—that
identify them as pilgrims.

Japanese Buddhist temples usually include a cluster of buildings
surrounded by a wall. Many have a two-story gateway, or *sanmon*, with

a curving tiled roof. Some temples have statues of *niō*, celestial guardians, on each side of the gate, their faces stretched into snarls to warn those whose motives for entering might be less than sincere. According to my guidebooks, one *niō* has his mouth open to say *ah*, while the other says *um*. The two sounds symbolize the beginning and end of the cosmos, alpha and omega. Combined they form the mantra *aum*, a word of power that, according to Buddhist doctrine, evokes the sound of the universe.

Inside the compound are the *shōrō* and the *hondō*, where the temple's primary deity, or *honzon*, is enshrined. A multi-tiered tower—a pagoda—may contain relics associated with the Buddha or other precious objects. There can also be lecture halls, administrative buildings, the head priest's home, and perhaps a cemetery. The temples on the Shikoku route, most of which are attached to the Shingon sect, also have the *daishidō* dedicated to Kōbō Daishi.[13]

Standing outside Ryōzenji temple as a would-be pilgrim, I was conscious of what I was about to do: cross a symbolic threshold from the profane to the sacred world. I recalled a phrase I'd read in Oliver Statler's account of his Shikoku pilgrimage in the late 1960s, where he described pilgrims entering the temple as crossing from "the secular realm to the sacred precincts within."[14] I stared at the two fierce-faced *niō* flanking the gate. They glared back, as though doubting the purity of my motives. Tradition holds that once a *henro* walks through the gate, he or she is committed to completing the pilgrimage even at the risk of death.[15] I'd read about pilgrims succumbing to heart attacks. As it happened, I would find numerous graves along the trail. In the old days, the pilgrim's white robe—in Japan, white is the color of death—was used as a burial shroud, while the broad straw hat was placed over the face as a symbolic coffin. The pilgrim's staff became a grave marker.[16]

For a moment, facing the gate at Ryōzenji, I imagined myself lying dead at the side of a mountain trail. But then I shook away the image, turned up the collar of my rain jacket against the drizzle, and splashed across the street. Half an hour later, I was an official *henro*. I'd signed my name in the pilgrim register, which I would sign again in two months if I could prove I'd completed the pilgrimage. I was also dressed for the part, having purchased a hip-length *hakui*, a packet of the five-inch by two-inch *osamefuda,* and a white shoulder bag for carrying maps and guidebooks. I also carried a five-foot *kongō-tsue.*

My most important purchase, however, was the pilgrim's passport, the *nōkyōchō.* I would fill it with black-ink-and-vermilion temple stamps as evidence of my pilgrim's progress. At every temple, a clerk would write the name of the temple's deity on the page. The name of the deity is crucial. In my research I'd read that in Shingon Buddhist tradition the word, or its written form, contains the deity's essential spirit. Thus *henro* carry the divine essence as they trek from temple to temple. Many Japanese pilgrims place the *nōkyōchō* in their household shrine when they return home. Some have their pilgrim books buried with them.[17]

According to tradition, the Shikoku pilgrim walks with the spirit of Kōbō Daishi as a guide and protector. That is why the walking staff is inscribed with the words "Namu daishi henjō kongō. Dōgyō ninin." "Homage to Kōbō Daishi. We two—pilgrims together." In using the staff as an aid for climbing steep slopes or mounting a long flight of stairs at a temple, pilgrims are literally, if also symbolically, leaning on the deity. They are supposed to wash the base of the staff each night out of respect for their spiritual companion.[18]

I looked at my newly purchased staff, a simple square-cut length of pine. I ran a hand along the smooth shaft. I knew from past pilgrimages that I would grow emotionally attached to it. I stroked the inscription by way of introducing myself. "Okay, Kōbō," I said, banging the base of the staff on the wet asphalt. "Let's hit the road."

For the next two days, I—we?—walked inland, following the Yoshino River valley. The first eleven temples are scattered on either side of the river. I found them in small villages, tucked into the folds of green hills and planted in rice fields and vegetable farms. It was the end of March. The cherry trees were coming into bloom. Winter camellias covered the ground with splotches of red. I spotted farmers wading across their muddy fields to plant rice seedlings.

Every Shikoku temple has a legend about its origins, along with artifacts or monuments attesting to its significance or popularity. A kilometer west of Ryōzenji was Gokurakuji, where women pray for a safe childbirth. Legend says that Kōbō Daishi planted the huge cedar tree that stands in front of one hall, and that touching the tree trunk while praying ensures a long life. There were dozens of coins stuck in the bark. I gave the tree a big hug and inserted a 100-yen coin—about a dollar. I figured I needed all the help I could get.

I "hit" five temples that first day, covering about fifteen kilometers before stopping at the Kotobuki Shōkudō *minshuku*, a guesthouse off the highway a few kilometers from Temple Six. I was the only guest, except for a shaven-headed young man I saw at dinner. We nodded to each other.

The rain had been the only spoiler to the day. My Gore-Tex jacket had leaked, as did my boots with their Gore-Tex lining. When I emptied my backpack in my room, most everything was wet, including my passport, airline tickets, money, and notebooks. Even my *nōkyōchō* was damp, causing some of the temple stamps to run. After dinner, I spread the contents of my pack on the tatami to dry. I studied my gear: a sleeping bag and water-proof emergency shelter; two pairs of fast-drying nylon pants and two nylon shirts; a T-shirt and a long-sleeved jersey, both made of Capilene that, supposedly, absorbs and wicks away sweat; three pairs of socks and three sets of underwear; a fleece jacket for warmth and a hooded nylon rain jacket. I had a medical-and-toiletries kit, including moleskin and tape to prevent blisters, and needles, thread, and iodine in case I got blisters. I also carried an under-the-shirt belt for money and passport and other valuables. But even that had gotten wet somehow.

I had notebooks, pens, and two cameras—digital and film. And, as usual, I had packed reading material, including Taisen Miyata's *A Henro Pilgrimage Guide to the 88 Temples of Shikoku Island*, an English-Japanese dictionary, and a couple of books for inspiration: Statler's *Japanese Pilgrimage* and Matsuo Bashō's *Narrow Road to the Interior*, which recounts the seventeenth-century Japanese haiku master's five-month pilgrimage around northern Japan. I knew I was carrying too much, but I always seemed to start out that way and then spend the early stages of the journey whittling down to the essentials. I repacked what I could and left the rest to dry overnight. Then I crawled onto the futon and fell asleep almost immediately.

The next day I was up at 6 a.m. After repacking my backpack and eating a breakfast of miso soup, some tiny dried fish that looked like slivers of curled wood, and some vegetables I couldn't identify, I was on the road an hour later. It was cool and sunny. That second day saw me all the way from Anrakuji, Temple Six, to Kirihataji, Temple Ten. The route cut across farm fields and along narrow roads lined by wall-enclosed houses. I passed roadside shrines where locals had set bottles of water or an orange at the feet of a small Buddha statue. The streets were clean and peaceful. Sometimes I came across an elderly man or woman shuffling along. Many of the women walked bent over, their backs bowed by years working in the rice fields. They greeted me with a nod and a salutation—"Ohayō gozaimasu," "Good morning"—and, more often than not, a look of surprise when they saw I was a foreigner. Of course, I returned the greeting and the bow.

A quiet village surrounds Anrakuji, the Temple of Everlasting Joy. The pagoda with its white walls and red pillars makes a colorful contrast to the green temple. According to legend, Kōbō Daishi founded the temple when he realized the hot spring's rust-colored water could cure disease. Yakushi, the Buddha of healing, is the patron deity of the hondō. At the temples where Yakushi presides, pilgrims rub his statue on the knees, hands, and back and then rub the part of their body that ails them, hoping for relief from arthritis, back pain, or even cancer.

By late morning I made it to Kumadaniji, Temple Eight, where I took a break and watched a man clean the carp pond. He stood on a small bridge that arched across the pond and leaned over to drag a long pole with a net through the water. The carp, all fat and brightly colored, raced back and forth across the pond trying to avoid the net.

Temple Eight also offered a panoramic view of the Yoshino valley. From the daishidō I saw the river winding like a shiny ribbon through the green plain. On the far side of the valley were the serried ranks of mountain ranges. Looking at the broad expanse of rice fields and farms, I tried to spot Hōrinji, Temple Nine, about three kilometers away.

The only thing ailing me that morning was caffeine withdrawal. After finishing my prayers at the temple halls and getting my pilgrim stamp, I was suddenly desperate for coffee. It occurred to me that I hadn't had a cup of coffee since leaving Tokushima two days earlier. Kōbō Daishi was quick to deliver.

Stroll the streets of Japan, even in the countryside, and sooner or later you'll find a series of vending machines lined up like shrines, offering snacks and drinks—from water and juice to coffee, beer, and sake. I couldn't imagine such things on a North American street corner; they wouldn't survive the vandals. But at Temple Nine, as if in answer to my prayers, I discovered machines that offered several varieties of canned drinks, hot and cold. From the hot side I settled on something called Georgia Café au Lait. On the cold side there was Pocari Sweat. The name alone demanded that I try it. The Pocari Sweat was icy and refreshing, tasting of limes. I read the label, part of which was in English: "An ion supply drink with the appropriate density and electrolytes, close to that of the human body fluid, it can be easily absorbed by the body." Linguistic flaws aside, I'd discovered not only the drinks of choice for my trek but a daily ritual as well. I would feel quite put out when I couldn't have a hot can of Georgia coffee in the morning and a cold Pocari Sweat at the end of the day.

After getting my *nōkyōchō* stamped at Temple Nine I dragged my pack and my body outside the gate. There was a grocery store across the street. A bank of vending machines stood soldier-like next to the store. I emptied my pockets of coins for three cans of Pocari Sweat and a couple of cans of Georgia Café au Lait. I hauled my booty back to the temple steps and sat down, letting the sun and a cool breeze dry my sweat-soaked shirt as I sipped the coffee. I figured that was as close to Nirvana as I was likely to get. Pilgrimages are made of such modest rewards.

Kirihataji, Temple Ten, was four kilometers—and two bottles of Pocari Sweat—away, the last temple on the north side of the Yoshino River. It was the first temple I had to climb to reach, offering a hint of what I would face the next day. I stopped at a small restaurant at the corner of the narrow lane leading to the temple to ask—or, rather, gesture—if I could leave my pack. Then I trudged up the lane past the souvenir shops and farmhouses to the temple gate at the foot of the mountain. I didn't get very far before my leg muscles twanged and trembled in protest. And that was only at the halfway point of the 333 steps leading to the main hall. I reached the top and limped across the courtyard to the *hondō* and the temple office. I sat on a bench in the temple compound to rest and read Statler's account of his visit to the temple. He, too, refers to "the first long flight of stone steps" and admits that his heart was pounding by the time he reached the main hall.[19] I took some comfort in the notion that I wasn't the only out-of-condition pilgrim.

According to legend, Kōbō Daishi founded the temple in honor of a beautiful young girl. Every day, while he performed his meditations in a mountainside hut, she interrupted her cloth-weaving—*kirihata* means "cut-cloth"—to bring him food. Eventually, she told her story: her mother had been a lady of the court in Kyoto and her father an officer in the court guard. With the father exiled before her birth for his part in a rebellion, the mother, fearing for her unborn child, prayed to Kannon, the bodhisattva of compassion. Kannon answered the woman's prayers, helping her to flee to Shikoku, where she raised her child. After the mother's death, though, the daughter was alone. Moved by the young woman's story, Kōbō Daishi carved her a statue of Kannon and, heeding the girl's wishes, ordained her as a nun. She immediately attained enlightenment, or Buddhahood, and changed into a statue of Kannon, joining the one that Kōbō Daishi had carved. Kōbō Daishi enshrined both statues in the temple he built.[20]

Kirihataji is understandably popular with Japanese women. Before Kōbō Daishi came along, women weren't thought capable of Buddhahood. They had to be reborn as men to gain that potential. Kōbō Daishi's teaching that every person has a Buddha-nature and is capable of attaining enlightenment in this life changed that attitude. Such influences have made Kōbō Daishi one of the most important figures in Japanese religious history.[21] In 828 AD, for example, he founded the first school for commoners, providing food, shelter, and education. This was unheard of at the time. Until Kōbō Daishi, only aristocrats could obtain an education.

At Temple Ten, I also gained my first inkling that there might be something to the tradition that Kōbō Daishi walks with every pilgrim. I was parked on a bench in the courtyard, admiring a statue of Kannon and trying to ignore my body's whining at the prospect of the afternoon's walk, nearly ten kilometers across the Yoshino valley, when I saw the shaven headed young man with whom I'd shared the dining room at the Kotobuki Shōkudō the previous night. He was walking toward me, accompanied by a thin-faced, middle-aged man wearing glasses and a ball cap and a younger man with long black hair. They bowed as a group. I stood up to return the gesture. The shaven-headed youth rattled off something in Japanese.

"Gomen nasai," I said, dredging up one of my memorized phrases. "Nihongo wa sukoshi shika dekimasen.""I'm sorry. I speak only a little Japanese."

"Ah, you are American?" he asked in halting English.

"Iie, Kanada-jin desu," I said."No, I'm Canadian."

The young man was Hiroshi Yoshida, a university student from Osaka. He was dressed as a pilgrim with a straw hat and white robe. The others were Shūji Niwano and his son Jun, from Tokyo. Neither of them wore *henro* garb. Nor did they carry walking staffs. They wanted me to take their picture. Niwano-san then asked if I would pose for a photograph with his son. The request would have considerable consequences for my pilgrimage.

After performing the required rituals and getting our pilgrim stamps, we walked together down the long flight of stairs to the Fujiya restaurant. It was little more than a few tables and half a dozen stools huddled around a counter. On one wall were faded pictures of *henro* and temples along with dozens of name slips. There was also a calendar, dated 1996, with a picture of the Toronto skyline and the CN Tower as its centerpiece. Takeko Hara and her daughter, Mayumi, ran the place. They fed me my first udon.

Udon is a classic Japanese dish: thick noodles made from white flour simmered in a broth in which other ingredients—soft-boiled eggs, beef, shrimp, or fish—are mixed. Served in a large, heavy bowl, it is delicious and filling, and no one objects to the loud slurping noises you make as you eat because everyone makes the same noises. I said "itadakimasu"—the Japanese form of grace, meaning literally "I will receive"—when the bowl was set in front of me. I had some difficulty picking up the long slippery noodles with chopsticks, which my companions thought was funny. Before we left, Hara-san had us sign name slips for her collection. She taped mine next to the Toronto skyline picture.

We walked the rest of the afternoon as a group, crossing the wide gravel bed of the Yoshino River and following the path through the town of Kamojima and into the foothills. I asked my companions why they were walking the Henro Michi. Hiroshi-san said he was taking a break from his university. Niwano-san explained that thirty years earlier he'd lived in Imabari, a town on the north side of Shikoku where he had met his wife, Ikuko, and where Jun was born. They'd moved to Tokyo for him to find work, but when he retired he decided to walk the Shikoku pilgrimage with Jun. Concern for Jun, the older of his two sons, also motivated him.

"Jun is not strong," Niwano-san said in stilted English. He looked up the road toward Jun and Hiroshi-san.

I'd already concluded that Jun's behavior was not normal for a young man in his twenties. While he was friendly and eager to talk—even at a distance I could hear Jun chattering away—he was impulsive, almost desperate, in his actions. Whenever we met another pilgrim on the road, Jun practically leapt at them to talk and ask questions. He wasn't being aggressive; he just lacked self-restraint or awareness that self-restraint was necessary on occasion. It was the same thing with dogs. Jun would inevitably run at any we encountered, wanting to pet them. The dogs, however, snarled and barked at his charging approach. He was always surprised, and hurt.

Over the next few weeks, walking together for at least part of each day, I heard more about Niwano-san, his hopes and fears regarding his son and family—confidences that both surprised and humbled me. Unlike North Americans, the Japanese don't readily pour out their private lives to strangers. For some reason, Niwano-san confided in me. I suspected he did so, in part at least, because I was a gaijin and thus, as a foreigner, provided a convenient sounding board for private things he couldn't tell other Japanese. But a pilgrimage also invites intimacy. The shared experiences of the trek, good and bad, foster an immediate empathy you wouldn't normally feel for those who aren't friends or family.

Jun, I learned, had suffered some kind of nervous breakdown several years earlier and never fully recovered. He'd had to leave school and was unable to hold a job. Now he lived at home, largely spending his time in his room listening to music and watching television. Niwano-san hoped the Henro Michi would help his son regain his health and self-confidence.

We reached Fujiidera, Temple Eleven, a few minutes before the office closed at 5 p.m. After getting our pilgrim books stamped, nobody felt like walking back to Kamojima, where everyone had rooms reserved in various hotels or inns. We decided to share a taxi. While we waited for the cab, I found a bench against a wisteria-covered trellis where I could gaze down the path leading into the mountains that I had to climb the next day on my way to Shōsanji, Temple Twelve. With the day's walking done, I felt my leg muscles twitching as they relaxed. I flexed my toes inside my boots, testing for hot spots that might be blisters in formation. A few places felt tender, but nothing approached blister status. I stared down the trail.

Shōsanji is one of six *nansho*, or perilous temples, that pilgrims find most difficult to reach. My guidebooks described the route as a long, hard climb. Indeed the trail climbs from an elevation of forty meters at Temple Eleven to about seven hundred meters just before Temple Twelve—the second highest elevation on the entire pilgrimage. Gravestones of fallen pilgrims are scattered along the route. The path is nearly perpendicular in places. Perhaps that's why the Japanese call the route to Shōsanji *henro korogashi*, or "pilgrim falling."

※※※

Stretched out in the *o-furo*, the back of my head resting on the wooden rim of the tub and the beer within easy reach, I replayed my third day on the Henro Michi. It had started pleasantly enough, with the weather sunny but cool. I left the Central Hotel at 6:30 a.m. My feet seemed fine—I'd wrapped them in moleskin just in case—and the stiffness in my legs disappeared after a few minutes of walking. I purchased a *bentō*, an all-in-one-box meal, for lunch, along with a can of Georgia Café au Lait, two bottles of Pocari Sweat, and two bottles of water, at a kiosk in the Kamojima train station.

The trail was a tease. It began with a slight incline that led past a wide field of tea plants and then climbed gently into the shade of a cedar forest. The air was cool, damp, and pungent. Nightingales noted my passing. But then I confronted a set of stairs cut into the ground, and the trail climbed steeply into the trees. It kept climbing and climbing. I eventually reached a plateau that offered a fine view of the Yoshino River valley, but I was huffing and puffing too much to truly appreciate the panorama. I dropped my pack and collapsed. I pulled out my map and looked at my watch. It had taken me thirty minutes to climb one kilometer. I knew then that I was in for a long day.

The route followed a series of peaks and valleys. I'd reach the summit of one mountain only to drop to a valley floor and then have to climb all over again. I filed along ridges that fell away in vertiginous drops. It was easy to imagine plummeting over the edge into a tangle of dark wood. The path, slippery and soggy from spring rain, was so steep in places that at times I was climbing almost perpendicular on my hands and knees, my face inches from the root-tangled earth. My boots grew leaden with mud. I had to clamber and leap over boulders—no easy task with a heavy pack. I was grateful for "Kōbō Daishi," my walking staff, which saved me from twisting an ankle or worse. After a few hours, my leg muscles whimpered, and my heart thudded like a bass drum. I envisioned a blood vessel bursting and my body lying at the edge of the trail.

It took me four hours to cover a little more than eight kilometers. By the time I reached the small temple of Yanagi-no-mizu-an, nearly halfway to Shōsanji, I was wet, weary, and ready to drop. I flopped in the dappled shade of a camellia bush to have my lunch. When my breathing and heartbeat returned to normal, I pulled the *bentō* out of my pack. Turning back the lid, I found three pieces of sushi; some tempura vegetables; several slices of *kamaboko*, a sausage-like fish-paste roll; slices of bamboo shoot and squash; and three *onigiri*, triangular chunks of rice wrapped in seaweed. It was gone in minutes. I drained a bottle of water and a bottle of Pocari Sweat.

I wondered what Statler thought about the climb and pulled his book from my pack. I liked his description: "We pass through tangled copses and stands of tall cedars, plumb valleys, and file along ridges from which the mountains fall away on either side to rise again in ranges green and blue as far as the eye can see."[22] Nice, I thought. But what about the climb itself? Statler conceded the trail was "hard going," but that was his only acknowledgment of its arduous nature. I felt disappointed, but I wasn't sure whether it was with myself or with Statler for not being more forthright. Either that or he was in much better physical shape than I was.

I sat in the shade, listening to the buzz of insects and watching the sway of the cedars. I was reluctant to continue the hike. But then I heard the tinkling of a bell, and two men came out of the forest into the temple clearing. Both wore *hakui* and walked with a *kongō-tsue*. The tinkling came from a small bell attached to the staff of one of the men.

The taller man had a long, lean face and walked straight-shouldered like a soldier. I guessed him to be in his late sixties. The other had dark, gray-flecked hair. He looked to be in his fifties. They bowed and greeted me but did not pause. When they disappeared around a corner of the trail, I stood up and then stumbled in pursuit of the bell I could still hear. If they could do it, so could I.

The path started to climb almost immediately, and I was soon wondering again if collapse was imminent. But then I found something to encourage me along, something to focus on other than myself. I had occasionally noticed little statues of Jizō here and there along the trail. The bald-pated deity is said to guard children, the souls of the dead, and travelers. He has the power of salvation.

In Japan, Jizō statues are everywhere—at roadside shrines and temples, on the edge of farm fields, at intersections, in cemeteries, and, as I discovered, along mountain trails. It seemed to me that I was seeing figures of Jizō more and more frequently as I staggered those last kilometers to Shōsanji. I happily adopted the deity as the guardian of out-of-condition gaijin pilgrims. I marked my progress by how many Jizō statues I saw, forcing myself to count three before taking a break. Each break lasted only long enough to let me catch my breath. I refused to look at my watch or calculate the remaining distance. You'll get there when you get there, I told myself, remembering what my father used to say to his impatient children on Sunday drives. It didn't help when I spotted the occasional grave marker—short, pillar-like stones on the side of the trail, often huddled around a Jizō statue. The stones were covered with lichen and half-sunk into the ground, and their inscriptions had long worn away.

There were times when I was desperate for the sight of Jizō peeping out from behind a tree or bush or hanging out on a corner. I stabbed the trail with my staff, put one foot in front of the other, and kept my eyes on the ground, refusing to look at the trail up ahead. When, coming around a bend, I almost tripped on a set of stone stairs, I looked up. At the top stood a six-meter-high statue of Kōbō Daishi behind a wrought-iron fence in the shade of a huge cedar. I recognized it from a pilgrim account I'd read when I researched the Henro Michi. The statue was considered a national treasure. According to tradition, Kōbō Daishi had planted the tree after having slept at the site and dreamed of a Buddhist deity.[23] Which one I couldn't remember, and just then I didn't care. I was more concerned with whether my ordeal was at an end. I looked at my watch—nearly 3:30 p.m. I had been on the trail for almost nine hours and still had a way to go.

I checked my map. I'd reached Ipponsugi-an, a small shrine about an hour's walk from Shōsanji. Praise Jizō, the trail was mostly downhill. The path dropped through orange groves and orchards of cherry trees. The pungent ripeness of the orange trees in bloom mixed with the sweet and softer perfume of the cherry blossoms. It was an open-air cathedral of scent. By the time I crossed a rushing stream at the foot of the mountain—elevation 422 meters—and began the final climb to Shōsanji, I was feeling more charitable toward the world.

But that final two-kilometer climb to Temple Twelve was one long slog. My pace was slow and staggering. My legs grew wobbly. My back ached from the strain of my pack. The path was worn to bedrock and the stone wet from rain. My feet kept slipping on the rocks, threatening to turn an ankle. I concentrated on technique. When the path became too steep to climb straight on, I zigzagged back and forth across the width of the path. It was more time-consuming, but it eased the strain on my legs. I tasted the salty sweat dripping off my forehead. Jizō sightings seemed farther and farther apart.

Then I heard a bell. It wasn't the annoying sound of a tinkling bell on a pilgrim's walking stick but one of those substantive sonorous bongs of a temple bell. It sounded too good to be true, and I wondered if I was having an auditory hallucination. I stood still and listened. Yes, there it was again. Somebody, bless Jizō, was banging away at the Shōsanji bell. Not long afterward, I emerged from the forest to climb a final set of stairs through the temple gate to whack that bell myself.

Two hours later, I was near to falling asleep in the o-furo. I felt as limp as a noodle in a bowl of udon. My legs wobbled when I hauled myself out of the bath. After drying myself and donning my yukata, I made my way down the quiet hallways of the lodge to my room. Instead of going to bed as I should have, however, I decided to stroll around the temple compound even though it was getting dark outside. I grabbed some change from my money belt and went outside, crunching along the gravel path toward the temple halls. Wouldn't you know it? I spotted a bank of vending machines against the wall of the administration building. I treated myself to a Georgia Café au Lait and found a bench that looked over the valley below the temple compound. In the distance, a series of saw-toothed mountain ridges marched away to the southwest, turning from blue to purple to black as they got farther away. I sat nursing my coffee as night fell and the mountains became one black mass silhouetted against a star-plastered sky.

The day had been hard, and I knew there would be others like it ahead. But I'd done enough long-distance hikes to know the first week was always the most difficult. The body needs time to adjust to walking for hours. So, too, does the mind. Anybody in reasonable health can walk thirty kilometers for a few days. But knowing you have to walk that distance every day for weeks throws up a psychological barrier. You're tempted to find any excuse to chuck it because you know it's going to get worse before it gets better. So why was I doing this?

Certainly the Henro Michi offered the lure of the exotic and appealed to my sense of adventure. Asphalt and concrete cover much of Japan, but Shikoku still possesses areas of near wilderness. Nor is the route on the foreign tourist itinerary. But surely there was more to my pilgrimage than exoticism and adventure. If all I was doing was visiting eighty-eight Buddhist temples, why do it the hard way? Why not be a bus pilgrim, which, as I'd read, was how the vast majority of pilgrims made the journey? I'd walked forty kilometers so far. I had more than 1,300 kilometers to go. What was I trying to prove? Come to that, to whom was I trying to prove anything? I wasn't a Buddhist, so I couldn't claim a compelling religious motive.

Sipping my coffee, I remembered a line from Donald Richie's travelogue of a boat journey he once made on the seaway separating the main Japanese island of Honshu from Shikoku. "A journey is always something of a flight," Richie wrote. "You go to reach, but you also go to escape."[24] Was I trying to escape from something or reaching for something? Maybe, as Richie suggests, it was both. A few years earlier I'd hiked across northern Spain, walking the eight-hundred-kilometer Camino de Santiago to the Galician city of Santiago de Compostela.[25] Memories of that pilgrimage still haunted me—the peacefulness of a sun-splashed forest path, the empty early morning streets of Pamplona, the far horizon of the Spanish *meseta*. But what I most remembered were those rare moments when, after my body—and my mind—had grown accustomed to the walking, a deep sense of peace and detachment descended on me. My mind emptied of the clatter and crush of everyday life, and I felt that some epiphany, some brief transcendence, was at hand.

I wanted something similar from Shikoku. But I also wanted something more. Just then, as I stared at the mountains I would cross in the coming days, I was too tired to think about what "more" might be. I took a last swallow of my now-cold coffee and returned to my room. I prepared my pack for the morning and opened the window, taking a deep breath. The mountain air was sweet with cedar. I turned out the light and crawled beneath the quilt on my futon. As I fell asleep I heard someone chanting the Heart Sutra.

2

Companions

With more companions
to pilgrimage with
we travel merrily.
—SHŪJI NIWANO

I was in the foyer of the Shōsanji temple lodge by six the next morning, trying to jam my feet into a pair of outdoor slippers for a pre-breakfast stroll to the coffee machine, when I saw Jun and his father approaching.

"You walk with us?" Jun asked.

"We would like that—to walk together," Niwano-san said. "Please, you call me Shūji. That is my given name."

"I will be your Japanese teacher," said Jun.

The Japanese tend to be very formal with strangers. Unlike North Americans, they don't presume the intimacy of using someone's first name unless invited to do so. Niwano-san was making a generous gesture, considering that I'd only met him and Jun a couple of days earlier. I knew this at the time, but only later did I realize how in that moment my Shikoku adventure took on a different direction or, more accurately perhaps, a different sensibility. I'd assumed I would meet other pilgrims and enjoy their company, but I'd also thought that given my inability to speak Japanese and my ignorance of the culture, I'd walk mostly alone and have to rely on my own devices as best I could. What Shūji and Jun offered was an unanticipated pilgrimage experience, a chance to join a pilgrim family. Part of me hesitated. I liked to walk alone, following my wandering thoughts. On the other hand, I wanted to absorb as much of Japanese culture as I could. Accompanying Shūji and his son would, I thought, open doors that would otherwise remain closed to me. Indeed, as it turned out, I learned much from Jun, who was eager to provide the Japanese word for objects we spotted as we walked or to identify items of food. And, as I would come to know later, Niwano-san had his own reasons, however inchoate, for wanting me to join him and his son.

"I would like that, Niwano-san," I said. "Dōmo arigatō gozaimasu." "Thank you very much."

"Dō itashimashite." "You're welcome." He asked me again to call him Shūji.

I bowed and repeated my thanks and said that he and Jun should call me "Robāto."

"Good. Better than Shiburī-san. Too hard to say." Shūji then invited me to join him and Jun for breakfast.

"Dōmo. Dewa go-isshoni," I said, abandoning my pursuit of some hot coffee. "Thanks. I will."

An hour later, after breakfast—I was getting used to miso soup, grilled fish, pickled vegetables, and a raw egg stirred into a bowl of steaming rice as our morning fare—we were back in the foyer, pulling on boots and shouldering packs. I mentally checked myself: my legs were a bit sore and stiff from the previous day's exertions, but otherwise I felt fine. There was no hint of blisters to come.

I pulled my walking staff out of the large stack that had accumulated against the wall of the foyer. It was easy to distinguish mine from the others. Three days on the trail had frayed the bottom of the staff. Rock scrapes had chipped the sides. The sweat of my palm had darkened the wood at the top. Most of the other staffs were in pristine condition with their bells and bright hand cushions still attached and the wood still shiny with varnish—a sure sign that their owners weren't walking pilgrims.

In my research I'd read that the vast majority of the 150,000 Japanese who undertake the Henro Michi each year do so by bus on group tours. Only a few thousand people—2,000 to 4,000 by some estimates—walk the pilgrim route. There are those who hold that people who take buses aren't serious pilgrims. Because they travel in comfort and don't suffer the rigors of walking, they are considered more tourists than *henro*.[1] I'd encountered this attitude on the Camino de

Santiago; walkers regarded those who took buses or trains as less pure in their spiritual motives. It struck me as rather silly, and narcissistic, that anyone would feel a need to disparage the motives and methods of other pilgrims to inflate their own status.

On the other hand, as my pilgrimage progressed I began to see an essential difference between those who took buses from temple to temple and those like me who walked. At the temples I'd see groups of bus pilgrims diligently going through the rituals and devotional rites. They were attentive to the place of worship because for them being at the temple was the whole point of their pilgrimage. As a walker I found myself largely ignoring the temples. To be sure, I performed the obligatory rituals. But after a while, I tended to devote less and less time to the temple rites and had to force myself to be more diligent. I was more interested in the space between the temples.[2] Indeed, as I eventually discovered, my memories of the Henro Michi would be mainly images of quiet forest paths, empty village streets, and stunning panoramic vistas. With only a few exceptions, the temples were a blur of tiled roofs, neat gardens, and the smell of incense.[3]

That morning, leaving Shōsanji was a case in point. It was a beautiful morning for walking. The mountain air was sweet and cool. The three of us were heading down the mountain to Dainichiji, Temple Thirteen, some twenty-six kilometers away. In early April the cherry blossoms were just coming into bloom on Shikoku, while the other deciduous trees possessed their first blush of green. Shafts of sunlight fell through the cedars, dappling the path in shifting patterns of light and shade. A woodpecker and a nightingale competed for the title of most haunting sound in the forest.

After about two kilometers, we reached a small trailside temple sheltered in a grove of cedar trees, where we took a break. According to tradition, it was here at Joshin-an, Cedar Staff Temple, that the Shikoku pilgrimage had its origins. Like many religious traditions, the Henro Michi begins with death and redemption—in this case, the death and salvation of the first pilgrim, Emon Saburō. One day, the story goes, a bedraggled monk repeatedly appeared at Saburō's home to beg for food. Saburō, a rich man known for his greed and cruelty, tried to hit the monk with a stick and smashed his begging bowl. The monk—Kōbō Daishi, of course—did not return. Soon afterward,

Saburō's eight children became sick and died. Full of remorse, Saburō set out after the Daishi to beg forgiveness but was unable to find him despite repeatedly circling the island. Worn out and near death, Saburō struggled to climb the path to Shōsanji. But at the moment of collapse, Kōbō Daishi appeared on the trail just in time to forgive Saburō and bury him, marking the trailside grave with Saburō's staff. That staff, legend says, grew into the tall cedar beneath which I stood drinking a Pocari Sweat.[4]

The trail markers that line the Henro Michi reinforce the Daishi's presence. All along the route, I would see signs showing a red-painted silhouette of a *henro* or stone pillars embossed with a pointing hand.[5] Sometimes, though, the markers are little more than a red ribbon tied around a tree trunk or a plaque hanging from a branch. Pilgrims have to pay close attention, especially on the mountain trails. Miss a sign or take a wrong turn and you can end up wandering a mountainside far from the pilgrim path. That's apparently what happened to a woman and two children whom we encountered that morning.

Walking with Shūji and Jun, I almost inevitably ended up ahead of them, at least early in the day, because my legs were longer. So it was on this morning, when I was the first to encounter the woman and her children. I'm not sure who was more startled: me, at the sight of a crouching woman holding two children in her arms in the middle of the trail, or them, at the sight of a gaijin stumbling toward them. The woman looked to be in her early thirties, her hair dyed with henna in the Japanese fashion. The girl, whom I guessed to be about five, was crying, and the boy, who was perhaps eight, seemed close to tears. They stared goggle-eyed when they saw me. I bowed and said good morning and tried to explain that I was a pilgrim.

"Chotto matte, kudasai." "Wait a minute, please," I said, making wait-a-minute gestures and smiling to show I was no threat. I pointed back in the direction of my companions. "Tomodachi." "Friends."

The woman said something to the children. The girl wiped her tears and stared at me. I wondered if I was her first foreigner.

A few minutes later, Shūji and Jun joined us. While Jun chatted with the kids and offered them candy, Shūji talked to the woman. It turned out, as Shūji later explained to me, that they'd been walking in circles, following a trail that kept returning them to the same spot.

The woman's name was Atsuko Yasuda. The boy was Hidetaka and the girl Mizuki. The family lived in Yokkaichi, a city south of Tokyo on the Honshu coast. They were visiting the Shikoku temples, walking those parts of the route the children could manage and taking buses and trains to temples that were too hard for them to reach. As we had, they'd spent the night in the *shukubō* at Shōsanji temple.

It's not unusual to see women as pilgrims on Shikoku, and it's common to see families visiting the temples. But this was the only time that I saw children walking the route. The family stayed with us for almost ten kilometers, Shūji and the woman talking together as we walked. While we took more breaks than usual, the children often ran ahead, laughing, to wait for the adults to catch up. I bought them ice-cream cones when we stopped for a rest in Nabeiwa, a village at the foot of the mountain we'd descended.

Yasuda-san and her children eventually left us in Hamyo, a village on the banks of a tributary of the Akui River. After Shūji, Jun, and I waved goodbye as they boarded a bus, we found a restaurant for lunch, ordering large bowls of udon. I asked Shūji why Yasuda-san was making the pilgrimage with her children. He tapped on the keys of his electronic dictionary, which we used to communicate when we couldn't speak the right words, and then passed it to me. I read: "Her husband was killed in a car accident last year. They walk to honor his memory."

We still had sixteen kilometers to go to Temple Thirteen, where we would spend the night. It was a lovely warm day, and although my feet were starting to feel sore I continued to enjoy the walking. I thought about the woman and her children and how she was using the Henro Michi to honor her late husband. That got me thinking again about my own motives and why I'd undertaken another pilgrimage. It was a topic I'd been mulling over since my journey on the Camino de Santiago.[6]

***

Years ago I came across a quotation from the German literary critic Walter Benjamin that I've adopted as a kind of reference point for assessing whether I'm living as fully as I'd like. In an essay on Marcel Proust's *À la recherche du temps perdu*, Benjamin wrote that at the center of the French novelist's book is "the insight that none of us has the time to live the true dramas of the life that we are destined for."[7] That's certainly been my experience—or so I discovered rather late in life. At a certain point I came to realize that what was most important to me wasn't any of the things I'd been taught to pursue—career, reputation, ambition, money—but rather the things of little consequence. What lingered in my memory were images of a particular place or a certain person, or brief moments of what I came to regard as epiphanies. In effect, I'd awakened to the spiritual life.

We all possess a spiritual life to some degree, a sense of inwardness shaped by personal experience, the climate of opinion in which we live, and our psychological dispositions. It's surely a mark of sanity to find a way to reflect on the spiritual dimension of your life, to discover, if possible, a thread of meaning and purpose in the tapestry of everyday experience. Many people appear to get along without a need for more than superficial reflection. They seem content with the diversions of consumption and entertainment offered by a technological society. But others don't seem satisfied with such distractions. The challenge, of course, once you're aware of your dissatisfaction, is finding the time, place, and circumstance that allow you to cultivate those habits of reflection and introspection that might open you to the "true dramas" of your life.

I was fortunate. I had stumbled onto pilgrimage and found a practice that allowed me a respite from the demands of my ordinary life, a chance to step out temporarily from the magic circle of the modern world and seek those "dramas." Indeed, my first pilgrimage on the road to Santiago had affected me a great deal, albeit in often subtle ways that I didn't at first recognize. There was no great revelation, no soul-changing epiphany, no sudden conversion to religious faith. Yet the journey turned me in a direction I hadn't anticipated. I was haunted for months by images from my walk, images that while inconsequential to anyone else seemed to resonate with great significance for me. I wondered if there was a discernible psychological pattern to those moments of epiphany. And if there was, might those moments provide a meaningful pattern to my life as a whole? Why did I remember some things and not others, and what did that selective memory say about my psychological state and, indeed, my spiritual longings? What did it all mean, if anything?

I certainly wasn't alone in asking these questions. Nor was I the first to find in pilgrimage a means for such contemplation. Pilgrimages are among the most universal of spiritual and religious phenomena. The word "pilgrim" derives from the Latin *peregrinus* and refers to those who wander beyond the security of the community. It's difficult to think of a religion or a culture that doesn't feature some form of pilgrimage. Irish Catholics climb Croagh Patrick on their knees in the hope of salvation. Every August, on the Feast of the Assumption, thousands of Greek Orthodox worshipers travel to Tinos to venerate a nineteenth-century icon of the Virgin Mary, performing acts of self-flagellation as they approach the shrine. Christians in general visit Rome and Jerusalem or trek the Camino de Santiago across northern Spain. Jews seek out the Wailing Wall in Jerusalem. Muslims perform the *hajj* to Mecca and Medina. Hindus wade in the shallow waters of the Ganges during the Kumbha Mela festival.

Secularists have shrines, too: Elvis Presley's Graceland mansion in Tennessee, Jim Morrison's grave in Paris, John Lennon's memorial in New York, Princess Diana's gravesite in England. I'd even read of a shrine in Mexico where drug dealers offer prayers to a dead trafficker, lighting candles and seeking his blessing for the marijuana harvest.

And now here I was on a Buddhist pilgrimage, throughout which symbols of spiritual journeying and metaphors of death, rebirth, and redemption proliferated. Everywhere along the route, as I soon came to see, there were iconic references to Kōbō Daishi as a spiritual hero worthy of emulation. It was easy to understand why. Kōbō Daishi was born in northeastern Shikoku in 774 AD. He left home at the age of seventeen to attend the university in Nara, which was then the political and cultural center of Japan. A Buddhist monk inspired him to reject his family's wishes that he become a court bureaucrat, and he returned to Shikoku to spend seven years visiting island temples. He eventually achieved enlightenment and took the name Kūkai. In 804, the emperor asked Kūkai, then thirty-one, to join a diplomatic mission to China, where he met the Chinese master Hui-kuo, the seventh patriarch of esoteric Buddhism. Hui-kuo recognized Kūkai as his successor and set out to impart his teachings. Two years later, with the great transmission of knowledge complete, Kūkai returned to Japan, establishing a version of Buddhism known as Shingon that today is one of the main Buddhist sects in Japan.[8]

Unlike some Buddhist sects, Shingon teaches that enlightenment is possible in this life. You don't need to go through repeated cycles of birth and rebirth. This core doctrine is *sokushin-jōbutsu,* attaining enlightenment while still in this earthly life. The height of enlightenment is to attain knowledge of absolute reality, or Buddhahood, as an individual while living in the world. It may be extremely difficult and require decades of effort, but salvation through esoteric practice is available to anyone, rich or poor, samurai or peasant, man or woman, who is open to the love of Buddha. This claim ensured that Shingon Buddhism was open to more than the aristocrats who had been Buddhism's main followers since the religion reached Japan during the sixth century.

Kūkai worked for ten years after his return from China to spread the word. In 816, Emperor Saga granted his request to establish the seat of Shingon Buddhism on the forested heights of Mount Kōyasan, near the city of Osaka. Mount Kōyasan is a large community even today, with 120 or so temple-monastery complexes. That's a far cry from the 1,500 temples that once spread across the mountaintop during the seventeenth century, but it's still a stunning setting of beautiful buildings surrounded by cedar-covered mountain slopes.[9] After my visit, I had to agree with a travel writer who said that if you can spend only one day in Japan, it should be at Mount Kōyasan, even if only to visit Kōbō Daishi's mausoleum deep in the forest cemetery.[10]

According to legend, Kōbō Daishi predicted the day on which he would die: March 21, 835. But his devotees don't believe that he's dead. Instead, they claim that he entered into "eternal meditation," or *nyūjō,* remaining alive in his mausoleum at Mount Kōyasan to act as a spiritual guide and to await the arrival of Miroku Bosatsu, the next Buddha who is to succeed Gautama Buddha, the founder of Buddhism. In 921, the belief that Kūkai is somehow still alive was reinforced. The imperial court that year granted him the title Kōbō Daishi, which means "great teacher who spread the law of Buddhism across the country." When news of the honor reached Mount Kōyasan, priests entered Kūkai's mausoleum. They claimed to have found his hair growing and his body warm. Holy men calculated that the Daishi has to wait 5,670,000,000 years for Miroku's appearance and the salvation of the world.[11]

By the latter part of the eleventh century, people were undertaking pilgrimages to Mount Kōyasan, and a huge necropolis grew up around Kōbō Daishi's mausoleum. People wanted their own graves nearby, believing that proximity to the saint would give them access to the future Buddha. Sometime after that, Kōbō Daishi descended the mountain, metaphorically speaking. Maybe it wasn't like Moses bringing the Ten Commandments, but priests and religious ascetics trekked across Japan promoting Kōbō Daishi "as a traveling pilgrim dressed in monks' robes, with a begging bowl, a staff, and a bamboo hat, wandering around Japan" to cure the sick, benefit the virtuous, and punish the wicked.[12]

Kōbō Daishi's well-documented journeys around Shikoku provided the guide and inspiration for other *hijiri*, or holy men, from Mount Kōyasan. Most temple visitors between the twelfth and the early fourteenth centuries were monks. But in the mid-1300s, at the beginning of what the Japanese refer to as the Muromachi era (1338–1573), people other than ascetics and religious mendicants began to undertake the pilgrimage. By the early years of the Edo period (1603–1868), as roads and economic circumstances improved, the Shikoku pilgrimage became increasingly popular. And by the late seventeenth century, the pilgrimage was so popular that a Buddhist ascetic named Shinnen, who spent much of his life walking the circuit, published a guidebook and erected dozens of stone markers to guide other pilgrims. Ordinary people began walking the Shikoku trails, stopping at the temples and praying for the souls of their ancestors, for good health for themselves and their families, and for abundant crops in the fields.[13]

***

By mid-afternoon I was praying for salvation myself. My early morning good spirits were fading fast. The balls of my feet felt hot and sore, a sure sign of blisters. I tried to ignore the pain, but it sliced into my feet with each step, slowing my pace. I took a few moments to pull off my boots and examine my feet. I didn't like what I saw. The moleskin I'd applied in the morning had bunched up against my toes. Blisters had formed on the pads of my toes and in between. A fat, thumb-length blister looped around the side and back of my left heel. The right heel was showing all the signs of an impending outbreak as well.[14]

I knew immediately what was wrong and why, and I was furious with myself. Feet swell when you walk long distances. If your boots are too small, your feet have no room to expand. That had been the curse of my previous pilgrimage on the Camino de Santiago. I'd had to take a couple of days off just to let the blisters heal sufficiently so that I could walk again. And even after that I still had trouble. I'd hoped that my Japanese pilgrimage would be different. I'd purchased boots a half-size larger than I normally wear, assuming that would be sufficient. It wasn't, or so it seemed. I pulled out my medical kit and bandaged my feet even though I knew it wouldn't do any good.

By late afternoon I was stumbling along, leaning heavily on my staff and praying for the day to end. We'd walked out of a narrow river valley into a wide plain filled with houses and factories. The trail had changed from a pleasant country lane to a narrow highway, thick and noisy with traffic. Passing cars and trucks buffeted me as I limped along the shoulder of the road. I was sorely tempted to flag down a cab, but the sight of Shūji and Jun stolidly trudging ahead kept me going, although Jun seemed to be struggling, too. At one point, he waited for me to catch up so that we could walk together. I appreciated the gesture, but I didn't want to learn any more Japanese words just then.

"No talk, Jun," I said, "just walk."

We arrived at Dainichiji, the Temple of the Great Sun, shortly before 5 p.m. I was weary and wobbling when we climbed the flight of steps off the road and entered the temple's small, gateless courtyard. We'd walked twenty-six kilometers. I had no inclination to perform the pilgrim rituals, so I sat on a low wall in the courtyard. But I was ashamed of myself when I saw Shūji light a stick of incense and stagger up the steps of the hondō to say his prayers. What kind of pilgrim was I? I hoisted myself to my feet and followed his example, even though I was only going through the motions. I presumed that Kōbō Daishi would understand. Surely even saints got blisters.

After getting our stamp books signed and inscribed at the temple office, we checked into the shukubō. When I got to my room, I stripped off my boots and soaking clothes, wrapped myself in a yukata, and rushed as fast as my aching, blistered feet would carry me to the o-furo for a pre-supper soak. I postponed dealing with my feet—or even looking at them too closely—until after supper.

Once I was back in my room, I finally confronted my feet. I'd had my share of blisters from other long-distance treks, but this batch was dismaying. Two-inch-wide blisters ran over the balls of both feet, from behind the second and third toes to halfway down the soles. There were blisters on or between every toe and curving around the sides and backs of each heel. It took an hour to perform the pilgrim surgery of sterilizing a needle with matches and pulling some iodine-soaked thread through each blister. I'd performed this on-the-trail surgery before, so I knew what to expect. Even so, by the time I finished, my jaw ached from gritting my teeth and I was soaked in sweat. My feet looked a mess with two reddened, iodine-stained soles cross-hatched with lines of black thread. Still, I was lucky: the outer skin hadn't torn to expose the raw layer underneath. When that happens, even the slightest pressure can be excruciatingly painful. I wrapped my battered feet in moleskin and bandages and hoped they'd be better by morning.

They weren't, at least not after a couple hours of walking. We left Temple Thirteen at 7 a.m., expecting to cover the eight kilometers to Temple Seventeen within three hours, including breaks. The temples in between—Fourteen, Fifteen, and Sixteen—are fairly close together, and the route is flat all the way across a lowland plain that follows the Akui River as it skirts the southern edge of Tokushima City. Nevertheless, thanks to my moving so slowly, we didn't reach Temple Seventeen until nearly noon. It was an awful morning. I'd expected to be hobbling like an old man, but that day my leg muscles seized up every time I stopped. I had to endure shafts of pain in my legs as soon as I started to walk again. I moved like a piece of rusty machinery.

I forced myself to keep on keeping on. I barely noticed the countryside. At each temple, I rushed through the rituals so that I could find a spot to rest for as long as possible. At least my rest periods allowed me some awareness of the temples themselves—Jōrakuji, Temple Fourteen, with its undulating bedrock that makes up the courtyard; Kokubunji, Temple Fifteen, with its sprawling compound and dignified halls; Kannonji, Temple Sixteen, a compact temple behind an old gate and a wall of stone pillars carved with the names of donors; Idoji, Temple Seventeen, with its rock garden and the Well of the Image, where, as legend has it, if you don't see yourself reflected in the water, you will have great misfortune. I didn't see myself in the well.

I knew I was slowing Shūji and Jun down. They would disappear around some street corner or drop out of sight behind the curve of a hill and then pull up, walking slowly, looking back for me. Sometimes they would stop and wait. At other times, Jun would walk behind me. I was touched and grateful. Knowing they were looking out for me allowed me to walk without having to check my maps or worry about getting lost. They also allowed me to rest at each temple for longer than usual.

I pulled the plug at Temple Seventeen. My legs were cramping, and every step fired a jolt of pain from heel to knee. When it was time to go, I used my walking stick to lever myself off the bench and hobble to a nearby restaurant for lunch. As we slurped our udon, Shūji and I looked over the maps: eighteen kilometers to go.

"You should not walk, maybe," Shūji said.

Maybe I should have soldiered on and worked through the pain, but I didn't. I accepted Shūji's advice with embarrassed relief. Just then, all I wanted was to take off my too-small boots and lie down and sleep. Shūji phoned for a cab and told the driver to take me to the Chibu *min-shuku*, the guesthouse where we'd booked rooms for the night. Taxis are expensive in Japan, and the ride cost 5,500 yen, or about $55. It was worth it as far as I was concerned. I arrived at the Chibu *minshuku*, near Temple Eighteen, shortly before 1 p.m. The woman who ran the place was waiting for me with a welcoming bow. Shūji had phoned ahead to let her know I was on the way. I don't know what he told her, but when I arrived the futon in my room was laid out, and as soon as I stripped off my clothes and put on the freshly laundered *yukata*, the *okami-san*, or housemistress, slid open the *shōji* to set a tea tray on the floor. Before I could say anything she'd grabbed my dirty laundry and taken it away. I didn't understand a word that she said but just kept bowing and mumbling like a ventriloquist's dummy, saying "Dōmo arigatō." "Thank you."

I hadn't even finished the cup of tea before I fell asleep. When I woke up, the room was awash with sunshine. The tatami mats glowed yellow in the bright light. I drew back the blinds and looked out across rice fields toward a copse of bamboo. The wind carried the scent of cedar and, I could swear, a whiff of incense. My watch said it was 4 p.m. I'd slept nearly three hours. I felt strangely lightheaded, as if a fever had broken.

I could see Onzanji, Temple Eighteen, from my window, a few hundred yards up the road. I decided to get my *nōkyōchō* stamped. During my time in Japan I often saw hotel guests walking the streets in their *yukata*. But I probably looked a bit odd, limping up the hill with my walking stick, wearing my boots and the too-small blue robe flapping in the wind. It seemed that a few hours off the trail and a nap had done me a world of good. It also helped that I wasn't carrying an overweight pack. I decided to unload as much as possible at the next post office.

I deliberately lingered over my pilgrim rituals at the *hondō* and the *daishidō*, lighting a stick of incense in the big urn in front of each hall before getting my pilgrim book stamped. Afterward I wandered around the temple compound, admiring the wall of miniature Jizō figurines and the statues of the ten disciples of Gautama Buddha. I moved slowly and cautiously, my feet tender and legs sore. I found a vending machine, bought a bottle of Pocari Sweat, and parked myself on a bench beneath the cherry trees.

Onzanji, the Temple of Gratitude Mountain, is a place where you can sit for a long time, soaking up the serenity. The breeze carried scents of cedar and incense. Sometimes the wind blew stronger, showering me with cherry blossoms. As I nursed my drink, I watched other pilgrims climb the stairs, ring the *waniguchi* bell, and stand with heads bowed, chanting the Hannya Shingyō. Most of them were women.

According to my guidebook, women once couldn't enter the temple precincts because they were believed to be spiritually impure. Even Kōbō Daishi's mother, Tamayori, couldn't visit her son during one of his stays at the temple. That restriction irritated the saint, and he spent seventeen days performing various rites and rituals at the temple gate, exorcising the prohibition against women. His mother eventually became a nun, and Kōbō Daishi changed the temple's name to Onzanji, which literally means "parental love as solid as a mountain." A hall dedicated to Tamayori is on the left side of the temple compound, next to the *daishidō*. Her bones supposedly reside there.

I was trying to convince myself—or, rather, convince my legs—to stand and hobble back to the *minshuku* when I spotted the banker from Sendai, Sayama-san, and the Hokkaido businessman, Murakoshi-san, coming toward me. I hadn't seen them since our meal together at Shōsanji.

"Genki desu ka?" asked Sayama-san. "How are you?"

"Mā-mā," I said. "So-so." I pointed to my feet, remembering the word for blister. "Mizubukure."

They seemed to understand. Sayama-san tapped a foot with his walking stick and said, "Watashi mo." "Me, too."

They bowed and went about their *henro* duties. Sayama-san, I noticed, was limping. I forced myself to waddle down the hill to the *minshuku*, where, as it turned out, all of us were staying. Just before I reached the inn, I saw Shūji and Jun coming up the road. They looked wiped out, especially Jun, who was limping badly. I felt ashamed. I should have walked with them.

***

The hike from Temple Eighteen to Temple Twenty-Three is about fifty-five kilometers, crosses two mountain ranges, and requires two or three days of hard walking. The greatest challenge, however, was psychological. I'd been on the road for nearly a week, and the impact on my body—blisters, aching legs, and strained back, for starters—had begun to take its toll. But I was also increasingly aware of what it really meant to tackle the Henro Michi: I still had seventy temples and 1,300 kilometers to go.

The morning we left the Chibu *minshuku*—my sixth day on the Henro Michi—it rained. There is nothing unusual in that, of course. It rains a lot on Shikoku. But this wasn't just a sprinkle, a drizzle, or a shower but a heavy downpour. We walked in it most of the day. Indeed, after only a couple of minutes on the road, I was soaked from head to toe, bemoaning my fate and scanning the terrain for a vending machine to buy a can of hot Georgia Café au Lait.

The trail from Onzanji to Temples Nineteen and Twenty, Tatsueji and Kakurinji, cuts across a flat landscape of rice paddies, vegetable farms, hothouse farms, and small villages until, just before Temple Twenty, it starts to climb. Shūji had made reservations for the three of us at the Kanekoya Ryokan in Ikuna, a hamlet at the foot of a mountain about three kilometers below Kakurinji. We intended to drop our bags at the *ryokan*, climb to the temple, and then return to our lodgings. Altogether the trek should have meant about twenty kilometers of walking—say, five or six hours, excluding time spent at the temples. It ended up being a nine-hour day that left us chilled and exhausted. Even after only a few kilometers, I felt the bandages and moleskin on my feet coming loose and curling behind my toes, exposing the blisters on the soles. By the time we reached Tatsueji—a four-kilometer hike—I was limping badly. So was Jun.

Despite my sorry state—and my self-pity—I could still admire the temple. It had an air of prosperity with its impressive halls, neatly trimmed gardens, and handsome statues of Kōbō Daishi and Kannon. But Tatsueji is also known as a "barrier temple," a psychological boundary that, according to tradition, a *henro* must cross in order to continue the pilgrimage. Here Kōbō Daishi judges whether pilgrims are worthy to continue their spiritual quest. If pilgrims can honestly tell themselves they're walking for spiritual motives and have no fear about what is to come, then they have passed the test.

On the way to Temple Nineteen I had to admit I was a poor candidate to pass the barrier test. I was faltering, physically and psychologically. At a convenience store, I bought a plastic rain suit, but it was no help. The plastic didn't breathe, and I soon felt as though I were walking in a portable sauna. The afternoon became one long slog. Rain was the enemy, mud a hateful presence, and the mountains a curse. I was no longer on a pilgrimage but on an endurance course. I was angry and resentful of the Henro Michi and the suffering it imposes. I asked myself why I was doing what I was doing. What I'd imagined would be a stroll along country lanes, an intoxication of cherry trees in bloom and panoramic vistas of misty mountains to inspire the spirit, had instead become a wearying march of blistered feet, aching legs, and soggy clothes. And it only promised to get worse: when—or if—I reached Temple Twenty-Three I faced a three-day, seventy-five-kilometer trek to Temple Twenty-Four. Many walking pilgrims, I'd read during my research, pack it in by the time they reach Temple Twenty-Three, in the coastal town of Hiwasa.

At times the rain came down so hard that we couldn't walk. We'd find shelter where we could—the open door of a garage, the eaves of a warehouse, a bus stop—and watch the rain hit the ground or asphalt with such a pulverizing force that it ricocheted upward to form a knee-high wall of water. The sound was like low rumbling thunder. Unfortunately, sheltering from the storm consumed a lot of time. We didn't reach the Kanekoya Ryokan until about 2 p.m. But the day wasn't over. We still had the climb to Kakurinji, the Crane Forest Temple.

The hike to Temple Twenty would have been hard even in good weather. The temple was on the summit of a mountain 550 meters above sea level. We followed the Katsuura River until the trail started to climb through groves of orange and cherry trees. The wind and rain had stripped the cherry trees of their blossoms, covering the path with pink petals. They were pretty but made the trail treacherous. In our slipping and sliding in the muck, pink cherry blossoms soon covered our boots and pants.

What saved me that day was my own previous pilgrimage experience. I'd done enough long-distance hiking to expect this psychological barrier. I knew I couldn't walk for two months filled with resentment. I couldn't rise at dawn every day and walk twenty or thirty kilometers if the prospect filled me with dread. The secret, as I'd learned, was to walk with my head rather than with my body. In the same way that a Zen master teaches acolytes to let the chatter of the mind pass by during meditation, I'd learned to let the hardships of the pilgrimage come and go without obsessing about them. There was no point fretting about or lamenting my blisters or my aching feet. Rather, I needed to be aware of the pain but not dwell on it, wish it were otherwise, or curse my lack of fitness. I reminded myself not to regard the walk as an endurance test, a challenge to my toughness, or a confrontation between ego and world. The way is the way; just proceed. The Henro Michi has existed for a long time, and it would exist long after I'd disappeared. My ego, that fantasy of myself as the center of the universe, had to humble itself before a reality it couldn't control. No excuses, no complaints; let the pain go and just walk. In short, I had to get over myself.

Of course this was easy to say and hard to do. Shedding the ego, especially its propensity for self-pity, is like trying to plug a leaking water pipe with chewing gum. You have to keep applying more gum. But that's what I did, and somehow it worked. I stayed in my head as much as possible and let my internal monologue on pilgrim psychology carry me through the day. I put one foot in front of the other, swung my walking stick with reasonable rhythm, and let the rain be rain and the blisters be blisters. I changed my wet socks and bandages when we stopped for a break, taking some comfort in seeing that at least no new blisters had formed and my feet looked no worse.

The passage of generations of pilgrims had worn the trail to bedrock in places, forcing us to wade through narrow gullies that ran fast with muddy rivulets. When we weren't splashing through water we slogged through mud. We stopped repeatedly to scrape the heavy globs from our boots, which of course transferred more pink blossoms to our pants and jackets. By the time we passed the two snarling *niō* statues guarding the gate to Temple Twenty, we looked like a trio of demented clowns, speckled in cherry blossoms from head to toe. Even without our packs it had taken nearly two hours to climb four kilometers.

Kakurinji was a lovely temple, spacious and quiet and redolent with age, set in a forest of cedar and cypress. Buddhist priests have trained here for centuries. The main hall is more than four hundred years old, and the three-story pagoda is nearly two hundred years old. I admired the two three-meter-tall bronze cranes on either side of the steps in front of the *hondō*. The crane, a symbol of long life and good fortune, is the national bird of Japan. Another pair of carved wooden cranes stood in front of the giant straw sandals that hung on the *niō* gate. One crane had its mouth open, and the other had its mouth closed; together they were saying "ah" and "um," or "aum." Pilgrims had jammed hundreds of coins into cracks in the wooden bodies of the birds, offerings for a long and prosperous life. The cranes looked as though they were dressed in armor. I added my three-yen worth, thinking of my wife and son as well as myself.

Luckily, it took less than an hour to descend the mountain. And the rain eased up to provide a pleasant end to an otherwise miserable day. Maybe the gods were pleased with our efforts. Although we'd climbed in mist and fog, our descent gave us panoramic vistas of terraced valleys and blue peaks. We walked through an orange grove where a murder of crows feasted on mandarins that had fallen to the ground. The gorging birds were loud and raucous, as if intoxicated. The air was ripe with the smell of shredded fruit.

Within minutes of our return to the Kanekoya Ryokan I was soaking in the *o-furo* and sipping a cold can of Kirin beer. Soothed by the steaming water and an easy-on-the-eyes view of the rock garden beyond the window, I let images from the day come and go. Remembering the wooden cranes, I recalled a spring break I'd spent at a Buddhist retreat when I was a university student. I'd been given a mantra for meditation. I hadn't thought of that mantra, much less chanted it, for years. But now, with only the drip of water to disturb the silence of the *o-furo*, it blossomed in my head again, and for a moment I was back in that meditation hall: the mothball smell of the cushions, the aching thigh muscles from sitting in a half-lotus position, and the haunting sound of young acolytes chanting the mantra in the dimly lit room. I took a sip of beer and tried uttering my mantra. It sounded strange from disuse yet at the same time familiar.

✻✻✻

I mumbled the mantra the next day as we trekked to Temple Twenty-One. It wasn't deliberate. My mind had unexpectedly tuned into some cosmic broadcast and "aum" provided the test pattern. At first it was annoying, and I tried to divert myself with other thoughts. But after a while I surrendered and chanted along—"aum, aum, aum." It was like that for most of the morning, and oddly enough I found that concentrating on the mantra seemed to lessen the pain in my feet.

We trekked around a mountain and crossed the Naka River and began the climb to Tairyūji, the Great Dragon Temple, one of the most beautiful on the Shikoku route. We wanted to reach two temples that day, Tairyūji and Byōdōji—a distance of about twenty-five kilometers. Tairyūji stands at an elevation of 618 meters. I remembered that the travel writer Ed Readicker-Henderson referred to Tairyūji as "a test of the *henro*'s dedication and stamina."[15] I passed, but barely. On the other hand, it was a beautiful day. The rain had surrendered to sunshine. We walked in green-tinted sunlight on narrow country lanes that ran along the edges of ravines rushing with spring runoff. The air was cool and sweet with cedar. As we climbed, the lane became a path cutting into a valley with tree slopes closing in on us. Buttercups, violets, and wild iris lined the path. The valley narrowed into a gorge that gradually sank into the ground until we were traversing a trench so deep in places that I could brush my hands along the wet, mossy rocks and bulking roots that protruded from the earthen walls. If I hadn't been able to see the slit of sky above me, it would have been easy to believe I was walking underground. I thought of the millions of pilgrims who had walked here before me, each generation digging the trench a little deeper with their passing.

The path to Tairyūji gradually steepened, becoming slippery and treacherous. We had to walk carefully, concentrating on where we placed our feet. By the time we reached the temple my legs were trem-bling. I saw spots before my eyes and found a bench to sit on before I fainted. I lowered my head between my knees and waited, imagining my body pitching face forward on the white gravel walkway, felled by a heart attack. But after a few minutes, focusing on my bootlaces, my eyes cleared and the lightheadedness passed.

Shūji and Jun hovered nearby. They, too, were tired, but they waited to see if I was all right. When it seemed that I wasn't going to pass out, Jun handed me a bottle of Pocari Sweat. I thanked him and swallowed most of the icy lime drink all at once. I'd consumed three bottles of water during the climb, but judging by my wet clothes, I had sweated it out. I suspected I was dehydrated and in need of an electrolyte boost. I assured them I just needed to sit for a while. Satisfied, Shūji went off to perform his rituals at the *hondō* and the *daishidō*, while Jun lay down to nap on a nearby bench. I skipped the rituals and settled for having my visit recorded in the *nōkyōchō* and listening to the mantra in my head. I told myself that Kōbō Daishi would understand. After all, he'd climbed this mountain himself in his search for enlightenment, and maybe he was hearing things, too, by the time he got to the top.

Tairyūji, founded in 789, is one of the few Shikoku temples where there is definite evidence of Kōbō Daishi's presence. I'd read that in one of his books, the *Sangōshīki*, he refers to the months he spent at the temple chanting a mantra one million times, hoping for satori. "I diligently practiced the Buddhist way in the mountain of Tairyū-ga-dake," he wrote. "The valley reverberated to the resounding echoes of my recitation until the morning star appeared in the sky."[16] One time, as legend has it, Kōbō Daishi threw himself off the mountain, believing that if he were fated to be a religious leader, the Buddha would save him. Buddha did. There was no way I was going to try the same test. My faith wasn't very strong.

When I felt better I gazed around the temple grounds. Tairyūji was lovely. Surrounded by a forest of huge cedars, the temple compound—with its stately, weatherworn halls, moss-draped statues, and pathways shaded by cherry trees—felt secluded and unworldly. The bench where I sat was on a gravel avenue lined by a row of ancient cedars. In front of me, built into a rock face, was a set of stairs that climbed to the main hall and the *daishidō* in addition to the two-story pagoda. Halfway up the stairs was a *shōrō*. Remembering my efforts in the bell tower of Temple Twelve a few days earlier, I got to my feet and climbed the stairs to ring the bell. It didn't hurt to remind the presiding deities that I'd made it this far.

The second temple of that day, Byōdōji, is on the outskirts of Aratano, a country town on the banks of the Kuwano River. Fortunately, we didn't have to walk. We descended Tairyū Mountain for Aratano the easy way. A kilometer from Temple Twenty-One is a cable-car system—the Japanese call it a "ropeway"—that drops down the mountainside to the town of Wajiki. It's the longest ropeway in western Japan, plunging 422 meters over a distance of 2,775 meters. The view was spectacular: forest-thick mountain peaks marching away to the blue horizon. When we got to the bottom, we had only ten kilometers to walk to Byōdōji, Temple Twenty-Two.

It was a pleasant walk despite the pain in my feet. We rambled along a series of mountain ridges that looked down on copses of gray-green bamboo. The trail eventually plunged into the bamboo forests. Smooth celadon trunks swayed overhead in the wind, their slender new leaves pale green against the sky. Again I chanted "aum" for the next few kilometers.

After two days of climbing mountains, those last few kilometers to Temple Twenty-Two were a stroll in the park. Still, by the time we reached Byōdōji late in the afternoon, I was dragging with fatigue, and my feet felt as if some demon were taking perverse delight in testing the sharpness of knitting needles. Shūji and Jun also showed signs of exhaustion. Jun limped as badly as I did. As soon as we performed the temple rituals and had our record books stamped, we staggered up the street to the Zazanaka *minshuku*.

We had a homecoming of sorts. Sayama-san and Murakoshi-san had arrived an hour earlier. But we also gained a new member for our loose-knit pilgrim family—Tomatsu Hasegawa, a metallurgical engineer for Toyota who lived near Tokyo. I guessed him to be in his mid-thirties. He was walking as much of the Henro Michi as he could during his vacation.

Supper that night was a kind of celebration. After surviving the trek to two hard-to-reach temples, everyone felt a mixture of relief, fatigue, and anxiety. There was only Yakuōji, Temple Twenty-Three, to get to before we left Tokushima Prefecture and entered Kōchi Prefecture, the second leg of the pilgrimage. Tradition says that Tokushima, with its twenty-three temples, is the province where pilgrims become aware of their spiritual longings. In Kōchi, with its sixteen temples, we're supposed to be engaged in ascetic discipline. The consensus around the dinner table was that Kōchi would be even harder than Tokushima. After our meal we sat in the dining room drinking Kirin beer, watching sumo wrestling on television, and comparing blisters. Although all of us had them, mine seemed to be the worst. Hasegawa-san offered me strips of the adhesive tape he had for wrapping his own feet.

I noticed that Jun had gone to bed. Usually he wanted a language lesson after supper. I asked Shūji if Jun was okay. He shook his head. I caught the word *tsukareta*, tired. He was worried that Jun was flagging. I remembered how important this pilgrimage was to Shūji, and I resolved to do what I could to encourage Jun.

Two local men came into the dining room, which also served as the neighborhood *nawanoren*, a traditional tavern or workingman's bar. The word means "rope curtain" and refers to the shop curtain, or *noren*, that hangs from a *nawa*, or rope, from the top of the doorframe of many Japanese shops, restaurants, and bars. After the introductions and bows, the two men—Iwano-san and Shigeno-san—insisted that I share their bottle of sake. They wanted to know what a gaijin was doing on the Henro Michi. Was I a Buddhist? Did I know about Kōbō Daishi? Did I recite the Hannya Shingyō at the temples? I deployed some of my stock responses: I was a journalist, a *jānarisuto*, and I worked for a daily newspaper, a *nikkanshi*, in Canada. I was interested in Japanese culture. I liked long-distance treks. Hasegawa-san, who spoke English well, came to my rescue for the more complex questions, making sense of and translating my mix of English and pidgin Japanese.

We finished the sake as they offered a toast and encouraged me, "gambatte kudasai," "do your best"—the standard exhortation among pilgrims. When I tried to pay my share of the bill, they waved me off, saying "settai."

Settai is the traditional practice on Shikoku in which locals offer hospitality to pilgrims—everything from gifts of food and articles of clothing to free lodging and money. Tradition obliges pilgrims to accept the donations. Those offering *settai* think of themselves as giving indirectly to Kōbō Daishi. Thus they share in the merits of the pilgrimage.[17] During my pilgrimage, I received cups of tea, oranges, towels, free meals, and in a few cases money. Once, a woman on a bicycle rode up to me, pulled a wallet from her bag, and thrust 1,000 yen—worth about $10 at the time—into my hand. Then she pedaled away without speaking. Behind the tradition of *settai* is the folk belief that the pilgrim might be Kōbō Daishi, and it never hurts to side with the saints.

The sake wasn't my only *settai* that night. The *okami-san*, the lady of the house, noticed that I was limping and insisted on inspecting my feet. She clucked her tongue and shook her head at the blistered, iodine-stained skin. She disappeared and returned with a pair of white socks that had separate sleeves for each toe in the same way that gloves have for fingers. I'd never seen such socks before. But as I soon discovered, they were great for walking because the toes didn't rub together. I would go through three pairs before the end of my trek. I thanked her and tried to pay for them, but she refused. "Settai," she said.

I bowed and touched the socks to my forehead in the traditional gesture for accepting *settai*. I also filled out an *osamefuda* and gave it to her, making sure to use both hands palms up as I held it out. The *okami-san* laughed, surprised that I knew the proper etiquette for acknowledging *settai*. She took my name slip and laid it at the foot of the Buddha statue in the small household shrine.

I took the socks to my room. It was only 8 p.m., but pilgrims go to bed early. Besides, I wanted to give my feet as much rest as possible. I was about to turn off the light when I heard tapping on the wooden frame of the *shōji*.

"Dōzo, ohairi kudasai." "Please, come in."

It was the *okami-san*, returning my clothes—washed, pressed, and folded. I noticed in the morning that my bill didn't include a laundry charge. More *settai*. I didn't know it then, but I would receive many such blessings in the weeks to come, *settai* and otherwise.

3

Blessings

A moss-worn Jizō
in a field—
pilgrim's road.
—SHŪJI NIWANO

I was parked on a bench beneath the *sakura*, or cherry trees, at Ya-kuōji temple, admiring my ugly new shoes, when a man carrying a little girl in his arms approached. He said something in Japanese that I didn't catch, but with a camera in hand, the child in the crook of his arm, and the cherry trees in bloom, it wasn't hard to figure out what he wanted.

"Gomen nasai. Nihongo wa sukoshi shika dekimasen. Wakarima-shita," I said, employing my minimalist Japanese. "I'm sorry. I speak only a little Japanese. I understand."

I snapped pictures of them posing beneath the trees. The child looked to be about three years old, and like many Japanese children she was extraordinarily pretty—almost doll-like. The man asked in passable English where I was from. I explained that I was a *henro* from Canada. He seemed impressed.

"Ah, henro-san," the man said, addressing the little girl in his arms. She wasn't impressed. She was grabbing at blossoms on the swaying branch of one of the trees. "I have been to Canada," he said. "I visited Vancouver, Banff, and Calgary. Very beautiful."

I complimented him on his English and tried to say how much I liked Japan. "Nihon wa totemo utsukushii desu," I said. "Japan is very beautiful."

We continued in this stilted fashion for a bit. I learned that he was a retired schoolteacher from Osaka and that he and his wife were car pilgrims, driving around the island with his son and daughter-in-law, visiting the temples. The child was his *magomusume*, or granddaughter.

He set the little girl at his feet. She clung to his arm, staring up at me with her dark eyes. He pulled out his wallet, extracted a 1,000-yen note—about $10—and handed it to me.

"Dōzo, settai," he said.

I was obliged as a pilgrim to accept the offering. I bowed and thanked him, touching the bill to my forehead in the proper gesture.

"I tell my granddaughter you are Kōbō Daishi," the man said. He then smiled and bowed, picked the child up, and walked away.

I probably shouldn't have been surprised at the reference to the founder of the Henro Michi. It was a common, if idealistic, way of referring to pilgrims. As the man walked away along the flagstone path with the child back in his arms, the girl watched me over his shoulder. I couldn't resist: I raised my arms and waggled my hands with my thumbs in my ears and stuck out my tongue. The child's eyes got even bigger. I imagined that for the rest of her life she'd be puzzled by this vague childhood memory of a hairy-faced "saint" making faces at her.

But if the child was disconcerted, so was I at my improbable spiritual elevation, even if it was a pilgrimage commonplace. It was the second time that day that someone had identified me with one of Japan's greatest religious leaders. Another tradition of the Henro Michi—and another reason that *settai* is both offered and accepted—is the belief that Kōbō Daishi walks with each pilgrim as a spiritual guide.[1] The unsaid message is: Be careful when you meet a pilgrim, you might also be meeting the saint himself, an encounter that could decide your karma for millennia to come. Watching the man and his granddaughter disappear down the stairs behind one of the temple pagodas, I wondered at his words and all the other coincidences of the day.

Yakuōji, Temple Twenty-Three, is perched on a hillside overlooking Hiwasa, a town halfway along the coastline toward Cape Muroto on Shikoku's southern tip. From the terraced courtyard where I'd been contemplating the marvel of my new shoes, I had a bird's-eye view across the red-and-gray-tile roofs of the town to the harbor and the Pacific Ocean beyond. It was pleasant to sit there in the late afternoon, absorbing the warmth of the sun, watching the green-hulled fishing boats puttering in and out of the harbor, and inhaling the smell of salt and kelp on the occasional breezes that shook the cherry trees and scattered blossoms like confetti around the red-and-white pagoda.

For the next week or so I would seldom be out of sight of the ocean. The pilgrim trail descends the eastern verge of Cape Muroto before rounding the cape to follow the coastline west to Cape Ashizuri. Sometimes the trail cuts inland, but mostly it hugs the coast. In the old days, the path went along the shoreline, and pilgrims had to scramble over what Statler describes as "jumping stones, bucking stones, tumbling stones."[2] These days, though, the pilgrim path generally follows Highway 55.

I watched the boats for a long time, thinking how the whole tableau before me—sea and sun, temple and cherry blossoms—was a cliché of ordinary postcard beauty. Yet the scene, like the entire day, felt extraordinary. It's not that anything spectacular happened on this day; I hadn't attained satori, much less Buddhahood. Somehow, though, the ordinariness of the day's events had heightened significance. Mundane occurrences, serendipitous situations, banal circumstances—they were all brushed with a patina of portent.

Was I slipping into spiritual solipsism? My education in Western scientific rationalism had taught me that the cosmos is contingent, without inherent purpose and devoid of ultimate meaning, and that the material world isn't saturated with or influenced by any spiritual essence or presence. Nonetheless, after nearly a week on the Henro Michi, I'd experienced a string of coincidences and beneficial occurrences that had me a bit spooked. Sitting on the bench as the cherry blossoms fell on me and staring across the town to the harbor, I realized that the whole day—getting to Hiwasa, acquiring my new shoes, receiving the blessing of *settai*—provided an example of how a pilgrimage turns the ordinary into the extraordinary and, in turn, deepens the pilgrim mind.

Shūji, Jun, and I had left the *minshuku* in Aratano around 7 a.m. We'd planned to head south to Fukui Dam and then hike through the maze of rice paddies and rural lanes to the coastal road that leads to Hiwasa, avoiding as much of Highway 55 and all its trucks and tractor trailers as we could. It looked to be perfect walking weather—hazy and cool, without the threat of rain—but our plans started to unravel almost immediately. Jun was not well. Normally he was chatty and eager in the morning, and he and I would walk together for the first hour or so, letting Shūji hike by himself. We'd swap words in our respective languages for things we saw along the road, or he'd teach me how to express particular sentiments. I even picked up a fair lexicon of Japanese swear words. As Jun endlessly repeated, "I am your Japanese teacher."

At other times, however, Jun trudged ahead by himself, sometimes wandering off the pilgrim route. Despite his age, Jun showed little ability to read maps and invariably got lost. Shūji regularly had to double back to find him, questioning passersby who might have seen his son. He carried out his searches with fatalistic good humor, one of the burdens of fatherhood. Almost inevitably, Shūji found Jun sauntering along with a can of soda or an orange he'd cajoled as *settai* from some shopkeeper. But for all his waywardness and lack of forethought, Jun's cheerfulness and desire to please gave him a certain charm that made it hard to judge too harshly his apparent irresponsibility and inattentiveness.

This morning, though, Jun wasn't his usual self. There were no language lessons. I wasn't doing that well, either. I still had a bad case of blisters and wasn't so much walking as lurching. Shūji, too, looked haggard and puffy-eyed, as if he hadn't slept. Jun, he said, had been sick to his stomach most of the night. We managed to walk five kilometers to the village of Awafukui before Jun collapsed.

Oddly enough, I would remember those few kilometers as one of the loveliest walks of my pilgrimage. The path wound along the edges of rice fields, slowly turning green with newly planted seedlings, and meandered down country lanes lined with groves of bamboo. In some places maples and oaks grew so close to the sides of the road that it was like walking in a green tunnel. Nightingales formed a choir in the trees, competing with a chorus of cicadas in the underbrush. Tendrils of moss crawled across the narrow lanes, using cracks in the asphalt as passageways. I stepped carefully, not wanting to mar the reclamation effort.

I was approaching the intersection of Highway 55 when I heard Shūji shouting behind me. I turned and saw Jun on his hands and knees on the shoulder of the road. I dropped my pack and ran back.

"Jun is very tired," Shūji said. "He needs to rest." Jun's face was slack and his eyes, usually bright and animated, glazed with fatigue.

"Kibun wa dō desu ka?" I asked, crouching beside him. "How are you feeling?"

"Fukutsu desu," he mumbled. "I feel sick to my stomach."

It was obvious Jun wouldn't be walking very far that day. While he rested, Shūji and I studied our maps. We were about a kilometer from Fukui Dam, where there was supposedly a large picnic area with a playground. We got Jun to his feet, and ten minutes later he was able to stretch out on a picnic bench and sleep. I dropped my pack at a bank of vending machines and bought cans of hot coffee for Shūji and me. We found a high concrete wall where we could sit out of the wind. I had to admit it was pleasant not to be walking and, instead, enjoying a can of coffee hot in my hands and the sun warm on my face and my outstretched legs.

"Robāto-san, you have been a good friend, walking with us," Shūji said.

"Dōmo arigatō," I said. "We are tomodachi, friends." I tipped my can of coffee to him.

Shūji smiled and nodded his understanding. Then he said that Jun needed to sleep for a couple of hours. "I am sorry," he said. "Jun is not strong. He cannot walk so far today. I am sorry for upsetting your walking."

I almost laughed. His son was sick, but Shūji was worried about messing up my schedule. I shook my head. I didn't know how to say the words in Japanese, so I spoke in English: "No need to apologize."

"Perhaps you want to walk alone," Shūji said. "You do not need to wait for us."

For a moment I wondered if he was trying to get rid of me, but looking at his sad-eyed face I realized it was an unworthy notion on my part. Shūji was genuinely concerned that Jun's difficulties were interfering with my pilgrimage. I thought back to a couple of days earlier when he'd told me about Jun suffering some sort of nervous breakdown a few years before and never fully recovering. In reading about the Henro Michi I'd learned that many Japanese pilgrims believe that walking the pilgrimage trail will cure sickness and restore health.[3] This was Shūji's hope for Jun. But now, looking at Shūji's strained face, I had the distinct feeling he was worried about how I would respond to Jun's latest collapse.

I remembered a scene from Oliver Statler's *Japanese Pilgrimage*, one of the few books I was carrying. Statler recounts that on his pilgrimage in 1971 a woman offered him a cup of coffee in her home as *settai* and then begged him to look at her daughter who was ill in bed. Statler knew the tradition behind the woman's request: Kōbō Daishi had miraculous powers of healing. Pilgrims who follow in his footsteps effectively identify themselves with the Buddhist saint and thereby acquire a hint of the Daishi's presence.[4] Statler, however, panicked and refused the woman's request, a decision he later regretted, realizing that he'd been thinking about himself, his own presumed inadequacies. Even if he believed he lacked any healing power, the woman thought otherwise. In rejecting her request, he'd succumbed to the selfishness and the egocentrism of his own Western skepticism.[5] At that moment, watching Shūji, I knew I didn't want to make the same mistake. I remembered how he and Jun had looked out for me, a stranger and a foreigner, when I was having difficulty walking. They could easily have left me to my own devices.

"Shūji, please, I do not want to be a burden to you," I said. "If I am, tell me. But I think of you and Jun as friends now. We began walking the Henro Michi together. I would like us to finish together. Wakarimasu ka? Do you understand?"

Shūji took off his glasses, looked at them in his hands, and then replaced them. "Hai, wakarimashita," he said. "Dōmo arigatō gozaimasu, Robāto-san." "I understand. Thank you very much." He put out his hand. "You are Kōbō Daishi."

"Iie. Tomodachi," I said, shaking his hand. "No. Friend."

We settled back against the wall, sipping our coffee. I thought about Japanese attitudes toward religion. According to some scholars, most Japanese are not particularly religious and even describe their society as one in which religion has largely died out. Yet, at the same time, the Japanese demonstrate high levels of religious activity and behavior. They might deny a religious sensibility and even be ignorant of Buddhism and Shinto. But each year millions of Japanese take part in *hatsumōde*, the traditional New Year's custom of visiting temples and shrines to pray for good fortune and happiness. During the summer festival of *o-bon*, they travel in equal number to be with their families to visit ancestral graves. Even if they aren't believers, they still go for social and cultural reasons, taking part in the prayers and making offerings. They buy numerous talismans and amulets as well as *o-mikuji*, the written divinations sold at shrines that foretell the future.[6]

The popularity of pilgrimages—there are hundreds in Japan, large and small—arguably reflects this instinctive spirituality. Those who undertake a pilgrimage, whether by car, bus, or on foot, don't necessarily do so for conscious religious reasons, at least initially. Several pilgrims I met on the Henro Michi told me they set out thinking of their trek not in religious terms but as a break from their everyday routines, an opportunity to reflect on their lives.[7] The religious sensibility, the awareness of a spiritual dimension to their pilgrimage, seemed to develop later. It occurred to me that with his linkage of Kōbō Daishi and me, joking or not, Shūji was starting to slip into the more spiritual aspects of pilgrimage. It wouldn't be uncommon if he did. As I knew from my own experience on the Camino de Santiago, you can start out walking on one kind of journey and end up on something completely different.

We let Jun sleep for a couple of hours and then trudged back up the road to Awafukui train station. It was getting too late for us to reach our next destination easily on foot with Jun feeling the way he did, so we'd decided to take the train. While we waited, Shūji and I ate bowls of udon in the decrepit café next to the station. Jun napped on a bench in the waiting room. We woke him up for the 11:56 departure for Hiwasa.

I felt guilty about not walking—I told myself a day's rest would give my feet a chance to recover—but I also had to admit that it was a treat to sit in a train car as it clacked and creaked through Shikoku's green coastal valleys. The car was nearly empty, with only a couple of girls in their dark blue school uniforms and an elderly woman carrying a bag of onions. Just before Yuki Town, I got my first glimpse of the Pacific Ocean. The sight of the ocean seemed an auspicious way to mark the completion of my first week on the Henro Michi. Two weeks earlier, in my cubbyhole at the office, I'd been anticipating my trip to Japan. Now I was on a Japanese train overlooking the Pacific. I felt displaced, dislocated, and divided, as though I were in two places at once or, more precisely, bouncing back and forth between them. I couldn't have been happier as images of my displacement—this place, then that place, then back again—filled my head. But before I could tie myself in metaphysical knots with fantasies about existing in multiple universes, the swaying of the train lulled me into a nap. I woke up just before 1 p.m. as the train pulled into Hiwasa. What would have taken most of the day to walk had taken an hour by train.

We were soon dropping our packs at the Funatsuki Ryokan. It was too early to check in, but the *okami-san*, a tiny woman with big black horn-rimmed glasses, let Shūji and Jun have their room so that Jun could sleep. I left them to find a post office where I could use the automatic teller to restock my supply of yen. I also wanted to lighten my pack by shipping a few items to a friend in Tokushima, David Moreton, who would keep them for me until I returned at the end of my walk. Afterward, I headed for Yakuōji, Temple Twenty-Three.

On the way to the temple, I stopped at a bar in the square near Hiwasa Station. "Bīru o kudasai," I said, ordering a glass of beer. The half-dozen tables were empty; I was the only customer. It was a sunny day, and I was happy to sit by the window, enjoying the warm sun and the cold beer. Maybe I should take other days off, too, I thought. I removed my boots, wrote some postcards, and drank another beer. Squeezing my feet back into my boots, I then paid the bill, bowed to my hostess, and stepped into the street, where I spotted another *henro* crossing the square. It was Tomatsu Hasegawa, the metallurgist I had met at the *minshuku* in Aratano the previous night. He spotted me and waved as I hobbled toward him.

"Your feet are bad?" he asked.

"Not too good," I shrugged in reply.

Hasegawa-san explained that he'd just checked into his *ryokan*. While Shūji and I had been waiting with Jun at the Fukui Dam, he'd walked from Aratano. Now he was heading to the temple for his devotions. I was welcome to come with him. We started walking, but I couldn't keep up.

"You need other shoes," he said, after having stopped to wait for me a couple of times.

It was the obvious solution but one I hadn't wanted to consider. I'd spent a lot of money on the boots—thick soles, ankle-high uppers,

Gore-Tex lining—and was reluctant to admit it had been a waste. Although my boots were a half-size larger than my normal shoe size, they should have been a full-size larger, and wider, to allow my feet to swell from long-distance walking without being squeezed too much. I'd hoped my feet and boots would find mutual accommodation. But after a week, it was clear that wasn't going to happen. The sensible thing to do was to buy other shoes, regardless of the cost.

Hasegawa-san led me through the narrow streets to a shoe store where—after listening to his instructions, which seemed to entail pointing to me and laughing a great deal—the clerk hauled out half a dozen pairs of running shoes. I tried several of them until I settled on a pair of Nike Air. They really were ugly—blue and gray with sickly splotches of iridescent yellow and that idiotic check-mark-like "swoosh" on the side. Normally I'd never wear something so gaudy. But they were wide and comfortable, and for the first time in days my feet didn't suffer needles of pain when I pressed down. My feet were still sore, but the Nikes—unlike my four-hundred-dollar, all-weather, walk-anywhere, climb-the-highest-mountain boots—didn't make matters worse. They were a real blessing, thanks to Hasegawa-san's intervention.

Another blessing was yet to come. The shoes were 8,000 yen, about $80. When I handed the money to the clerk, he shook his head. I thought he meant I needed to pay more, so I started to hand over more cash. He waved this off, too, and handed me back 3,000 yen.

"Settai," he said.

"Dōmo arigatō," I said, bowing low in gratitude.

***

After getting my new shoes, I walked with Hasegawa-san to the temple to complete our devotions and have our pilgrim books stamped. He then headed back to his *ryokan* for a nap. I decided to linger at the temple. It occurred to me that he'd saved my pilgrimage. I would continue to limp for days to come and would still feel footsore at the end of each hike, but for the first time in a week or so I was confident that my feet would heal and I'd complete my pilgrimage. Perhaps Hasegawa-san was Kōbō Daishi, I thought, as I sat there beneath the cherry trees after the departure of the man and his granddaughter. It had certainly been a stroke of luck on my part to have bumped into him. Or was it "luck" at all, I asked myself.

Yakuōji was the right temple for such questions, rational or not. It is known as a *yaku-yoke* temple—that is, a temple for "danger-banishing prayers." During the first two weeks of every new year, thousands of people visit the temple to pray for good fortune. Traditionally, the Japanese believe there are certain critical ages when men and women need to take extra care with their health and conduct. One of the most dangerous ages for men is forty-two. For women it is thirty-three. Kōbō Daishi supposedly visited the temple grounds when he was forty-two and enshrined a statue of Yakushi Nyorai, a Buddhist deity possessed of wisdom and mercy, in the main hall in the hope of avoiding misfortune. Inside the main gate are two flights of stairs—or *yakuzaka*, "misfortune slopes"—leading to the *hondō*. One set of stairs has thirty-three steps; the other has forty-two.[8]

I wasn't taking any chances. I was older than forty-two, but there are always misfortunes ahead. I climbed the forty-two steps to the main hall, placing coins on each step. I also dropped extra yen in the donation bins in the main hall. And on the off-chance that Kōbō Daishi might have had something to do with the acquisition of my new shoes, I bowed extra low to his statue in the *daishidō*. You never know.

Back on my bench beneath the cherry trees, I thought about the coincidences and circumstances of the day, how each seemingly ordinary event—Jun's illness, the chance meeting with Hasegawa-san, the shoe-store clerk's *settai*, the encounter with the grandfather—had by some alchemy of cause-and-effect culminated in what felt to me to be an extraordinary day. I was, as I well knew from research and past experience, in the grip of a psychological phenomenon common to pilgrimage: ordinary events and situations acquire a significance that belies their ordinariness. Catching a train in the nick of time, having minor aches suddenly disappear, unexpectedly meeting someone who takes care of a particular need— such banal occurrences can seem almost miraculous, encouraging you to imagine that someone or something is watching over you. Pilgrims even come to regard such events as gifts or personal messages from Kōbō Daishi, in the case of the Henro Michi. This is perhaps not surprising, given the symbolism of the pilgrimage—namely, the notion that the pilgrim embodies the saint's presence.[9]

As I pondered my Nikes for spiritual significance, I remembered a haiku the Japanese poet Bashō wrote in his travel journal, *Narrow Road to the Interior*, which I had with me. The journal recounts a journey that Bashō and a companion made in the spring of 1689 as they trekked from Edo, or old Tokyo, along the eastern coast into the then-remote and mysterious northern regions of Honshu. At one point an admirer gave Bashō two pairs of sandals as a gift. The sandals had dark blue laces. The poet was inspired to write: "It looks as if / Iris flowers had bloomed / On my feet."[10]

As I looked at my shoes and their gray laces, I saw nothing to inspire a poem. But that probably said more about my capacity for perception than anything else. It occurred to me that, like Bashō, I needed to learn how to grasp the extraordinariness of the ordinary, to perceive the poetry of the banal.[11] Wiggling my toes and flexing my feet, I knew that the shoes would be sufficient for walking, if not for poetry. With twenty-three temples and about 150 kilometers under my belt—under my feet?—I was happy just knowing the blisters would heal sooner or later. Take care of the physical, I figured, and the blessings of the spirit will sooner or later appear. Besides, given this extraordinary day, maybe Kōbō Daishi was watching over me.

✳✳✳

The next day, as I was tramping past the police station on the outskirts of Mugi Town, a woman in a green hat rushed up to me. Her Japanese was incomprehensible. I could only grin and nod, repeatedly saying, "Wakarimasen." "I don't understand." Spotting a couple of policemen looking at us from a window, I wondered if I had broken some obscure law. Was this woman, waving her hands and gesturing for me to follow her, supposed to fetch me for the police? For one panicked moment, I thought maybe there was an emergency back home, that the RCMP had contacted the Japanese police to be on the lookout for me.

Shūji and Jun came to the rescue. They'd been a few hundred meters behind me all morning since we left Hiwasa. As they approached, the woman turned to them with obvious relief. Shūji explained to me that she was a member of a local group dedicated to serving the walking *henro*. So instead of hauling me into the police station, the woman led us into a parking lot behind the building where a couple of picnic benches were set end-to-end beneath a large awning. The tables were stacked with bananas and apples and oranges. There were plates of crackers, nuts, and candy. A pot of water bubbled on a propane stove. I headed for a cooler filled with soft drinks, fruit juice, and water.

"Settai," said the woman, whose name, as I learned, was Teruko Asaka. She ushered us over to the awning where two other middle-aged women—Fusako Tomida and Yukō Juyako—waited.

To our surprise, Goki Sayama, the retired banker from Sendai, greeted us as we stepped beneath the awning. We hadn't seen him on the trail for a couple of days. He was sitting at the table drinking a cup of tea and peeling an orange. I noticed that he'd pulled his boots off and that tape was wrapped around the balls of his feet. I asked how he was doing.

He looked at his feet and shrugged. "Okagesama de. Sochira wa?" he said, popping a wedge of orange into his mouth. "Very well. And you?"

I shrugged. "Mā-mā." "So-so." I pulled up my pants legs. "I have new shoes." He laughed.

The women urged us to sit. I noticed a can of coffee on a shelf and begged for a cup: "Kōhī, kudasai." A few minutes later I was enjoying my first cup of freshly brewed coffee in more than a week.

We'd covered nearly twenty kilometers since leaving Hiwasa at about 8 a.m., and the walking had been good. I still limped, but the new shoes were much more comfortable than my boots. It was an immense relief to walk without stabs of pain. I sometimes even forgot about my feet, which was a good sign.

I'd almost forgotten about Jun, too. He was still feeling weak, so we planned to walk while he was able and then, if necessary, take a train or bus to Kaifu, where Shūji had reserved rooms at the Saba Daishi temple. I glanced up from my coffee at Jun lying in the shade of a nearby fence. After downing a bowl of miso soup, he told Shūji he wanted to nap.

One of our hostesses took out a register containing the names of passing pilgrims. I couldn't read the Japanese, but flipping through the pages I noticed that most of the henro were in their fifties or sixties. The oldest I saw was eighty-one; the youngest was nineteen.

I asked Sayama-san how old he was.

"Watakushi wa nana-ju san." "I am seventy-three."

"Why do you walk?"

Sayama-san tried his English but reverted to Japanese when he couldn't express himself clearly. Shūji translated: Sayama-san was walking the Henro Michi to think about his family. "He has trouble at home," Shūji said, struggling to find the English words. "Family trouble. He prays for his family."

I remembered reading that for many pilgrims, particularly those who walk, the Henro Michi has little to do with religious faith and more to do with finding a way to escape the pressures of their lives, especially for those middle-aged men who lost their jobs during the recessionary years of the 1990s and 2000s. A few even drop out of society to become permanent pilgrims who repeatedly walk the temple circuit, living off odd jobs and *settai*. Still others, and this I thought applied to Sayama-san, undertake the pilgrimage as a way to think through and sort out personal problems.[12]

I never found out the nature of Sayama-san's troubles—something having to do with one of his sons—but I noticed that as Shūji and Sayama-san talked amongst themselves, they kept glancing at Jun. Maybe they had something in common.

By the time I finished my second cup of coffee, Sayama-san had put on his shoes and shouldered his pack. He bowed to us and then, dignified as ever, walked back to the road, around the corner of a building, and out of sight. I never saw him again. Shūji, Jun, and I left a short time later, after thanking the women and adding our names to the register. Mine was the only non-Japanese name, so far as I could tell.

We walked for an hour, following the highway above the ocean, before Jun pleaded for another break. We found a path that led down to a strip of beach. We set our packs on a small knoll beneath some palm trees. Jun curled up to sleep. Shūji sat near him and took out his notebook. Someday, I thought, I had to ask Shūji what he was writing. I trundled down to the beach, propped myself against a gnarled piece of driftwood, and stretched out on the sand.

I watched a kite riding the air above a distant headland. A freighter moved slowly across the blue horizon. Then, out of the blue, a memory came to mind. I remembered another ship on another horizon and an afternoon in the fall of 1970 with a woman I'd been seeing, Nilla Brown, on the rock-strewn beach below Point-No-Point on the western coast of Vancouver Island. We'd huddled together out of the wind and watched a ship churn through the Strait of Juan de Fuca toward the Pacific Ocean. The memory surprised me. I hadn't thought of Nilla for a long time. Older than I, she'd been separated from her husband when we met. We'd had a short affair before she returned to him. Watching the passing ship, I wondered what had happened to her.

I must have drifted off because when I heard someone shouting my name, I thought for a few disoriented seconds that I was at Point-No-Point again. I looked back up the slope of the beach. Shūji and Jun were on their feet, with packs on their backs. Standing beside them was Tomatsu Hasegawa. Walking up the sloping beach to join them, I paused to look back at where I'd been lying. I wanted to remember the spot where a long-forgotten memory of another place and another time returned to me.

"How are your feet?" Hasegawa-san asked.

"Good. Thanks to you, I can walk," I replied. "You are Kōbō Daishi."

I walked with Hasegawa-san for the next few hours. He told me he was using two weeks of his vacation to walk as far as he could. He'd been on the trail for nearly a week and expected to reach Kōchi City and Temple Thirty-One before having to return home. Next year, he would do another two weeks of pilgrimage.

"In my job everything is quick, quick," he said. "Walking gives me time to think about things that are important to me."

We reached Kaifu about 4 p.m. A stone marker sent us down a narrow lane to Saba Daishi temple. The temple is one of dozens of *bangai*, or unnumbered temples, scattered across Shikoku. While they aren't officially part of the temple circuit, they still attract pilgrims. Saba Daishi is one of the more famous. Twice a year, the temple stages an outdoor *hiwatari*, or fire-walk ceremony, during which the priests and willing visitors walk barefoot the length of a five-meter pit of hot coals. The fire walk is one of the great rituals of Shingon Buddhism.

Unfortunately—or perhaps fortunately, since I would have been tempted to try it, blisters be damned—there was no fire walk scheduled during our stay. But after a supper of kelp soup, bonito sashimi, mushroom-and-shrimp pudding, and vegetable tempura, Hasegawa-san asked if I wanted to attend the next best thing, an indoor *goma*, or fire ritual, early in the morning.

I said yes, so he took me to see a temple priest to register for the ceremony. With Hasegawa-san translating, the priest asked if there was anyone I wanted to commemorate in the ceremony. "Watashi no otōsan," I said, hoping I'd used the correct phrasing. "My father."

I selected a narrow strip of cedar known as a prayer stick and spelled out my father's name, Albert, on a piece of paper for the priest to follow. Hasegawa-san also wanted to commemorate his father. The priest dipped his brush into an ink well and painted our fathers' names on prayer sticks before placing them on a pile of others at the side of his desk. During the *goma*, as I would find out, priests would toss them one by one into the fire as they chanted prayers for the souls of the departed.

We bought two cans of Kirin beer from a vending machine in the lobby of the *shukubō* and went to my room. Sitting on the tatami at the low table, Hasegawa-san explained that he and his father had planned to walk the Henro Michi, but his father had died two weeks before they were to leave.

"Now I am walking alone in his memory."

"You will always miss him," I said, telling Hasegawa-san that my father had been dead for twenty years, but there probably hadn't been a day since his death when I didn't think of him.

Hasegawa-san nodded. "Hai. Itsumo." "Always." He lifted his beer in a toast. "You and me, the same. No father."

We drank to ourselves and to our absent fathers.

Hasegawa-san rattled the *shōji* panel of my room at 5 a.m. Half an hour later I was sitting cross-legged on a tatami-covered floor in an octagonal room with two dozen other pilgrims in the near-darkness of the Fudō hall. Around the perimeter, flickering candlelight picked up several large black-and-gold statues of Fudō Myōō, the fierce-faced deity who defends the Buddhist faith and represents "fatherly strictness." I could also see between the larger figures hundreds of foot-tall statues of Ashura the Guardian lining the walls. The service began when four priests in burgundy robes silently entered the room. The head priest climbed a raised platform and sat facing the glowing embers of an open fire pit below the dais. The other priests took positions around the dais. One stood in front of a kettledrum and a gong hanging from a rope, while the other two lit sticks of incense and candles in the small urns that sat along the edge of the dais. Silence settled on us.

The sudden chime of a bell startled me. The sound seemed to take a long time to fade. Then the gong sounded, its echo filling the room. The priest on the dais began to chant, spreading and folding his arms over the smoldering fire as if gathering the smoke to himself. The other priests joined the chant. The head priest then started to drop thin sticks into the fire. As the flames grew, the drumming became steady and insistent, louder and louder, and the chanting fast and urgent. The sounds filled my chest and head. As the fire leapt high out of the pit, the priest inserted the *gomagi*, the prayer sticks, one by one into the flames. With each stick, he read out a name. If I'd understood Japanese better I might have caught my father's name being uttered. I watched the thickening column of smoke, imagining the ascension of souls. I glanced at Hasegawa-san beside me. The candlelight caught the gleam of tears on his face. I was near tears myself.

After the last of the *gomagi* went into the flames, the priest allowed the fire to die. As it subsided, so did the chanting and drumming. When the prayers were over, the priest gave a short sermon—none of which I understood except the final phrase, "gambatte kudasai," "do your best"—after which our group was invited to walk around the smoldering fire. We imitated the priest by waving our hands through the tendrils of smoke and rubbing those parts of our bodies that we believed needed divine blessing. I rubbed my head.

Leaving the *goma* room, I took a last look at Fudō Myōō, the light from the fire and candles playing across his fierce face. He carries a sword to smite those who surrender to delusion and evil and reserves his hostility for those who continue to live in arrogance and ignorance. But he also assumes the sufferings of human beings. A good model for a father, I thought. I offered a final nod to the deity and followed my fellow pilgrims through a dimly lit tunnel, lined with small pictures of temples, and back to the *shukubō*.

Shūji and Jun were waiting for us in the foyer. Jun was slouching half-asleep beside his backpack. Shūji looked apologetic as he explained that Jun was not up to walking again. In my less charitable moods I sometimes thought that Jun was goofing off and just lacked the will to overcome his weaknesses. I squatted beside him.

"How do you feel?" I asked.

He looked at me, making an effort to focus his attention. "Tired."

The lack of focus in his eyes told me Jun wasn't faking. The thought came unbidden: What would Fudō Myōō do? Smite the weakness or make allowances? I'd read about a social phenomenon plaguing Japan: young people turning away from society, including friends and parents, refusing to leave the house, and sinking into self-isolation. This can last for weeks, months, and even years. Japanese psychologists have labeled the phenomenon *hikikomori*, social withdrawal. It is especially prevalent among young men in their late teens and twenties. Typically, they live the reverse of normal life, sleeping during the day and then watching television, playing video games, or surfing the Internet through the night. For the most part, they aren't violent. There have been reports, however, of *hikikomori* sufferers attacking family members, including their parents.

Some authorities link the phenomenon to Japan's economy. There aren't enough jobs or university placements for the young, and the competition is too stiff for the openings that do exist. Still, I wondered about the point made in an essay by the novelist Ryu Murakami, who argued that it was because of the affluence of the older generation that the younger generation was able to withdraw from society.[13]

Was Jun a victim of *hikikomori*? He didn't seem to show symptoms of "social withdrawal." His gregarious behavior and desire to befriend others seemed almost desperate at times, but more as a sign of immaturity than as a form of social pathology. True, he took no responsibility for planning each day, and he smoked incessantly, lighting up a cigarette when we took even the shortest break. But he was always friendly and helpful when called upon. He was always offering me something to drink or eat. And the only aggression I saw, at least to that point, was the occasional shouting match with his father.

Crouched beside Jun, I thought that perhaps I could strike off on my own or, glancing up at Hasegawa-san, continue with my new friend. The walking was beginning to absorb me despite the aches and pains. Taking buses and trains marred the purity of the pilgrimage. But I knew I couldn't abandon Shūji. I'd come to like him, admiring his stoicism and his patience with Jun. I remembered my own words from the previous day: we'd started the Henro Michi together and we would finish together. Wasn't that what Fudō Myōō would do?

Looking at Shūji, I asked, "Can we take a train or bus part of the way and walk when Jun feels better?"

The relief on Shūji's face was palpable. "Yes, that would be good," he answered, bowing. "Thank you."

To my surprise, Hasegawa-san said he would like to join us. "I could use an easy day," he added.

The four of us walked to Kainan and caught the 7:51 a.m. commuter train to Kannoura, where we boarded a bus to Cape Muroto and Hotsumisakiji, Temple Twenty-Four. We reached the cape about 9:30. In less than an hour we covered a fifty-five-kilometer stretch that would have taken at least two days to walk. I felt guilty yet also relieved. I wasn't the purest of pilgrims, but my feet were grateful.

***

I also enjoyed the bus ride. Highway 55 curved along the top of cliffs above the Pacific Ocean, winding through fishing villages, crossing forested hills, and diving into shadowy gorges. The ocean appeared in sudden gaps, the shore meeting the sea in a clash of rock and water. The eastern side of Cape Muroto was especially rugged, a long scarp of serrated rock plunging into the sea. From my window seat I stared straight down on the white froth of water as it lashed rocks as big as houses. Dozens of Jizō statues lined the edge of the road. It was like seeing an old friend.

When we reached Cape Muroto, Shūji had the driver drop us at a bus stop across from the caves where, according to tradition, Kōbō Daishi had holed up between the ages of nineteen and twenty-one as he struggled to attain enlightenment, the true nature of his mind. The caves were set at the back of a horseshoe-shaped cove. Inside, they were damp and claustrophobic, and the sound of the ocean seemed far away. There was barely room to stand upright, and the rock seemed to press down on us. Neat piles of stones surrounded a series of small shrines at the back of each cave. I tried to imagine what it was like for the young Kōbō Daishi—then known by his family name of Mao—to live alone for months in these caves, seeking something my modern mind, trained to regard the world as spiritless matter, denied as real. Poking around the caves, I remembered that Statler had written about Kōbō Daishi's sojourn in the caves. I pulled his book from my pack and read.

In his first book, *Sangōshiki*, written when he was twenty-four, Mao described climbing the hill where Hotsumisakiji now stands and deciding he wouldn't leave until he achieved enlightenment. One morning, after three years in the caves, the spirit of Kokuzō Bosatsu, the deity who represents the wisdom of the Buddha, filled Mao as he watched Venus on the horizon. He achieved enlightenment and took the name Kūkai, which means "sky and sea together."[14]

I slouched out of the caves and down the sloping frontage through the palm trees to the ocean. The sea was perhaps three hundred meters away, booming louder and louder as I walked toward it. The waves roared up the shingle, grating and grinding the stones like cement in a mixer. Cape Muroto is where many of the typhoons that hit Japan come ashore at their most violent point. It must have taken immense discipline—as well as immense longing—to live in a dim and damp cave, while nature groaned and howled just meters away, and hope to hear that quiet inner voice of the divine. I had to admire Kūkai—and envy him. I picked up a stone from the shore and returned to the cave to add my contribution to the makeshift shrines.

The path to Hotsumisakiji, Temple Twenty-Four, was a short distance from the caves. It climbed steeply 165 meters above sea level to the temple compound. The view was panoramic, but I was disappointed in the temple. I expected a monument more in keeping with the place that commemorates Kōbō Daishi's attainment of ultimate wisdom. The Temple of the Cape reminded me of a house in need of renovation. The courtyard with its gravel-and-flagstone paths was neat and tidy, but the pagoda's red paint was faded to a dull pink. The wooden walls of the *hondō* and the *daishidō* were gray and weatherworn from the storms that lash the cape. But then it occurred to me that maybe the wear and tear imposed by climate and geography hinted at some of the insights that Kūkai gained from his years in the caves—namely, the futility of human illusions in the face of nature's power. As we left the temple, descending a series of switchbacks toward Muroto City, I realized that my view of the green fields and the vast ocean—"the open Pacific, the limitless horizon," as Statler put it—would have been familiar to Kōbō Daishi, and for a moment I imagined him standing beside me.[15]

Beyond Cape Muroto, the coastline of southern Shikoku loops for three hundred kilometers in a crescent to the black-rock headland

of Cape Ashizuri. Numerous indentations of beaches and fishing villages scallop the crescent all the way to Kōchi City. Shūji had booked
rooms for the four of us at a *shukubō* attached to Temple Twenty-Six,
Kongōchōji, on a hill west of Muroto City. It was sixteen kilometers
from Temple Twenty-Four to Temple Twenty-Six.

Wandering through the narrow streets of Muroto City, we passed
a lumberyard. The sharp tang of freshly cut wood reminded me of my
grandfather's work shed at the end of the garden at his house, where I
spent summer afternoons as a boy. The memory was so sharp and vivid
that, for the briefest moment, I smelled the fresh pine boards and saw
the curled shavings covering the dirt floor.

Pilgrimage generates many psychological phenomena, but one of
the strongest is its out-of-time quality when, as sometimes happens,
seemingly forgotten events resurface. It's as though through the reduc-
tion of life to walking, eating, and sleeping, the mind finds time to rum-
mage around in the nooks and crannies of memory. Recollections of
long-ago girlfriends and long-dead grandfathers meant that I was slipping into the pilgrim mind. This was as it should be. My mind was
starting to wander on its own, even as my body walked. Or perhaps
Kōbō Daishi was being generous.

Indeed, I was tempted to think we'd received another blessing from
the saint when, at Shinshōji, Temple Twenty-Five, we added another
member to our *henro* troop, Harumi Nakatsuji. She was a nurse from
a town in Nara Prefecture near Osaka. I guessed her to be in her early
thirties. She'd just finished her devotions and was resting in the temple
garden with its miniature pagodas and little red bridge across a pond
when we showed up. Shūji and Hasegawa-san introduced me.

"Hajimemashite," I said. "How do you do."

She said something I didn't understand. Hasegawa-san translated,
explaining that Harumi-san was surprised to see a foreigner on the Shikoku pilgrimage and even more surprised that I could speak Japanese.

"Sukoshi," I said. "Watashi wa nihongo ga sukoshi hanasemasu." "A
little. I speak only a little Japanese."

Harumi-san, it turned out, was between nursing jobs and had spent
the last two weeks on the pilgrimage route as a break before finding
another job. We all liked her, but she was a godsend for Shūji. She was
patient with Jun, willing to listen to his chattering for hours as they

walked. Shūji later told me that she'd given him good advice about Jun. I walked with her sometimes, even though we couldn't speak each other's language. I asked her why she chose the Henro Michi.

She said something I couldn't follow. Hasegawa-san translated: walking helped her to feel peaceful. She was unsure what she wanted to do with her life, and the Henro Michi offered her a chance to think about her future.

On that first day, Harumi-san joined us later for supper in the dining hall at Kongōchōji. She applauded my ability with chopsticks, or *hashi*, although I suspect she was being polite because she then insisted on teaching me how to hold them properly. It seems I was gripping the chopsticks too close to the narrow ends. I should hold them about a third of the way down from the top of the shaft. My mishandling cost me leverage, which explained why I had difficulty picking up smaller morsels of tofu and rice. I was supposed to set the bottom stick in the crook of my thumb and on the third finger, while the thumb, first, and second fingers managed the movement of the upper stick. Spearing food with chopsticks was improper. Also, Harumi-san told me, when food is set before me, it was a matter of politeness to bow to the server and say "itadakimasu," "I humbly receive." At the end of the meal, I should again bow and say "gochisōsama deshita," "I have been treated."

Harumi-san walked with us for the next three days on the way to Kōchi City, so I had plenty of opportunity to improve my *hashi* skills— and my manners.

From Kongōchōji, Temple Twenty-Six, the pilgrim trail cut through a mix of forests and farms, suburbs and factories. We trundled past rows of greenhouses filled with flowers and fruit, climbed sun-dappled forest paths, and leaned over seawalls to watch fishing boats unload their catches. We trudged past scrap yards and across rice fields. We wound through village lanes so narrow that I could touch the buildings on both sides. Normally, because some walked faster than others, we were strung out along the road throughout the day, coming together in the late afternoon at a temple or hotel. Shūji handled the reservations—our map books contained hotels, *ryokan*, and *minshuku* that catered to *henro*—and phoned each morning to book rooms for the night.

The first two days after Temple Twenty-Six were long, leg-aching hikes—twenty-eight and thirty-eight kilometers, respectively. The hardest stretch was to the coastal town of Yasuda and Temple Twenty-Seven. Kōnomineji is on a mountain summit about three kilometers inland from Yasuda, and it's considered one of Shikoku's difficult temples. To my surprise, I found it not that difficult.

On the second day, traveling from Yasuda to Temple Twenty-Eight, Dainichiji, in the town of Noichi, we slogged through farm fields and rice paddies, meeting in the evening at the Hotel Kiraku just below the temple. To everybody's relief, especially Shūji's, Jun walked largely without complaint, although he was staggering with fatigue by the end of the day. We made a point of praising his efforts, but I suspect his willingness to walk had more to do with Harumi-san's presence than any cajoling from Shūji or me.

Despite my aching legs and sore feet, I was learning to appreciate the blessings of pilgrimage: a pretty girl by the name of Yumike Saite, who insisted on having her picture taken with me in the sculpted garden at Kōnomineji; the long stretches of seashore, with the ocean spread out blue and limitless; the Tokutoku restaurant, where I got a pot of freshly brewed coffee and a half-hour of Mozart; and those few moments descending the mountain from Dainichiji to a chorus of frogs in the rice fields.

The third day's walk took us to Kōchi City, with Temples Twenty-Nine and Thirty, Kokubunji and Zenrakuji, along the way. Both were long hikes. By the time we reached the last temple we were so bushed that the prospect of walking into downtown Kōchi was too much. We squeezed into a cab for a three-kilometer drive to the Kōchi Hotel No. 1. That night, we had a farewell dinner with Harumi-san and Hasegawa-san.

The next morning, Shūji, Jun, and I said goodbye to our two companions in the hotel lobby. I gave Hasegawa-san a set of prayer beads I'd purchased at Temple Twenty-Six and to Harumi-san a fan trimmed with black lacquered wood. When the fan spread open, it spelled out the pilgrimage motto: dōgyō ninin, "two pilgrims together." I tried an awkward goodbye with phrases I'd memorized from my Japanese dictionary: "Gokurōsama. Goshinsetsu ni dōmo arigatō gozaimashita." "Bless you. Thank you very much for your kindness."

Harumi-san accepted my stilted Japanese with good humor and

gave me a hug, slipping a tube of salve into my hand. "For your feet," she said.

As they disappeared around a street corner, it struck me that to have met them entailed the synchronicity of a great many events. I knew I was drifting close to the shoals of mysticism—the red flags of rationalism warned me away—but it was tempting to imagine Kōbō Daishi or Fudō Myōō taking an interest in my pilgrimage. I wondered if I would have even stranger thoughts as I continued to walk. I hoped so. I sensed I was developing a pilgrim mind.

4

Spirits

*Just climb
the mountain pass
spring wind.*
—SHŪJI NIWANO

I'd been lying on Katsurahama Beach, absorbed in the grating wash of the Pacific Ocean along the gravel shoreline, when Shūji crouched beside me. He held out his arms and opened his hands to reveal a stone in each palm.

"Please, which one do you like?" he asked.

I sat up, wondering if this was some kind of Japanese game. I studied the stones for a moment. Each was the size of a large egg. The one in Shūji's left hand was light gray and ovoid. His right hand held a darker, slightly elongated stone with glints of mica. My impulse was to pick it up and press the ends to regain an egg-like perfection.

"Kore," I replied. "This one." I tapped on the darker stone.

Shūji dropped it in my hand. "It is for you," he said. "To remind you of this place."

Shūji said he would add the other stone to his bonsai collection. "This will remind us of our visit here," he explained. "This will be Robāto-san's stone."

As he declared his intentions, I recalled the Japanese tradition of naming stones to commemorate an event or a person. "I am honored, Shūji," I said. "And I will call this Shūji's stone."

We sat for a few minutes in companionable silence, rolling the stones in our hands and watching the wide sweep of the ocean. Over the course of the last couple of weeks, we'd grown comfortable with

each other and often had felt no need to talk. But then Katsurahama
Beach was the kind of place where words seemed superfluous. It was
about 7:30 a.m. An early morning haze blurred the distinction between sea and sky. A cool breeze came off the water as a long line of
waves rolled one after the other onto the shore. A couple of freighters
churned slowly westward across the horizon. We watched them until
they went around a headland and out of sight.

We'd spent the night at the Sekinoya Ryokan, an inn on the outskirts of Kōchi City near Sekkeiji, Temple Thirty-Three. It was an old-
fashioned *ryokan* with a rock garden and a pond full of fat, colorful
carp. I'd slept well after the previous day's long walk through the suburbs of Kōchi and was looking forward to this day's hike to Shōryuji,
Temple Thirty-Six, in the foothills of Utsuga-san some thirty kilometers away. Before we headed out, though, Shūji wanted to take a short
detour off the pilgrim path to show me one of his favorite places: Katsurahama Beach.

The Japanese have long celebrated Katsurahama as a place of singular beauty. Located on the south coast of Shikoku near Kōchi City, the
area's deep-green pine forests, its multi-hued pebble shore, and the blue
Pacific water inspired the poet Keigetsu Omichi to write this haiku:

> Watch the moon rise from the surface of the sea,
> drawing the attention of all
> on Katsurahama.[1]

The place is also famous for its statue of one of Japan's great heroes,
Ryōma Sakamoto, the son of a nineteenth-century samurai family who
fought to end the two-hundred-year reign of the Tokugawa Shōgunate
and restore imperial rule in the 1860s.

In 1853, U.S. Commodore Matthew Perry arrived with his Black
Ships and forced Japan's rulers to open the country to trade with the
rest of the world. That event effectively ended two centuries of self-
imposed isolation during which Japan had banned foreigners, except
in a couple of port cities, and barred its own people from traveling to
other countries. Sakamoto was one of the first Japanese intellectuals
to argue that Japan had to learn the ways of the barbarians if it was to
flourish. He studied Western political institutions and drafted a blue-

print for a constitutional government and parliamentary democracy. He also wore European-style boots instead of sandals, arguing that since a samurai must always be ready to fight, boots were better than sandals. A fanatic assassinated the thirty-three-year-old Sakamoto in 1867, making him a martyr to Japan's modernization. Statues throughout the country honor him.

At Katsurahama, Sakamoto's statue stands on a tree-covered bluff overlooking the beach. Shūji wanted me to see it, so we walked some distance down the beach in order to climb the bluff, leaving our packs with Jun while he napped on a bench on the sidewalk that ran along the top of the beach. The statue was half-hidden in a copse of trees at the top of the bluff. A stern-faced Sakamoto stood six meters tall. Dressed in traditional robes, gripping his swords, and of course with boots on his feet, he stared out to sea. Standing at the foot of the statue, I followed his sightless gaze over the long curving crescent of the shoreline. On the far side of the beach another steep-sided headland jutted into the ocean. A small red-and-white Shinto shrine perched on the top of the headland. Farther west, a series of jagged headlands thrust like extended fingers into the water, the nearest dark green, the more distant faded to blue. I felt as though I were looking at one of those Oriental prints with tiny figures walking through an overwhelming landscape. And for the first time in a long while, as I peered through a gap in the boughs of a pine tree to view the cliff-top shrine, I fell in love with a place.

In my years of travel I've collected several favorite places: the Kentish countryside of England, the west coast of Vancouver Island north of Victoria, the south coast of Crete, the Kootenay Lake region around Nelson in British Columbia, the Languedoc region of France, and stretches of the Yukon Highway between Whitehorse and Dawson City. Of all the other places I've been, these in particular continue to haunt me. I think of them as my what-if places. Nothing special or extraordinary happened in them, but for some reason they have embedded themselves in my psyche, popping into memory more often than any other places do, as if calling me back. As best I can fathom, they are all places where for a few brief moments I was intensely aware of my surroundings and of myself in those surroundings. And when I remember one of them or, more precisely, when an image of the place flares in my mind, I can't help but imagine myself living another life there.

Looking down on Katsurahama Beach, I knew I had added another what-if place to my collection. I heard the wind in the tall cedars overhead and the muted crash of waves on the beach below. A wide-winged kite rode the air currents like a kid on a roller coaster. Fragments of light danced in the troughs between the ocean waves. The wind carried the smell of the sea. I inhaled long and deep, wanting to absorb it. Again the image of the cliffs above Point-No-Point on the coast of Vancouver Island rose clear and vivid in my mind. For a moment I was transported to the other side of the Pacific to see a younger version of myself as he watched a freighter plowing west through the Strait of Juan de Fuca, the long arm of the Olympic peninsula on the other side of the strait hazy in the distance. Then the image disappeared, and I was back in the present, staring at a Japanese beach as Shūji tugged gently on my shoulder to ask if I was okay.

"Mōshiwake arimasen. Hakuchūmu," I said. "I am sorry. Daydream."

Shūji nodded. "This is a place of dreams," he said. "Long time ago, I was here. With my wife. Before Jun was born."

I glanced at him as he stood beside me, gazing out to sea. I was willing to bet that he, too, was seeing things that weren't there. "You haven't been back since?"

Shūji shook his head. "First time in thirty years," he said. "I gave my wife, Ikuko, a stone, too. She still has it in the garden."

I asked him why he never visited Katsurahama.

He shrugged. "I had a job in Tokyo. I was always working. We never came back."

I gestured down the bluff to the beach where we could see Jun on the sidewalk bench. "Is Jun okay?" I asked.

"Maybe. He tires too much. It is a worry."

"We'll just have to keep him going, ne? Dōgyō ninin."

Shūji laughed. "Yes, pilgrims together."

The Japanese don't generally display their feelings or affections publicly, particularly the older generation, so I was surprised when Shūji put his hand on my shoulder. "I am glad to share this return with you, Robāto," he said.

"Arigatō. Kōei desu." "Thank you. I am honored."

And I was. I thought of how Shūji, Jun, and I had been together for nearly two weeks. We seemed to reinforce each other's willingness to walk, encouraging each other to continue despite the fatigue and soreness and drenching rain. Even Jun occasionally perked up and outpaced both of us, although at other times it seemed to me that Jun's "condition" wasn't improving as Shūji had hoped. But now, with his gift of a stone and a moment of intimacy, I understood that Shūji's pilgrimage also had a personal dimension. I liked him even more for his nostalgia.

"I will remember this place," I said. "And our time here. I am grateful. Wakarimasu ka? Do you understand?"

"Hai, I understand," Shūji said with a bow.

We took a last look at Katsurahama Beach and then descended the bluff to awaken Jun and set out for the next temple.

***

The eight-kilometer hike to Temple Thirty-Four, Tanemaji, wound through the suburbs and into the countryside around Kōchi City. We marched between long rows of plastic greenhouses with crops of potatoes, cabbage, eggplant, and green peppers. Of course there were also the ubiquitous sun-sparkled rice paddies, squeezed between housing tracts, warehouses, and factories. Farmers in high rubber boots waded across soggy fields, hauling trays of rice seedlings to women standing calf-deep in the muddy water. In their brightly colored smocks and sunbonnets, the women looked like cheerful scarecrows.

Rice has been the food staple of Japan for millennia. Every meal I had in Japan, including breakfast, came with rice. The only exception was when, out of curiosity, I tried a McDonald's meal. To my surprise I couldn't eat it. It seemed I'd become used to a regime of rice, vegetables, and the freshest of seafood—bonito, tuna, squid, eel, octopus—and eating a Big Mac and fries was like trying to swallow a ball of lukewarm grease. My palate, and my stomach, objected.

Rice also has symbolic importance in Japan. The type of farming I saw that morning was wet-rice farming, or *taue*, "to put rice in the field," and it involves transplanting seedlings from their winter beds to the irrigated paddies. Some commentators have argued that the tradition of *taue* remains at the center of Japanese culture and identity. The company loyalty for which Japanese workers are famous rests on a deep-seated sense of being members of villages that once planted rice together. The water necessary to sustain the rice crop and to feed people was too valuable to be controlled by any individual or institution, hence the need for everyone to cooperate. According to this view, the traditions of a rice-farming culture that relied on interconnected irrigation systems have carried over into the kind of group-mindedness and cooperation that suits the modern corporate world.[2]

The tradition of *taue* was evident at Tanemaji, a pretty temple known as the Temple of Sowing Seeds. Local women regard the temple, built on a landfill in the middle of a rice field, as a fertility site. The temple's main buildings, the *hondō* and the *daishidō*, were set in a courtyard surrounded by a low wall in front of which there were dozens of weatherworn statues of Jizō. But there was also a small structure in front of the *hondō*. It held an image of Yakushi, the Buddha of medicine and healing. Dozens of water ladles, a common household item of wood or metal, hung on racks in the shrine. But these ladles are special. Traditionally, when a woman becomes pregnant, she brings one of her household ladles to a temple priest who punches a hole in it, sets it on the altar, and offers a blessing. The woman then takes the perforated ladle home and keeps it in the household shrine. After her child is born, presumably healthy, she returns the ladle to the temple as a gesture of thanks to Yakushi. The symbolism is obvious: in the same way that water pours effortlessly through a bottomless ladle, the woman hopes for an easy birth. I counted seven women praying at Yakushi's shrine when we stopped at the temple.

We had lunch two hours later, shortly after noon, in the courtyard of Kiyotakiji, Temple Thirty-Five, a mountainside temple that offered a panoramic view of rice fields and the Pacific Ocean. Parked on a bench in the shade of a maple tree, absorbed in the glinting patchwork of fields far below, and feeling the ache of the morning's walk leach from my leg muscles, I was suddenly and self-consciously aware of just how much I was enjoying myself. The blisters were nearly healed, my legs were stronger, and, best of all, my mind seemed to be slipping into the rhythms of pilgrimage. I remembered a line attributed to the Buddha: "You cannot travel on the path before you have become the path itself."

For me, the deepest pleasures of travel, indeed what makes it worthwhile, seldom involve dramatic situations, extraordinary sights, or epic efforts. Rather, the true gifts of travel, and of pilgrimage, are to be found in commonplace situations, uneventful stretches of time, and small events—Shūji's gift of the stone, for example. There were several such moments on this day.

Two Buddhist monks blessed us when we met them on the trail. A group of women insisted that I pose for a picture with them. A white-haired fruit seller at Kiyotakiji gave me an orange as *settai* and told me he'd been a soldier in an American prisoner-of-war camp and was forever grateful to the United States for how well he'd been treated. A medical student from Kyoto, Tashiro Masahiro, who was walking part of the pilgrimage route on his holiday, provided a glimpse into contemporary Japanese attitudes. "After the war, we followed Western ways in everything," he said, as we walked together between Temples Thirty-Four and Thirty-Five. "But now many young people want to know about Japanese ways."

The event I most remember from that day, however, was a ten-minute rest I enjoyed while squatting on a street-side curb outside a Tosa City postal station while Shūji used a cash machine inside and Jun phoned his mother. It was a narrow street of houses set behind whitewashed walls and largely empty of traffic. The only passersby were two middle-aged women who nodded and said "konnichi wa," "good afternoon," as they passed. Nothing happened, and yet there was poetry in the images before me: the green No. 32 bus rumbling past, with children in their dark blue school uniforms leaning out the windows; the rain-wet yellow curb lines running down the length of the road, bright under the sun; a spider's web of electrical wiring, silhouetted against the pale sky; tiled roofs and tidy shrub gardens, shining after the rain; a woman's lilting voice from the dark interior of a nearby house—everything seemed to hum and glow with intense significance, the ordinary transformed into the extraordinary. And for a few moments I imagined myself as a stone Jizō, cemented to the curb, forever watching over this street, my street. By the time Shūji and Jun came out of the post office, I was close to tears.

Of course what the deities give they just as readily take away. The morning's weather was perfect for walking—cool and overcast—with only a few sprinkles. This was not so after Temple Thirty-Five. It began to rain in the afternoon. As if that wasn't bad enough, we also endured one of the downsides of the Shikoku pilgrimage: trudging along a highway thick with car and truck traffic. It was sometimes scary with those roaring vehicles whipping by only a foot or two away from us. And it was worse in the rain. Passing vehicles sprayed us in their wake, and we were soon soaked from head to foot. We had to stay alert just in case some businessman who'd had a bit too much to drink for lunch at the local *nawanoren* wasn't seeing straight. Worst of all was breathing in the diesel exhaust fumes. I acquired a throbbing headache.

I'd read that pilgrims often complain about having to cope with the pilgrimage route on roads heavy with traffic.[3] I understood the sentiment and had enough experience of those roads myself. But oddly enough, it wasn't the asphalt and concrete that lingered in my mind but rather the mountain trails and quiet villages. That could be due to selective memory, I suppose. Either that or I was settling so deep into my own pilgrim mindset that having to walk on highways made little impression on me, much in the same way that after a time I paid less attention to the temples. Asphalt was just something to endure and then forget about.[4]

In any case, such was our afternoon hike to Shōryuji, Temple Thirty-Six. The temple is on the eastern end of an extended finger-like peninsula that runs parallel to Shikoku's southern coast. We had to tramp in the rain across a long wind-swept bridge over a river and then follow the highway as it curved around the eastern tip of the peninsula toward the temple. The wind coming off the water blew the rain straight into our faces and made for some hard walking. We reached Shōryuji barely in time to perform our rituals, offer our prayers, and have our pilgrim books stamped before the office closed at 5 p.m. It had been a wet and noisy—and sometimes nauseating—slog for most of the afternoon. We were soaked and sore-footed. But after a few moment's rest, I quickly recovered from the strenuous walk and was eager to explore one of the loveliest temples on the Henro Michi.

The Temple of the Green Dragon is in the foothills overlooking the Bay of Usa. The tree-shrouded compound occupies two levels linked by a stone staircase that ascends one hundred meters under a canopy of cedars to the main temple and the Daishi hall. As I climbed to the red-and-white pagoda, I entered a grove of cherry trees. The blossoms were in full bloom, and it looked like the pagoda above and ahead of me was floating in a cloud of pink-and-white petals. Behind the main gate, there is a small waterfall that *henro* use in an ascetic ritual in which they stand beneath the cascading water, for as long as they can, to pray and meditate. Already cold and wet, I skipped the ritual. I wanted to meditate over a can of Georgia Café au Lait or, better still, a *tokkuri*, or bottle, of hot sake.

It seemed that Shūji and Jun felt the same way. None of us wanted to walk another four kilometers to our night's accommodations, especially since it was raining again. Shūji used a temple phone to call the hotel. The manager was willing to come and get us. Self-prescribed *settai*, I thought. Why not?

***

The Tosa National Lodging House was one of the few places I've encountered that lives up to the tourist-brochure description: tranquil, relaxing, friendly, and offering a splendid view. Thirty minutes after checking into my room, exchanging my wet clothes for a dry *yukata*, and equipping myself with two large cans of Kirin beer, I was lounging in the steaming water of the lodge's open-air *o-furo*, gazing at the distant headlands of the Yokonami coast.

I had the bathing pool to myself. Set on a deck built into a patio at the rear of the lodge, it measured about six meters long by maybe three wide. One side of the bath was open, like a picture window without glass, to a wide-angle view of the Bay of Usa. I lay stretched out, chest-down in the water and chin resting on my folded arms on the narrow ledge, the beer within easy reach. The scene before me was both beautiful and frightening. A narrow ledge of stone slabs separated the bath from the precipice. When I pulled myself forward, I could peer over the edge and look down the craggy cliffs that dropped sharp and steep into the foaming ocean far below. It was almost as if I were hovering in mid-air above the water-thrashed rock, which was scary yet exhilarating. A hundred or more meters below me, almost straight down the cliff face, fingers of black stone probed the surging sea. Solitary pines, bent and contorted into grotesque shapes by salt spray and wind, clutched the rocky ledges and fissures. Here and there isolated lumps of black volcanic rock appeared and disappeared with the ebb and flow of the crashing tide. Out in the bay, bulbs of small islands poked from the water like stranded passengers from a sunken wreck.

Staring down at the black rocks and white swirl of water, I felt a surge of vertigo that made me close my eyes and push back from the edge of the bath. I sensed the lure of the plunge, the temptation of release, of letting go forever. One quick surge out of the water, using the leverage of my arms to hurl myself over the edge of the bath, and I would disappear into the foaming sea. I could see why the southern coast of Shikoku was a favorite place for suicides as well as the haunt of mystics and wandering holy men, including Kōbō Daishi. This was a landscape for visions and nightmares. I took a long pull on the beer and opened the other can.

My mind drifted like one of the hawks soaring over the distant headlands. I thought of Bashō. He would have been familiar with this kind of landscape. How would the poet-pilgrim have responded to this panorama of sea and sky, I asked myself. I remembered, from reading his *Narrow Road to the Interior* so often these last couple of weeks, the descriptions of his travels and the haiku he wrote about them. He, too, found the breathtaking views of rivers and mountains awesome. He, too, suffered for his spiritual inclinations. On a nighttime climb on a mountainside, he groped through forests of thick bamboo, waded across streams, climbed rocky slopes, and was tired, sweaty, and full of fear.[5] Another night, after bedding down in a decrepit inn, he was plagued by "old infirmities" when the roof leaked during a downpour and the room filled with fleas and mosquitoes, producing a "long, sleepless night."[6] I bet he even suffered blisters.

Nevertheless, Bashō made every effort to stay poetically attuned, taking in the world—cicadas and cuckoos, chestnuts and cherry blossoms—and translating that experience into poetry. As I floated in the *o-furo*, fragments of his poetry came to mind: "Ah, speechless before / these budding green spring leaves / in blazing sunlight." I remembered another haiku about how a long soak in a hot spring left him pleasantly weak and wobbly. "After hours of bathing / in Yamanaka's water— / I couldn't even pick a flower."[7] The lines made me smile. I felt the same way after my baths.

That's what I admired about Bashō. He was right there in the thick of things, enduring sore feet and aching legs and hard climbs. Yet he still attended to the frogs and the woodpeckers, the wind in the trees and the falling chestnuts. And from this attention to the everyday world, he turned ordinary experience into poetry. Bashō attempted to capture the effervescent quality of that everydayness. And that, I thought, is what made his poems a kind of pilgrimage. His long walks were an attempt to foster moments of vision. He sought to break free of the mind-numbing habits of daily life in order to reawaken to the extraordinariness of the ordinary, the "sheer Isness of Being," as I'd heard one of my philosophy professors once say.

As I lounged in the o-furo, sipping the second can of Kirin and half-hypnotized by the white froth of the sea crashing below me, my senses seemed to rush out to absorb the world. The vertiginous cliff, the heaving ocean, the isolated islands, the twisted trees, the low gray sky, the salty smell of the sea, the ticking sound of rain on the cedar roof of the o-furo, the cool wetness of the beer can—I took it all in with a surge of delight and an intense awareness. When a gust of wind blew the rain into the o-furo, I relished the sharp needles of cold water on my skin.

But it wasn't just my senses that were humming. My mind was buzzing as well. I felt I was on to something. Bashō not only described what he encountered and then responded to it as a poet; he also showed me how I should travel as a pilgrim. Bashō traveled as a means of letting his poetic sensibility encounter the landscape and thereby opening himself to the kind of epiphanic experiences that might produce poetry. He journeyed not only to the interior of Japan but also to the interior of himself.[8] For Bashō, genuine knowledge required entering the things he encountered—whether cherry blossoms, the wind in the trees, or the fleas flitting around his sleepless head. Thus, for him, pilgrimage and poetry went hand in hand. While pilgrimage forced him to be attentive to the everyday things he encountered, that deeper awareness of the everyday things of life inspired poetry.

Could this be my motive, too, I wondered. Or, more tentatively, was this the kind of motive I wanted for my pilgrimage? If so, then it seemed to me that Bashō was offering me a way to conduct my pilgrimage. Yes, the kilometers ticked over, the temples added up, and the blisters healed. After two weeks on the road I was even settling into the mental rhythms of the pilgrimage, my mind slowing down as my body adapted to the slower pace. But so far I had yet to attend to the walking in a focused and concentrated manner. Now, though, as the day's aches and pains floated away in the o-furo, it seemed to me that Bashō provided the example of an aesthetic of pilgrimage, a way of walking by which I could possibly achieve moments of epiphany that would lend my Henro Michi a deeper resonance, even if I wasn't a devoted Buddhist.

I recalled how, on my pilgrimage along the Camino de Santiago a few years earlier, I'd experienced several epiphanies, moments of sharpened awareness. They'd always been rooted in an intense consciousness of the world around me—a forest pathway, sunlight on a rain-wet wall, echoes of a church bell as I walked a cobblestone street. In those moments, I seemed to slip below the surface of things to perceive the underglimmer of reality. Those moments never lasted long, but they gave my Camino pilgrimage a sense of meaning that I hadn't originally anticipated. For months after returning home, images of those moments came to mind unbidden, transporting me back to the Camino. I came to think that my recollections of and reflections on my pilgrimage had produced subtle shifts in my psyche. These were shifts more of perception than of behavior. I took more long walks simply to feel an echo of my pilgrimage journey. I was more sharply aware of everyday things—the dining room dappled with sunlight streaming through the curtains, the drift of the scent of lilac across the backyard, the creak of the house late at night when everyone except me was in bed. Thanks to the Camino, the everyday world was more enchanted.[9]

Of course it proved difficult to maintain that sense of enchantment. After a time my Camino sensibility began to fade away—not completely, but enough to make me want to go on another pilgrimage. The first pilgrimage had unlatched the doors of perception. My Shikoku pilgrimage, I hoped, would push those doors open.

I took a last swallow of beer, saving some to pour over the edge of the o-furo to the rocks and water below—a small gesture of thanks to the deities of Japan for introducing Bashō as a ghostly walking companion. From now on, I thought, I would conjure the poet's presence in the morning before setting out on the day's walk. Maybe I would learn to walk like him.

***

The gods, however, seemed to have their own plans for me. After I hauled myself out of the hot water, well, I didn't have the strength to pick a flower. I managed to dry myself with one of the washcloth-sized towels the Japanese consider adequate for the job. I looked in the mirror at my sunburned, wind-whipped face. My hands and lower arms were brown. The soles of my feet still looked as though they'd been flayed, but they no longer hurt. I may even have lost a few pounds. Now, I thought, if I could only get my head in tune with my body.

I wrapped myself in the *yukata*, squished my feet into the too-small slippers, and headed for the lobby, figuring to get several of the little bottles of sake I'd spotted in the vending machines there. I thought I'd take the stash back to my room and get pleasantly drunk while staring out the window at the crashing sea. But that idea went out the window when I bumped into Shūji and Jun in the lobby. They wanted me to join them for dinner. I hesitated for a moment. I really wanted to be alone, but I did need to eat. I decided to go with them and save the sake for later. The lodge offered a set meal that included *ton-katsu*, or pork cutlets, a broth with tofu and clams, pickled vegetables, and of course rice. The waitress even agreed to make a fresh cup of coffee just for me.

After supper, Shūji and I sat cross-legged around the low table in my room, drinking the sake and plotting the next day's walk. Iwamotoji, Temple Thirty-Seven, was sixty kilometers west along Highways 47 and 23. It would take at least two days to get there. We figured we would walk as far as we could on the first day—depending on Jun's "condition," as Shūji put it—and find a *minshuku* for the night in one of the fishing villages. If we were lucky and the weather was good, it would be a lovely walk along the coast with the Pacific Ocean almost always in view.

But luck was not with me that night. After Shūji left I went to bed with the remainder of my sake. I felt a little woozy, but I attributed it to the long day and the alcohol. I fell asleep readily enough, but then sometime after midnight I woke up, knowing instantly that I was going to be sick to my stomach. I assumed the clams were to blame. I spent the next hour shivering and vomiting and swearing to Kōbō Daishi that I would never eat clams again. What I most feared was being laid up for a few days with food poisoning. That had happened to me on the Camino.

This time, though, the vomiting seemed to clean out my system, leaving me with only a bad bout of acid indigestion. I remembered there was an ice-cream machine in the lobby. I staggered down the stairs in my flapping *yukata*. A young woman behind the reception desk eyed me with alarm as I shoved coins into the vending machine. I tried to smile at her—as if to say, pay me no mind, I'm just a crazy gaijin with an early morning ice-cream craving. Back in my room, I realized I didn't have a spoon. I thought of going back to the lobby to ask for one but didn't know how I'd get that across to the desk clerk without making her hysterical. I found my jackknife at the bottom of a side pocket on my backpack. I cut the containers open and sliced the ice cream into bite-sized cubes that I could spear with the blade and pop into my mouth. I ate several four-ounce containers of Häagen-Dazs—two vanilla, one chocolate, and a strawberry ripple, as I recall. I took care not to slice my tongue but wasn't always successful. After sixteen ounces of ice cream, the pain in my stomach was reduced to a dull ache and I was able to sleep.

I still wasn't feeling well when I came downstairs at 6:30 a.m. to pay my bill. I was bleary-eyed and shaky and furious with myself. It didn't help that Shūji was waiting to tell me that Jun had also been sick in the night. Unfortunately, he hadn't tried ice-cream therapy and still felt nauseated. I didn't see any point in trying to explain my own sickness. Shūji wanted to let Jun sleep and then take a taxi back to Tosa to catch a bus to Kubokawa. Was I willing to do the same? He was apologetic; we'd been taking too many trains and buses. But when Jun was sick, Shūji had little choice. I was tempted. The prospect of a thirty-kilometer walk when I still felt weak and wobbly didn't thrill me. And yet I knew my weakness would pass once I started walking. To give in now would be unjustifiable and, no doubt, lead to future surrenders. Or so I told myself. But I was also aware that if I insisted on walking, it would mean the break-up of our *henro* troop. If I walked and they caught the bus to Kubokawa, it was unlikely we would meet up again unless they waited for me somewhere—but that would be hit-or-miss at best. If I didn't go with them now, we might as well say goodbye.

Shūji had a hangdog look. I suspected he knew what was going through my mind and was afraid that if our little trio broke up, Jun wouldn't be willing to complete the pilgrimage. He and Jun sometimes argued—the paper-and-wood walls in *ryokan* don't allow a lot of privacy—and Jun sometimes said he wanted to quit. There'd been a few times when Shūji stood back while I cajoled Jun into walking a few extra kilometers, using the excuses of needing a language lesson or wanting his companionship in an effort to get him moving again.

What would Bashō do, I asked myself. Surely he wouldn't abandon a sick friend. Nor was he a prissy pilgrimage purist. He didn't reject the occasional horse ride or a spot on the back of a farmer's cart. Was I just being bloody-minded, angry at my own weakness, and taking it out on Shūji? Perhaps. But I also like to think there was a good instinct at play, too. After nearly three weeks on the Henro Michi, I was, finally, really walking, physically and psychologically—maybe even spiritually. Bashō was waiting for me down the road. I didn't want to miss him.

"I'm sorry, Shūji-san, but I need to walk," I said. "Wakarimasu ka?"

He nodded. "Hai, I understand, Robāto-san."

Shūji helped me hoist my pack after I put on my rain gear and paid the bill. I said that I hoped Jun would be better soon and that I would look for them later on. Maybe he could leave messages at the temple offices. The priests could keep an eye out for me—there couldn't be that many foreign henro on the trail—and pass them on. Shūji kept nodding and agreeing and saying he understood. And then I left. I looked back once. Shūji was standing in front of the door. He bowed. I bowed. Then I turned and walked to the highway, even though I knew I was being really, really selfish.

***

Two hours after saying goodbye to Shūji I was almost convinced I was being punished for my un-Bashō-like behavior. Highway 47 winds along the southern edge of a fifteen-kilometer peninsula that parallels the main Shikoku island like a tine on a two-pronged fork. The road eventually connects to Highway 23 at the base of the peninsula, about eight kilometers east of the town of Susaki. I walked about halfway to the highway intersection before I was ready to admit that I'd been foolish. It had started to rain half an hour after I left the lodge. Only this was no ordinary rainfall. It was the downpour of doom, coming down so hard that rain ricocheted off the asphalt. In seconds I was soaked. The wind whipping off the Pacific Ocean didn't make it any easier. It was like walking through a combination carwash and wind tunnel.

I'd hiked about seven or eight kilometers, mostly climbing, when I came to a large roadside rest area that overlooked the Bay of Tosa. Two shuttered wooden kiosks stood beneath a line of pine trees at the far side of the parking lot. Their overhanging eaves offered some shelter from the wind and rain. I pulled off my pack and sat on a bench against a wall under the eaves. The rain thrummed on the cedar shingles.

I stared through the curtain of rain and down the steep slope of the cliff to the gray water lashing the rocks below. In the distance, half-obscured in mist, the black arm of another headland thrust into the ocean. Once in a while a car or truck whooshed past on the highway behind me, the tires making a ripping sound on the wet road. Nobody stopped. The rain fell. I looked at my watch. It was just after 9:30. I still had maybe twenty kilometers to go to reach Susaki. Normally that meant about five or six hours of walking, plus time for breaks. I knew I should get moving—get up, shoulder my pack, and hit the road, rain or no rain.

Yet I lingered. It wasn't because of the rain, or at least not completely. Bashō got wet. I could be wet, too. Nor was I feeling sorry for myself. My earlier weakness had passed. True, it would have been a comfort to have companions, and a warm, dry bus would have been nice. But something else held me. I was suddenly aware that for the first time in nearly three weeks, I was alone. There was only me—surrounded by the drumming rain, the air pungent with the smell of wet cedar, the heaving ocean, and the gray-bellied clouds shredding themselves on the tops of the surrounding hills.

The reality of being alone in the rain, on a hill overlooking the ocean, in an obscure corner of a Japanese island, was somehow extraordinary. A sharp, sweeping sense of *thereness* swept through me. I exulted in the sheer awareness of myself being in the place. It was as if I were merging osmosis-like with what I saw, heard, and smelled, as if there were no veil of self-consciousness to separate me from the experience, no gap between self and world. For the first time since starting on the Henro Michi, I felt like a real pilgrim.

The sensation didn't last long. My bladder reminded me there was more to pilgrimage than spiritual matters. I pulled my rain jacket over my head and ran to a convenient tree at the edge of the parking lot. When I got back to the kiosk, thinking I'd best get moving, I saw a Toyota van swerve off the highway. It pulled up beside the kiosk. The driver—on the right side of the van, since, like the British, the Japanese drive on the left side of the road—rolled down the window. I was looking at the bright, black eyes of a jowly, middle-aged woman with cropped, graying hair. Beside her in the passenger's seat was a tiny, bird-like elderly woman. From the looks on their faces they were surprised to see a gaijin.

"Gomen nasai. Nihongo wa sukoshi shika dekimasen. Watashi wa henro desu," I said, drawing on my repertoire of memorized phrases. "I am sorry. I can speak only a little Japanese. I am a pilgrim."

The woman said, "Chotto matte." "Just a minute." She turned to speak to someone in the back seat. Another window rolled down, and I was looking at a bespectacled young man with sleep-messed hair.

"You are a gaijin," he said.

I agreed that was the case. "Eigo ga hanashimasu ka?" "Can you speak English?"

He could. He spoke to the driver. I stood there getting wet while the three of them launched into conversation. Finally the young man stuck his head back out the window.

"You ride with us, ne?" he said. "Too much rain for walking."

How could I take a ride now after refusing to take a bus with Shūji and Jun? What would Bashō do? Didn't he ride horses when available?

"Settai desu ka? Kubokawa e ikitai desu," I said. "Are you offering settai? I want to go to Kubokawa."

I must have made sense because the driver smiled and said, "Hai, settai."

A couple of minutes later, after stashing my pack in the back of the van, I was scrunched in the front passenger seat. Despite my objections, the elderly woman moved to the back seat. "You are bigger," the young man explained. "Longer legs." When faced with typical Japanese politeness, I knew it would have been rude to protest.

The van driver, I soon learned, was a Buddhist nun who went by the name of Misiun. The young man was her nephew—I think his name was Joji—and the elderly woman, whose name I never caught, was her mother. They were driving around Shikoku visiting temples. They'd spotted me running across the parking lot to the kiosk and assumed I was in need of help. That I was a foreign *henro* was a surprising twist of karma. All this was related to me by Joji, who translated his aunt's questions—Who was I? Where was I from? Was I a Buddhist?—and then delivered my responses to her in Japanese.

Normally it should have taken an hour, maybe an hour and a half at most, to reach Kubokawa following Highway 47. But Misiun took it upon herself to be both tour guide and spiritual instructor, frequently turning off the highway to drive through some of the smaller villages. She also insisted on stopping whenever there was a panoramic view of the coastline and the water. Regardless of the rain, we stopped quite often.

There was one place that offered a sweeping view of the Pacific Ocean beyond a curving, gray-sand beach pinched between two rocky, anvil-like headlands. When we clambered out of the van, Misiun carried a bag of oranges. She pointed to a line of Jizō statues on a ledge behind a low chain-link fence between the parking lot and the edge of the cliff. Joji translated her words: In the old days, parents threw unwanted babies or those they could not support off the cliff into the sea. Elderly people who felt they had become a burden to their family and broken-hearted lovers also made use of the high cliffs. I counted about a dozen red-bibbed statues of Jizō, who watched over the souls of children in the afterlife. Misiun walked along the line of statues, placing an orange at the foot of each one, and delivering a short prayer and a bow. Her mother followed, setting 100-yen coins—about $1—on top of the oranges.

I'd adopted Jizō as my pilgrimage guardian during my first really hard climb to Temple Twelve. Was he watching over me now? Had he arranged this ride? I shook away the notion, but I wasn't taking any chances. I followed the mother's example and emptied my pockets of change. Not knowing what else to do, I crossed myself and genuflected before each Jizō.

Misiun seemed to approve. As I finished with the last statue, she gestured toward me with a mudra, one of the many stylized hand movements used by Buddhists as a symbolic spiritual expression. I didn't know what it meant, but I noticed that as she drove, she blessed the drivers of oncoming cars with the same mudra. Those who spotted the gesture bowed their heads in thanks. I wondered what drivers back home would do if I offered a mudra as I passed them. They'd probably think I was making an obscene gesture. I laughed to myself at the thought. I turned to Joji in the back seat and asked him to thank his aunt for showing me the Jizō statues.

"Dō itashimashite," she said, glancing at me, her eyes bright and laughing.

We ate the remaining oranges as we drove. The van filled with their scent. It was pleasant to be in a warm vehicle and to watch the green hills and the hamlets tucked into the folds of steep-sloped valleys, their gray-tile roofs shiny in the rain. The windshield wipers provided a metronome to my mood. I was near to nodding off when Misiun spoke.

Joji translated: "My auntie asks do you know the Hannya Shingyō? All *henro* should know the Hannya Shingyō."

According to scholars, to chant the Heart Sutra's 260 characters is to recite the whole of Buddhist scripture since it encapsulates the essence of Buddhism. Its constant recitation, whether alone or in the company of others, is supposed to open your mind to its Buddha-nature and to help free you from the suffering of this world. It takes only a few minutes to recite, and most pilgrims chant it at the temple shrines.[10] Hearing the sutra at the temples in the last few weeks had embedded fragments of it in my mind, although I'd made no conscious effort to learn it, much less to understand what I was hearing. Now I had to make the effort, even if only to be polite. Perhaps it would do me some good. I told Joji to tell his aunt that I would be pleased to learn the sutra.

And so for the next hour, as we drove through the rain to Kubo-kawa, I followed Misiun as she chanted the Heart Sutra. Eventually I picked up some of the phrases that had become familiar. "Gyate, gyate, hara gyate, hara so gyate, boji sowaka." I would later look up an English translation. "Gone, gone, gone beyond, gone altogether beyond, O what an awakening."[11]

Misiun seemed pleased that I followed along so readily. She said something to Joji. "My auntie says this must be karma. A gift from Kōbō Daishi," he said.

I had to wonder. What are the odds of meeting a Buddhist nun who wanted to teach me the Heart Sutra while giving me a ride? It was sheer serendipity that I'd been running across the parking lot when they drove past. I wouldn't have met Misiun if I hadn't left Shūji and Jun. My mind chased after an ever-receding swirl of what-ifs and what-might-have-beens. Was someone trying to tell me something?

I wondered about this even more after what happened in Kubokawa at Iwamotoji, Temple Thirty-Seven. The Temple of the Rocky Root huddles amidst a cluster of stores and shops just off Highway 56, near the town's railway station. Misiun parked down the street, and the four of us walked in the drizzling rain to the temple gate. I made sure to bow before I stepped through the gate into the temple compound. I was conscious of Misiun's presence as I performed the *henro* rituals. I wanted to do them right—payment of sorts for the ride and for the instruction. I was careful to wash my hands and rinse my mouth at the cistern. I rang the *waniguchi* bell on the veranda at both the *hondō* and the *daishidō*. Since the temple has five Buddhas as its deities—Fudō Myōō, Kannon, Jizō, Amida, and Yakushi—I genuflected before each. Then I dropped coins in the offering boxes. With Misiun beside me, I chanted the Heart Sutra. Or, more accurately, I tried to keep up as she recited it.

"Kekko desu," she said afterward. "Very good."

"Goshinsetu o makoto ni arigatō," I said. "Thank you very much for your kindness."

After getting my *nōkyōchō* stamped at the temple office, I walked across the courtyard toward the gate. It had stopped raining, but I decided to call it quits for the day even though Misiun invited me to continue on with them to Temple Thirty-Eight, another eighty kilometers away. As comfortable as that would have been, I knew I couldn't take another ride. That would have been too un-*henro*-like. I decided to find a room at a *minshuku* and have a short day. But then as we left the temple, I received more evidence that the gods really liked to play mind games with mere mortals. How else could I explain the sight of Shūji and Jun coming up the street? They were just as surprised, and judging by Shūji's handshake and Jun's chattering, they were equally pleased to see me.

"Kōbō Daishi, ne?" Shūji and I said in unison, laughing.

Shūji explained that he and Jun didn't leave the lodging house until late in the morning, taking a taxi back to Tosa City to catch an afternoon bus to Susaki. From Susaki, they had taken the train to Kubokawa and only just arrived.

"We shall walk together again?" Shūji asked.

"Hai," I said. "Dōgyō ninin."

I tried to introduce Misiun to Shūji and Jun, but my Japanese was inadequate. They did the job themselves. We decided to have lunch at a nearby udon shop before Misiun and her family departed. Misiun and Shūji talked together during the meal. I noticed Misiun occasionally glancing at Jun, who was oddly subdued in her presence. I was content to have my companions back, slurping the fat noodles in a dry place out of the rain, and pondering what seemed to me to be an extraordinary day.

After lunch we said our goodbyes at the van. "Taihen osewa ni narimashita," I said to Misiun. "I am very much obliged to you for your help." It was inadequate but the best I could do.

"Gambatte kudasai," she said, offering the traditional farewell among passing pilgrims. "Do your best."

Misiun looked at Shūji for a moment in silence and then offered him a parting mudra, extending her right arm out the van window with the arm bent at the elbow and the palm of her hand toward him, like a policeman halting traffic. She held that pose for a few seconds while Shūji bowed deeply. Then Misiun and her family drove away.

That night, as Shūji and I plotted the next day's walk, I asked about Misiun's mudra. Shūji explained that she'd offered him the *semui-in*, the mudra of fearlessness, by which the Buddha tells us not to fear suffering and death because nobody can avoid either one. Buddhism asserts that the universe is in constant flux, and we must learn to accept that everything is transient and that suffering is born of the egocentric desire to hold onto things—possessions, health, friends, even love—that can't be held fast. Only in accepting the transience of life and shedding the ego can we overcome fear and gain peace. It struck me as a strange message for Misiun to give Shūji. But then I didn't know what they'd talked about. Besides, Shūji seemed to derive some benefit from his brief encounter with the nun.

"She was a gift from Kōbō Daishi," he said.

***

The next week of walking brought other gifts. It took us three days to reach Kongōfukuji, Temple Thirty-Eight, in Tosashimizu at Cape Ashizuri, and another two days to make it to Enkōji, Temple Thirty-Nine, in Sukumo City. They were good days, mostly bright and sunny without being too hot. I would be weary and footsore by the end of a thirty-kilometer day, but after a night's sleep—and I slept soundly—I looked forward to being on the road again. Even Jun seemed livelier, and that made Shūji happy.

The pleasure of those days was also rooted in the spectacular landscape. Between Temples Thirty-Seven and Thirty-Eight the *henro* path largely followed the coastline to Ashizuri, a distance of eighty-five kilometers, and for much of that we were in sight of the Pacific Ocean. In several places the path ran across sandy beaches or along headland heights that offered stunning views of the sea and vertiginous drops to the water-scoured rocks. The clash of the sea and land had carved strangely shaped shafts of stone, distorted arches, and deep furrowed inlets. The pounding water swirled savagely across the black rocks before falling back into quiet gray pools. I could see why Cape Ashizuri was also famous for attracting suicides.[12]

The route after Temple Thirty-Eight took us along the west coast of Cape Ashizuri through small towns—Tosashimizu and Misaki, Otsuki and Kozukushi—before turning inland across the green mountains to Sukumo, a small town a few kilometers before Temple Thirty-Nine. The Temple of Emitting Light was half-hidden in the forest at the foot of a mountain slope—a lovely, quiet temple with a pond of turtles and a large symbolic stone turtle in the courtyard. Pilgrims stroked the stone turtle as a way of wishing for a long life. I did, too.

Following the green-tunnel roads that twisted along the Ashizuri coast, climbing the mountain paths, and descending the valley slopes, I was captured by vignettes: a woman in a red bonnet digging for clams on a beach; thickets of bright red camellias on the mountain slopes near Otsuki; fish rising when I tossed pieces of rice into the water during a leisurely lunch on a riverbank. They were commonplace scenes, perhaps, but I felt that I'd gained a glimpse of *Yamato-damashii,* the soul or spirit of Japan.

My reaction to the Shikoku landscape was not unusual. Japan's ancient spirit resides in nature.[13] Indeed nature is the source of Japan's indigenous religion, Shinto. Once upon a time, forests of *sugi* and *hinoki,* Japanese cedar and cypress, covered the mountains and hills that make up 70 percent of the Japanese islands. Sadly, nature isn't what it once was in Japan. Coastlines, hills, rivers, and fields—they all reveal a human presence. Only a handful of Japan's thirty thousand rivers and streams remain free of dams. Tunnels channel most rivers, and those that remain open have had their banks layered in concrete. Logging, pollution, and acid rain have devastated the forests.[14] In the national parks and the more remote regions such as southwestern Shikoku, however, you can still glimpse the glory that was once Japan's forests. Climbing along a steep-sided mountain ridge or through a narrow gorge thick with old-growth trees, I could see why the ancient Japanese believed in the existence of *kami*, spirits-in-the-world. Even along the coastlines, where the forests are hard to reach, there is something palpably haunting about the pine trees that cling with talon-like tenacity to cliff sides or perch like contorted birds on the rocky islets that jut from the sea. I imagined those trees as the souls of those so reluctant to leave this world that they grab onto anything, take any shape, suffer any hardship, in order to stay in this life. Sitting on a beach or a headland, watching the trees, I began to think they were dancing, that in the swaying of their gnarled and twisted branches I was seeing the *kodama*, the spirit of the trees.

The ancient Japanese didn't give a name to their ancestral belief system, with its fertility cults and its nature and ancestor worship. But they referred to the *Kami no Michi*, the Way of the Gods, as distinct from the *Hotoke no Michi*, the Way of the Buddhas, after Buddhism arrived from China in the sixth century. The word *kami* is difficult to translate into English, but it roughly approximates the Western concept of spirits. More important is to understand the *Kami no Michi* as a positive worship of life itself, a religion that appreciates life's blessings and, at the same time, abhors death and defilement.[15]

In this regard, Shinto is inherently optimistic, unlike Buddhism, Christianity, or Islam. For Shinto, this world is not a pale reflection of a more substantial reality. It is neither a realm of exile for souls migrating through innumerable lives, as Buddhism teaches, nor a fallen world where we wait for judgment in the afterlife, as Christianity and Islam propound. Indeed Shinto lacks the concept of sinfulness. Humans are by nature good, and the world in which they dwell is also good. Evil belongs to another realm and comes from outside. Thus Shinto rites emphasize warding off disaster and defilement by seeking the help of the *kami* to promote peacefulness and happiness for the individual and the community. And since Shinto regards the material world in all its manifestations as a living entity, a *kami* can be a deity or a sage, a poet or a pauper, a forest or a field, a thunderstorm or a butterfly. Or maybe even a gaijin.[16]

Standing on a mountain ridge, looking over a dense green valley, I found the notion of a world teeming with *kami* tempting—if only my rationalist heritage didn't get in the way of such fanciful concepts. Surrounded by the haunting forests of Shikoku, I might imagine a re-enchanted world. But I couldn't ignore the little golem of modernity that whispered in my ear against such foolish sentimentality. I might feel nostalgia for the enchantment of a lost world, but I could no more believe in *kami* than I could recover a childhood belief in Santa Claus. At the same time, though, it seemed to me that a world devoid of *kami* was a lonely world for human beings, a world in which humans can't feel at home in any deep sense. Being able to master nature with technology can't substitute for feeling at home in the world.

As we followed the pilgrim path through western Shikoku, I kept thinking of Bashō's treks around Japan in the late seventeenth century. He, too, was awed—and inspired—by views of rivers and mountains, land and sea. Maybe I'd been reading too many of his poems, but there were times, while wandering through a copse of bamboo or looking down a vertiginous cliff to the surging sea, when I was close to convincing myself of the poet's presence, maybe a step or so behind me—a shadow at the periphery of my vision. It seemed to me that if I turned my head fast enough, I would catch a glimpse of him.

This sensation—hallucination?—was especially strong when I was hiking through gorges so narrow that the rock face on each side seemed ready to fall on me. I would hear the echo created by the tapping of my walking stick; but the sound seemed slightly unsynchronized, not quite matching the swing-and-step rhythm of my walking. There were moments when, after I lifted the stick, I was sure I heard another pilgrim staff tap the ground. It was spooky. I imagined that only a diaphanous barrier separated present and past, the living and the dead. It seemed, for a second or two, Bashō's world and mine were so close that, like some *kami* wandering the cosmos, he was haunting my steps.

Surrounded by the play of sun and shadow and the silence in Shikoku's forest, I was only too willing to indulge such fantasies. It was a landscape for the fantastical. It seemed to me that my pilgrimage was getting rather crowded with spirits, both real and not-so-real, living and dead: Shūji and Jun, Jizō, Bashō, Misiun, and the occasional *kami*. And as my walking stick constantly reminded me, there was always Kōbō Daishi, eternally supportive. In those moments, it hardly mattered which was real and which was not real. I wondered what other visions might be in store for me.

5

Dreams

Pilgrim's staff
I fill my mind
with emptiness.
—SHŪJI NIWANO

I draped the wet cloth on my head, closed my eyes, and lay back to let the *Kami no Yu*, the Water of the God, soothe me. Hot water lapped across my chest as I rested the back of my head against the rim of the pool. My sigh of pleasure must have been audible to the half-dozen other bathers in the Dōgo Onsen. I'd learned the pleasures of Japanese bathhouses a month earlier, and now, with fifty-one of the Henro Michi's eighty-eight official temples visited, I was no longer self-conscious about sharing an oversized bathtub with a bunch of men. I now regarded *sentō*, or public bathhouses, as the hallmark of civilized life.

The sun poured through the skylight, bouncing off the gray marble walls and tiled floor, saturating the spacious room with light. Shards of sunlight danced on the surface of the bathing pool, a semi-circle rimmed with blue granite that stretched half the length of the room. A large stone fountain at one end overflowed into the pool. On the wall above the fountain a blue-tile mosaic depicted an ascetic-looking old man sitting in a forest grove with a couple of children at his feet.

Shūji and Jun, along with our new traveling companion, Yukuo Tanaka, a retired engineer from Tokyo, were squatting on stools in the washing area a few meters from the pool. Following Japanese bathhouse etiquette, they were scrubbing and rinsing off soap and shampoo before joining me in the water.

It had been a hot and muggy day, and the four of us had arrived drenched in sweat after a fifteen-kilometer hike from Joruri, a village on the outskirts of Matsuyama where we'd spent the night. Tanaka-san and Shūji had decided there was no way I could visit Matsuyama, one of the larger cities on Shikoku, without enjoying a bath and tea at the famous Dōgo Onsen. It is one of Japan's oldest natural hot springs. The existing wooden bathhouse dates to 1894, but the *onsen* has been in use in one form or another since the sixth century when it was popular with Japanese nobility.

I was grateful to my companions for introducing me to it. And as far as I was concerned, the Dōgo Onsen was as close to heaven as I was likely to get on this side of the grave. Opening my eyes, I gazed around the pool. Three white-haired men sat across from me on the opposite side. I'd bowed to them earlier before stepping into the water. They'd smiled and returned the gesture, my politeness acknowledged and reciprocated. On my right, a muscular young man lay on his back, his stretched-out legs half-submerged in the water. He, too, had propped the back of his head on the rim of the pool and placed a washcloth over his face. On my left, another man sat on the pool's edge, holding a baby on his knees. Every once in a while he leaned forward and lowered the infant into the water, smiling as she kicked her chubby legs. I doubted I'd ever see anything like that in a North American city, since the mongers of political correctness would be hysterical at the thought of naked men and naked children together in a bathhouse.

The Japanese, however, still regard the neighborhood *sentō* as a community-gathering place, an institution where young and old, friends and family, can soak and gossip together. I'd read that houses and apartments in Japan began to include private baths only after the Second World War, and only then did men and women start bathing separately. The Dōgo Onsen, for example, has a separate section for women. Judging by the laughter coming over the wall that separated the two sections of the pool, the women were having a good time.

I watched a bald, round-bellied man walk into the *onsen* and across the tiled floor to the washing area. Two little boys, maybe six and eight years old, followed. All three were naked. The man—their father, I presumed—carried a rolled-up towel. He sat on one of the small stools in front of the taps, turning to say something to the boys. The younger boy filled a plastic bucket from the tap while the older one unfurled the towel and extracted a white washcloth and a bar of soap. Together they scrubbed their father's back. They laughed when the older boy dumped the bucket of water on his father's head. When the man finished rinsing himself, he soaped his sons and made sure they'd rinsed thoroughly before he led them to the pool, the two boys then sitting quietly at their father's side while he slid into the water up to his neck.

I glanced at the clock on the wall above the frosted doors that led to the bathing room. It was 11:13 a.m. As I gazed around at the other bathers and heard Jun's laughter as he splashed into the pool, I was suddenly and sharply aware of my pleasure in being where I was and in seeing what I did. It seemed to me that in the last month, my life had become marvelously straightforward, a minimalist calculation of moving between two geographical points each day, interspersed with simple requirements for walking, eating, and sleeping—and bathing, I thought to add, as the water lapped under my chin.

I closed my eyes and pulled the washcloth down over my face, filing in my memory bank the bathhouse tableau I'd just witnessed—another image from an extraordinary week. Indeed the past several days had been especially enjoyable. I walked without complaint, my legs strong and my feet blister-free. Sure, I would be weary and sore by the end of each day, but after a hot o-furo, a supper of sashimi, a bottle or two of cold Kirin beer, and a solid night's sleep, I was eager to walk the next morning.

In the past eight days we'd trekked 180 kilometers and visited eleven temples. The hike had taken us across a series of mountains and valleys in southwestern Shikoku that were as remote as modern Japan has to offer. With the physical demands of the pilgrimage no longer preoccupying me, I'd felt myself letting go, absorbed by the walking and sinking into the landscape. There were moments when my "real" life—family, job, mortgage—seemed unreal. I'd crossed into that psychic landscape where the pilgrimage had become my reality. I was too far from the end of the journey to begin thinking about returning home and, at the same time, too deep into the pilgrimage, chronologically and psychologically, to feel the remnant tug of having left. Indeed I felt a sense of arrival, as though in some way I'd come home to Japan.

Other Shikoku pilgrims I'd read about experienced something similar. For example, Ian Reader describes one of the "most striking experiences" he had during his 1984 Shikoku pilgrimage with his wife, Dorothy: how having "one simple routine to do each day—effectively, get up, eat, leave, put one foot in front of the other, visit the temple, get to the next lodge, eat and sleep—liberated us from the normal issues of daily life and the trials and stresses of work and provided a clear focus to everything we did. Life became simple and the world beyond the pilgrimage, beyond the simple process of walking, ephemeral."[1]

In my case, I was grateful for this shift in psychology. It meant that I was finally approaching pilgrim mindfulness. I'd acquired such a state of mind about halfway through my previous pilgrimage on the Camino de Santiago. Now, halfway along the Henro Michi, I was increasingly conscious of myself disappearing into the peripatetic existence of a pilgrim. I was entering what anthropologists have described as a "liminal state" in which I moved beyond the normal strictures of my everyday life and into a psychological condition in which I no longer felt bound by the constructions of my normal social order or by the sense of identity and belonging that I derived from that order. In this state of displacement I had acquired a new, if temporary, sense of identity and belonging.[2]

I sometimes fantasized about becoming a perpetual pilgrim. Give me a couple of years in Japan to acquire a credible grasp of the language and customs, and I would feel right at home, or as at home as any non-Japanese could ever feel in Japan. Why not just keep circling the island, relying on *settai* to provide food and shelter? I'd read about Japanese who did this, men who after a lifetime of work in the beehive of the corporate world spent the last years of their lives following Kōbō Daishi around Shikoku, sometimes dying at the side of the trail. Why couldn't a gaijin do it, too? I imagined myself going around and around the island, growing gray and bent, hobbling along with my battered pilgrim staff, my clothes a patchwork of donations. I'd become an object of mystery and veneration, the strange foreign pilgrim who disappeared into the forests of Ehime never to be seen again, except as a ghost that sometimes walked with pilgrims and urged them on—gambatte kudasai, do your best. Maybe they'd plant a marker at the spot where I fell, and over time the elements would rearrange it to resemble a moss-covered Jizō.[3]

Beneath the washcloth, I smiled at my perpetual pilgrim fantasy. The odds were greatly against me that I would ever become a deity, even a small one. I also knew full well that I owed my liminal leanings, such as they were, in large part to my companions. First Shūji and Jun, and now Tanaka-san, provided me with a little community. My small repertoire of Japanese words and phrases might carry me through most encounters, but my companions made things a great deal easier by arranging nightly accommodations—one of the great insecurities of pilgrimage—or by locating a drugstore on my map and even by pointing out local monuments that I would otherwise have passed by in ignorance. I certainly wouldn't have discovered the Dōgo Onsen without them.

Submerged in the *Kami no Yu*, I mentally scrolled through the past few days—especially the day at Kanjizaiji, Temple Forty, when Shūji began dressing as a *henro*. That was the day after we met Tanaka-san. Of course the two events were connected. But then after a month on the Henro Michi, I was beginning to think that everything was connected.

***

When I first met Shūji, he'd worn a baggy blue sweater, a shirt, khaki slacks, running shoes, and a baseball cap. Jun dressed much the same. Neither one used the *kongō-tsue*, the walking stick that symbolizes the presence of Kōbō Daishi. Until we reached Kanjizaiji—the Temple of Kannon, the Buddhist deity of mercy who saves people from disaster—the only *henro*-related item that Shūji had was a brocade-covered stamp book and a green *kesa*, the three-inch-wide, two-foot-long strip of cloth that pilgrims drape around their necks like a prayer shawl.

Shūji began to change after he met Misiun, the Buddhist nun, at Temple Thirty-Seven. He began more seriously chanting the Heart Sutra at the temples, along with the specific temple mantras and a *kigan*, a concluding prayer that invoked the influence of the temple deity. He told me later that the nun had taught him a particular *kigan*, and he'd promised to recite it as often as he could. The day Tanaka-san joined our pilgrim family, however, was the day when Shūji really changed.

We met Yukuo Tanaka at Enkōji, Temple Thirty-Nine. It was late morning. After finishing my pilgrim rituals and getting my *nōkyōchō* stamped, I grabbed my pack and walked out through the temple gate. I bought a cold bottle of Pocari Sweat from a kiosk and sat on the top step to wait for Shūji and Jun. I cracked the cap on the drink and drained half of it. I gazed down the narrow shop-lined street that sloped toward the main road through Mishō. There were few pedestrians and even fewer cars. I wondered what day it was—Saturday, Sunday, Monday perhaps—but I couldn't be bothered to work it out. I was happy sitting in the sun and eating an orange.

"Sumimasen, henro-san." "Excuse me, pilgrim."

I looked up at a balding, round-faced man in glasses. He looked to be in his late fifties or early sixties. He wore the *hakui* and held a pilgrim hat in his hand. He was neat and dapper, his white vest clean and unstained—unlike mine. I immediately assumed he was a bus *henro*, a member of some tour group driving the temple route. His English was good, if stilted.

"You are American?" he asked.

"Iie," I answered. "Kanada-jin desu." "No, I'm Canadian."

"I have never been to Canada. I have always wanted to see the aurora borealis," he said, stumbling on the Latin.

The reference to the northern lights startled me. I'd spent much of my boyhood and youth in the Northwest Territories and the Yukon where the aurora borealis was a common sight. It seemed strange to hear from a pilgrim in Japan a reference to this childhood image. But then in my state of mind at the time, I no longer believed in mere coincidence. Too many things had happened—a taxi driver who offered a free ride when my legs ached the most, an out-of-the blue smile from a little girl at a train station that cheered me up, a Buddhist nun who showed up to provide religious instruction—for me not to regard this man's reference to the northern lights as somehow significant.[4]

I said that I had often seen the northern lights, and yes, they were "totemo utsukushii," "very beautiful."

"Watakushi no namae wa Tanaka Yukuo," he said, following the Japanese practice of placing the family name before his given name.

I stood up to bow and to introduce myself. "Hajimemashite." "I am pleased to meet you."

Tanaka-san looked surprised by my bow and my use of Japanese. He said he'd been walking the Henro Michi for about four weeks, but I was the first gaijin he'd seen.

I soon disabused him of any false notions about my language skills as I stumbled through my memorized responses about my job and my interest in Japanese culture and my coming to Japan for the pilgrimage. Shūji and Jun came out of the temple at that moment. "Tanaka-san o goshokai shimasu," I said to Shūji. "May I introduce Mr. Tanaka."

They bowed to each other and began to talk. From the way they kept glancing at me, I assumed that Shūji was explaining how he came to be walking with a foreigner. Afterward, Tanaka-san asked if I objected to his walking with us. Not at all, I said, suspecting my Shikoku pilgrimage was about to take another turn. And so it did. Our foursome would endure all the way to Temple Eighty-Eight—and beyond, as it happened.

We all benefited from Tanaka-san's presence. He spoke better English than Shūji or Jun, so he was able to translate their words to me and mine to them. Our dinnertime conversations became lessons in Japanese history, culture, and current events, as well as an education for me in food, drink, and table etiquette. I would ask such questions as "Are Japanese people religious?" and "Are young people turning away from Western influences?" to which Shūji and Jun could respond, thanks to Tanaka-san.

Shūji, I think, benefited the most from Tanaka-san's companionship. That became evident at Kanjizaiji, Temple Forty, the first temple in Ehime Prefecture, which is the most westerly of Shikoku's four provinces. By tradition, Ehime is the *bodai no dōjō*, "the arena for the attainment of wisdom." After walking through the two previous prefectures, Tokushima and Kōchi, and visiting their thirty-nine temples, the pilgrim is supposed to become aware of his or her longing for enlightenment. Ehime Prefecture, with its twenty-six temples, is where you are supposed to achieve some sort of enlightenment, the true nature of your mind.

It took the four of us most of a day to hike to Kanjizaiji, following a thirty-kilometer path that led across mountains and valleys between Sukumo and Mishō. Shūji and Tanaka-san walked most of the way together, while Jun and I hiked on our own—sometimes together when we continued our language lessons, and sometimes apart. Tanaka-san told me later that he and Shūji mostly talked about Jun and what Shūji might do about his troubled son.

It was a hard walk with a lot of steep climbing. By the time we reached Mishō and found the temple, we were sweaty and sore and weary. After finishing the temple rituals—I was still trying to recite the Heart Sutra—I strolled through the courtyard past the line of stone Buddhas below the main hall. The eight Buddhas stood in alcoves above a cistern equipped with wooden ladles. Each Buddha corresponded to a particular part of the calendar, and pilgrims were to splash with water the one that corresponded to their birth date. I watched two women dressed as *henro* perform a birthday ritual. One woman ladled the water and flung it at her chosen Buddha, while the other woman chanted the Heart Sutra. When they were finished, they walked away chatting and laughing.

I bought a couple of fat oranges at a fruit stall. I was eating them, section by section, enjoying their juicy sweetness, when my companions came out of the temple gate. Shūji had been transformed. He was decked out in the full *henro* kit: the *hakui*; a straw hat, or *kasa*; plastic boxes for carrying the *osamefuda*, incense sticks, and prayer candles; and, of course, the *kongō-tsue* with the motto that symbolizes Kōbō Daishi's presence, "Dōgyō ninin," "We two—pilgrims together." He had a big grin on his hound-dog face.

As Shūji and Jun approached, I stood and bowed and addressed him as *o-henro-san*, or honorable pilgrim. Jun, I saw, had also acquired the walking stick but none of the other pilgrim garb. He lost the staff a few days later.

Tanaka-san, it seems, had convinced Shūji that if he wanted the benefits of the pilgrimage, then he had to be more diligent as a *henro*, which included dressing the part. He must also be diligent about reciting the Hannya Shingyō. Judging by Shūji's appearance, it seemed that he was following Tanaka-san's advice.

That night we stayed at the Isoya Ryokan on the outskirts of Mishō. At dinner I asked Tanaka-san why he was walking the Henro Michi.

He looked at me for a few seconds before answering: "There is a vacant space in my heart. My last big assignment before I retired was in Beijing. I lived in China for a couple of years, always working."

One day, he said, he came across a book of Buddhist writings. "They spoke to me. I felt emptiness in my heart. I started to think about who I was and how I have spent my life."

In Japan, he explained, men of his generation, those who came of age in the 1960s when Japan was still recovering from the Second World War, devoted their lives to the company. He became an electrical engineer. Family life—a wife and a son—came second. "This was the way of life in Japan after the war. Family was secondary."

One of the Buddhist scriptures he read while in China was the Heart Sutra. He tried to recite it at least once a day.[5] The constant recitation supposedly awakens one's Buddha-nature, one's potential for enlightenment. In Tanaka-san's case, the sutra stirred spiritual longings that his career had suppressed. A year earlier, at sixty-one, he had decided to retire. And one of the first things he decided to do in retirement was walk the Henro Michi. After a year of research and planning and putting his affairs in order, he set out.

"I want to find out if I can fill this empty place in my heart," Tanaka-san said, taking a final sip of tea. "Every day I walk and think and pray."

"Has your heart been filled?" I asked.

Tanaka-san laughed, adjusting the folds of his *yukata* as he stood up to go to his room. "Not yet. I will let you know."

***

Soaking in the Dōgo Onsen, sightless beneath the washcloth and vaguely aware of the splashing and laughter of other bathers, I replayed in my mind images of the pilgrimage since Temple Forty. Each day's walking had certainly been fulfilling as far as I was concerned. I was eager to return to the road each morning, eager to disappear into the walking. The cherry blossoms were in full bloom in the mountains. The rice fields in the valleys showed green shoots. Best of all, I was no longer walking the Henro Michi; it was walking me.

We had left Mishō early in the morning, following Highway 56 along the western coastline for about ten kilometers before we turned inland and started climbing into the mountains. It was a long, hard climb. It took two hours to hike four kilometers. We didn't reach the 470-meter peak until close to noon. Just beyond the peak, as we began our descent, the forest opened onto a wide escarpment overlooking the coastal plain. The dark trees fell away, marching down a series of ridges to the brown-and-green rectangles of farm fields. A small village, the buildings in the distance like the bright cubes of dice, huddled at the edge of the sea. Overhead a castle of cumulus clouds, gray-bellied and white-fringed, opened like a drawbridge to let a broad shaft of sunlight pour onto the blue waters of Bungo Strait. Kyushu, the southernmost island of the Japanese archipelago, bulked gray and hazy on the horizon across the strait.

We dropped our packs, pulled out our lunches, and sat strung out along the trail facing the sun-bright sea. We ate in silence, taking in the panorama of sea and sky and land. I still remember the food: two seaweed-wrapped rolls of sushi with pickled plums in their centers, an orange, and for dessert some pumpkin donuts I'd picked up at a convenience store we'd passed on the way out of Mishō. A bottle of warmish chocolate milk finished off the meal. It was delicious. After lunch, we lingered in the sun, sweat drying and muscles twitching in relaxation. I would have fallen asleep had we stayed longer, but we still had three hours of walking to reach the town of Tsushima, where we'd booked a *ryokan* for the night.

It was a lovely three hours. Peonies and rhododendrons drooped over the banks of mountain streams. Black butterflies fluttered above them. Loquat trees, their spring blossoms still wrapped in white paper bags to protect the ripening fruit, marched in orderly lines along the terraced sides of narrow valley slopes. Lizards lounged on sun-exposed rocks, their heads lazily swiveling as we passed. The occasional snake slithered across the path and over the edge of the slope to disappear in the bracken and bushes. I noticed they were green, which was a relief; the poisonous *mamushi* snakes that inhabit Shikoku are brown.

We reached Tsushima about 4 p.m., checking into the Yoshinoya Ryokan. We had walked only twenty-four kilometers, but that included a lot of climbing.

The next day we hiked thirty kilometers, encountering yet another of western Shikoku's numerous mountain tunnels. The Matsuo Tunnel is widely considered one of the worst, even though at a mere 1,700 meters—slightly more than a kilometer and a half—it isn't the longest. But what it lacked in length it made up for in being dark and narrow and scary. It took us thirty minutes to get from one end to the other—half an hour in an echo chamber filled with the steady roar of big Isuzu trucks whipping by only a couple of feet away. My hands and the sleeves and front of my white pilgrim vest were soon streaked with black soot as I tried to stay as close to the tunnel wall as possible and away from the thundering traffic. By the time we emerged, I had a throbbing headache from inhaling diesel fumes.[6]

The headache faded by the time we reached Uwajima, a pretty city with wide, clean, tree-lined streets. We rested at a park and watched a few innings of baseball. We had our lunch at a horrible strip mall just past the railway station, with a choice between McDonald's, a KFC outlet, a Mr. Donut, and a Mer-de-Napoli. I again tried a Big Mac and fries but couldn't eat them. Instead, I found a Lawson convenience store that sold the all-in-one *bentō* boxes with morsels of sushi, *nori-maki*, and a couple of shrimp tempura.

"You are becoming Japanese," Jun said, finishing my hamburger and fries.

Beyond Uwajima, we tramped another ten kilometers, following the incline of Highway 57 to Ryūkōji, Temple Forty-One, in Mima Town. Temple Forty-Two, Butsumokuji, was another four kilometers down the road. The two temples lie in a narrow valley surrounded by mountains, and both of them reflect the concerns of farming communities. Ryūkōji is dedicated to rice growing, while Butsumokuji is devoted to animal husbandry.

According to legend, Kōbō Daishi visited the two temples in 807. At Temple Forty-One, he met Inari-myojin, the Buddhist deity of fertility, in the form of a white-haired old man. Inari, originally a Shinto divinity, is an agricultural deity. Hence Ryūkōji is dedicated to rice growing. At Butsumokuji, on the other hand, Kōbō Daishi rode on a cow, so the temple is devoted to animal husbandry. The main deity, Dainichi Nyorai, the cosmic Buddha who loves all beings, reflects this dedication to animals. All creatures, it seems, great and small, can attain the Buddha's enlightenment.[7]

Not surprisingly, the two temples encourage these ideas, selling charms to local farmers to keep their crops and animals healthy. They must make money. The shelves in the offices of both temples, as well as the souvenir shops outside the gates, are well-stocked with protective amulets and talismans—prayer beads, figurines of Kōbō Daishi or Jizō, key chains promising healthy feet, pencils assuring success in exams, and prayer boards in brocaded cloth bags that can be carried or hung from a car mirror. These little pieces of wood offer prayers for anything from success at school to safe driving. Pregnant women can acquire a *hara obi*, a long strip of cloth worn around the stomach to ensure an easy birth.[8]

The temples also sold fortunes written on narrow, rolled-up strips of paper known as *o-mikuji*. If you don't like the fortune you receive, then you tie the paper strip to a tree, bush, or trellis on the temple grounds and leave it behind. *O-mamori* are strips of wood, paper, or plastic in small brocaded bags. These objects are charged with spiritual power.[9] They're supposed to bring good luck and to fend off misfortune.

I certainly wasn't going to mock this marketing of spiritual longing. Indeed I surrendered to an atavistic impulse and bought wooden votive plaques known as *ema*. You inscribe your name, the date, and your prayer—a cure for gambling, payment of a debt, acceptance into a university, the health of aged parents—on the small wooden plaque and hang it on a special rack in the temple courtyard.[10] I bought five *ema* boards at Butsumokuji. My first *ema* petitioned the *kami* to grant my son, Daniel, a long and fruitful life; another sought health and happiness for my wife, Margret; while a third expressed the same hope for my mother, Diana. I dedicated my fourth *ema* to old friends and lovers, wherever they might be. The fifth was for my deceased father, wherever he might be. I hung them on the prayer rack near the bell tower. Afterward I sat in the courtyard and listened to the soft clack of *ema* caught in the wind. I imagined all those prayers, mine included, rising to some ethereal realm where *kami* sat around a conference table laden with bottles of sake and got drunk as they debated the merits of mortal dreams and desires.

This is perhaps not a completely absurd notion. Everywhere I went in Japan, whether mountaintop temples or suburban streets, I saw statues, shrines, or other markers that implied some nearby spiritual presence. This omnipresence of the spiritual, as I'd read in my research, reflects both the Shinto notion that Japan is the dwelling place of *kami* and the Buddhist notion that since the world's Buddha-nature is all-pervasive, that nature is present anywhere at any time. And since enlightenment itself is nothing more than the full illumination of everyday experience, then every time and place offers the potential for realizing one's Buddha-nature. In other words, the divine can appear anytime or anywhere.[11]

Maybe this explains why, as I trudged along a mountain path, I increasingly felt that I wasn't alone, that someone—Bashō, Kōbō Daishi, Jizō—was watching over me. A fanciful notion, no doubt, but after so long on the road, surrounded by the quiet of the temples and the haunting forests of Shikoku, it was easy to let my Western rationalist heritage slip-slide away like a loose sheet of shale breaking from a mountainside.

When we left Butsumokuji we walked about a kilometer down the highway to the Toubeya *minshuku*, where we had rooms already reserved. Lying on the futon in my room that night, I heard the wind come up and the rain rattling on the tiled roof. Just before I fell asleep, I imagined my *ema* rattling on the rack, their messages wafting upward to the waiting deities, wherever and whatever they might be.

The next day we climbed in the rain over Long Tooth Pass and through a forest of cedars, arriving at Temple Forty-Three, Meisikiji, late in the morning. It was a ten-kilometer hike. A month earlier I would have cursed the rain; now it didn't bother me so much. Coming across the peak, we broke out of the forest onto a plateau. There was a small shrine at the top of the pass where we rested to get out of the rain and to take in the view. Ridges of dark mountains, the lower slopes obscured by mist, spread out before us in the distance. Clouds peeled off the peaks like calving icebergs. Through gaps in the clouds, we could make out the dark patches of islands in the Bungo Strait. The villages in the valley below looked like clusters of small white buttons scattered across a giant green quilt. A line of loquat trees escorted us as we made our descent on the other side of the mountain. The edges of the trail were thick with wild iris, and cedar branches hung so low that we sometimes had to walk hunched over.

Meisikiji is half-hidden in the forest above the town of Uwa. The main hall, decorated in gilt and bright paint, sits at the top of a flight of granite steps. After getting my pilgrim book stamped, I stumbled back down the stairs to shelter under the eaves of the *shōrō*. Watching the rain and waiting for my companions, I remembered the story of a young Japanese woman who, accompanied by an elderly man, walked the Henro Michi in the summer and fall of 1918, starting at Temple Forty-Three. Itsue Takamure wrote a series of newspaper articles about her trek, including a description of her first night sleeping at the temple. I pulled my research journal from my pack and read: "We found shelter under a tree beneath the crags, arranged three rocks to make a grate, and cooked rice in a small pot. We gathered edible grasses to put in our soup. This was our meal. Then, removing only sandals and gaiters, we each rolled in a blanket and slept. During the night I woke to find ants, lizards and hairy caterpillars crawling on me."[12]

I wandered around the temple compound, wondering what tree might have sheltered the young woman all those years ago. It was a far cry from where I would shelter that night.

We left Temple Forty-Three and trudged into Uwa, a suburb of Seiyo City. It was barely noon, and we'd walked only twelve kilometers since leaving the Toubeya *minshuku*. But it was raining so hard that we decided to call it quits for the day. Shūji and Tanaka-san consulted their guidebooks and started making phone calls. Half an hour later, after a quick but soggy march through the streets of Uwa, we reached the Uwa Park Hotel.

That night I slept on a double bed beneath clean sheets—my first Western-style bed after more than a month of futons. It rained all through the night. I woke up about 5 a.m. to the sound of rattling windows and rain lashing the glass. I didn't know if it was the rainstorm or my dreams that awakened me. I'd dreamed I was walking through a forest when I saw Itsue Takamure ahead of me on the trail. She wore a long white pilgrim robe and carried a walking stick. I shouted to get her attention and ran to catch up to her. But she didn't hear me, and somehow I couldn't reach her. I was desperate to tell her to watch out for the brown snakes. Never mind the lizards or insects. It was the brown snakes that were deadly. Then I thought, why am I chasing her? She's dead. The snakes couldn't hurt her. Still, I wanted to catch up to her and ask if she'd found what she'd been looking for. Did she even know what it was she was looking for so that she would know to look for it? The incline of the forest path became incredibly steep, and I crawled on hands and knees as I scrambled after her. I tried one last time to yell her name, and this time she heard me. But just as I was about to see her face, I woke up.

For a moment I was unsure of where I was. The bed was utterly foreign. A wave of panic came over me. I kicked away the covers and sat up. I was drenched in sweat. The rattle of the windows returned me to the here-and-now, and gradually my panic ebbed. My watch said it was 5:13 a.m. I thought of going back to sleep, but I knew sleep wouldn't come. I showered and dressed for the day's walk. Then I sat on the window ledge, sipping the remains of a bottle of Pocari Sweat. It was still too dark to see anything beyond the rain-streaked reflection of my own face in the window. But I could hear the rain as it beat against the windowpane. It sounded like someone was shaking a jar of bone fragments.

✳✳✳

Floating in the Dōgo Onsen, I mentally shook away the image of the dark window, preferring to replay our three-day hike from Uwa to Taihōji, Temple Forty-Four, in the mountain town of Kuma. The pilgrim trail largely follows a river through a deep valley. Even when we had to walk along the highway, it wasn't too bad because there was so little traffic. Certain images from that hike rose in my memory: Mozart on the stereo and the early morning smell of coffee in the Pechka coffeehouse on the road to Ozu; a lunch of sushi as we rested on the banks of a river; a sun-dappled clearing in a bamboo forest; the startling sound of the "Ode to Joy" from Beethoven's Ninth Symphony on loudspeakers as we walked through Oda Town; the drumming rain on the roof of a village gazebo while we crouched inside eating ice-cream cones.

On the afternoon of the third day, after climbing a series of ridges, we crested a mountain summit to enjoy a sweeping view of a wide plain sloping to the Inland Sea. The town of Kuma was directly below us. The gray-tile roofs of Taihōji showed above a wall of cedar and cypress on the mountainside behind the town. Our plan was to find the Fugataki *minshuku*, where we had reservations, and call it a day. In the morning, we intended to leave our packs at the guesthouse and walk to Temple Forty-Four and then on to Temple Forty-Five, Iwayaji, before returning to Kuma for a second night. While Taihōji was only a couple of kilometers from Kuma, Iwayaji was a steep and arduous ten-kilometer climb into some of the highest mountains on Shikoku. The temple itself was 670 meters above sea level.

The real pleasure in reaching Taihōji was the knowledge that we had visited half of the eighty-eight temples that make up the Henro Michi. But the hike to Iwayaji, the Temple of the Rocky Cave, was special. The pilgrim path wound through dense forests of cedar that formed tunnels over our heads. The bamboo had come into leaf, forming bright green cathedrals. Along the edge of the trail, rows of flowers—iris, rhododendron, azalea, camellia—filled the cool air with a confusion of scent. The *sakura* were in bloom. To walk into a grove of pink-and-white cherry trees was to walk into enchantment.

Now and then we came out of the forest and into a tiny hamlet. The villages, surrounded by citrus groves and rice fields, were little more than clusters of half a dozen wooden houses. If not for the utility poles and the drooping tangle of power lines, I could have been walking through ancient Japan.

Walking twenty to thirty kilometers a day for weeks on end affects you not only physically but also psychically. The enforced slowness of walking likewise forces the mind to slow down, and you feel a shift in the relationship between your inner and outer worlds. You hear another self, the self of memory and loss, of sadness and joy—the self you don't hear amidst the diversions of the technological world. The constant presence of the physical elements—stones and asphalt, mud and water, trees and flowers, rain and sun—induces a psychic journey. And sometimes, on these interior sojourns, you take strange detours.[13]

The hike to Iwayaji was an example of such a journey. After leaving Temple Forty-Four, I was content to let my companions get ahead of me. I walked slowly, placing one foot in front of the other without paying much attention to where I was going. Somehow I ended up approaching Temple Forty-Five by the backdoor, stumbling down a steep incline through the forest to the rear entrance of the temple. About a kilometer from the temple, near two moss-covered wooden shrines, I found a small graveyard. The gravestones had all but disappeared into the earth beneath a blanket of moss.

I'm not sure what impulse made me do what I did next, except that as I stood there I remembered a trip I'd made with my mother to her hometown of Hanna, Alberta, a few years earlier. One hot afternoon, we drove out to the cemetery. We spent a couple of hours cleaning my grandparents' graves, trimming the caragana hedge and washing the headstones.[14] And now, facing this trailside graveyard, I slipped off my pack, took my knife from a side pocket, and crawled on my hands and knees between the closely packed gravestones. I picked a small obelisk half-tilted into the ground and scraped away the moss until I saw the cold stone. I crouched lower, trying to see the ideographic marks, but they were barely visible. I grabbed a bottle of water from my pack and washed the stone, rubbing away the remnants of moss and dirt until I could make out the faint markings. I couldn't decipher them, of course, but they would at least be visible now to anyone who could. I imagined the pilgrim whose gravestone I'd cleaned being pleased at having his resting place restored to the eyes of some passerby, who might offer a prayer in remembrance. I thought that Itsue Takamure would also be pleased.

Ten minutes later I found my companions patiently waiting for me at the temple. Iwayaji, founded in 701, literally hangs on the side of a cliff above the valley of the Omogo River. The temple halls are set in the cliff face. Above the roofs of the temple, pocking the rock face, are caves where ascetics and holy men once lived. Ladders set into the stone connect the caves. I climbed one in order to squat in the opening of the cave and stare at the rolling mountain ridges and the river below. I tried to imagine the men and women who had come to this mountain for hundreds of years in the hope of gaining a glimpse of eternity.

As we ate our lunch on the benches in front of the temple, I pulled my copy of *Japanese Pilgrimage* from my pack and read Oliver Statler's description of the Temple of the Rocky Cave: "There are places along the pilgrimage route where we can almost feel the presence of those holy men of long ago. Such a place is Temple Forty-Five." No doubt, I thought, the modern world would certify them as delusions, but I preferred Statler's point of view. "One cannot stand dwarfed before this towering natural altar without knowing that it has been a sacred place since man first found it. A god resides here. And holy men have come to sojourn with him."[15]

That night back at the Fugataki *minshuku*, we celebrated our half-completed pilgrimage in Tanaka-san's room with a couple of bottles of *shōchū*, a cheaper alcohol than sake. Jun went to bed after only a couple of glasses. The rest of us stayed up past midnight, talking and drinking. Despite the language difficulties, we probably said more than we intended—Shūji, in particular. Halfway through the second bottle, he started talking about Jun—his despair at his son's condition, his grief at his wife's unhappiness, and his fear for the future, especially as he and Ikuko got older. I sensed that he'd been waiting a long time, maybe years, to say these things to someone. He was speaking in Japanese, but he was looking at me even as Tanaka-san translated.

"Shūji is thanking you," Tanaka-san said, "for being such a good friend to Jun."

I was embarrassed and replied with unintended glibness—that's what friends are for.

Shūji, however, had more on his mind. Again Tanaka-san relayed the words, although this time there was a startled look on his face. "Shūji says that he begs for forgiveness in his heart."

I wasn't following this. Forgiveness from whom? Not me, surely. "Wakarimasen." "I don't understand."

And that's when Shūji opened his heart. Tanaka-san was as surprised as I was. As he told me later, "Japanese do not reveal their private lives outside the family." But that night Shūji gave me a glimpse of his private life. One reason he had taken Jun on the pilgrimage was because his wife felt that she could no longer cope with Jun's behavior at home, especially his violence toward his younger brother, Makoto, who, as I then discovered, was autistic.

Ikuko had told Shūji that she sometimes thought of poisoning Jun and then herself. Shūji said he'd persuaded her that she mustn't do such a thing, especially since her own mother was still alive and Makoto needed her. No, he told her, if it came to that, it would be his duty. He was the father and was responsible for Jun.

Part of me didn't want to hear this. I was here to have a few modest epiphanies and enjoy the adventure. I didn't want to be a witness to another man's despair. Yet, like it or not, Shūji had chosen Tanaka-san and me to receive his secrets. I had no words of comfort, much less any wisdom. But maybe it was enough that Shūji had been able to share his burden. Watching his sad face, I detected the relief of a man who had just had an immense weight lifted from his shoulders. What could I say that wasn't trite or inane? But then Shūji relieved us of the need for a response. "I am praying for forgiveness for these thoughts. I am saying Hannya Shingyō for forgiveness."

It seemed to me that I now knew the motive for Shūji's conversion to the pilgrim role and his sudden devotion to praying at the temples. Tanaka-san had told me it didn't matter if you couldn't understand the words to the sutra because the words are the embodiment of the Buddha in sound. To utter the words is to make the Buddha present in your mind. Shūji, I realized, was a more genuine pilgrim than I would ever be. For the first time in my life, I was face to face with a man who had a desperate need for divine guidance and a deep desire to know there was some purpose, some reason, for his suffering and, I suppose, some kind of justice out of it. I felt helpless and useless. But then, looking at Shūji and the palpable relief on his tear-streaked face, I thought maybe it was sufficient to bear witness to his pain and to be his friend. What else was there to do?

Back in my own room, before crawling under the futon cover, I went out on the balcony to clear my head, draining a bottle of water. The moon floated across the sky, wrapped in a corona of mist. The lights of Kuma glittered. I looked into the dark in the direction of the temple, with the image of the *henro* cemetery and its one moss-free gravestone floating across my mind. Words formed in my head: "So much death." Then another image, a vision really, superimposed itself: I was standing in the graveyard with Itsue Takamure. She was looking at me as she had been trying to do in my dream the other night. She was beautiful. She smiled. And clear as a bell, I heard her repeat the words with which she ended her pilgrimage articles: "Let everything be as it is." And suddenly, like Shūji, I was crying; I was in love with a ghost.

I don't know how long I stood on the balcony staring at the moon as it moved across the sky, but after a time I noticed I was shivering. I shook my head. Hallucination? Vision? Too much *shōchū*? Fantasies are common to the pilgrimage experience. Hallucinations, too. That such an image would rise unbidden and yet be so vivid suggested that I was dropping down the pilgrim rabbit hole. Shūji's story echoed in my head. I wondered what I'd gotten myself into and how deep that hole might get.

Two days and six temples later, I was asking myself those questions again as I wallowed in the Water of the God at the Dōgo Onsen. I must have soaked for nearly an hour before Shūji splashed over to me to say that he and Jun were going shopping. Jun needed a new pair of shoes. We would meet them later and walk to Temple Fifty-Two. In the meantime, Tanaka-san and I had a post-bath pot of tea and engaged in *chabanashi*, or tea-sharing talk.

We took tea in a spacious room on the second floor of the bath-house. An elderly waiter placed on the table a lacquered tray with a tea-pot and two cups and a plate of *taruto*, a sweet bean-paste wrapped in a cake roll. The black surface of the tray gleamed. The teapot and cups, squat and dark brown, seemed almost to float over the glossy reflective surface of the tray. Two slices of the *taruto* lay delicate and delectable on a small round saucer, also brown, that had been placed on the far side of the tray away from the teapot and cups. Two sets of pale chopsticks in white paper wrappers rested on either side of the saucer. Tanaka-san poured the *o-cha*, or tea, with care.

I glanced around the room. There were eight people, men and women, at other tables. They, too, were enjoying tea. Everybody wore their bathhouse *yukata*. Tanaka-san picked up a set of chopsticks, pulled them out of the wrapper, and snapped them apart. "We eat the cakes before having *o-cha*. Wakarimasu ka? Do you understand?"

"Hai, wakarimasu." "Yes, I understand."

I ate my cake. "Oiishi," I said. "Delicious." And it was. The mix of pastry and sweet paste melted in my mouth. Tanaka-san ate, too, and then he picked up the cup of tea. I followed suit, imitating him, cradling the handle-less cup against the palm of my right hand while resting its base on a platform of the fingers of my left hand and then bringing the cup to my mouth to take a careful sip of the scalding tea. It occurred to me that this was as close as I would likely get to a *cha-no-yu*, the tea ceremony, which is one of the most esoteric rituals in Japanese culture.

During my pre-pilgrimage researches, I'd read that *o-cha* symbolizes three dimensions of Japanese social life: relaxation, hospitality, and consolation. In times of distress, the Japanese will prepare a cup of tea as a psychological palliative. Tanaka-san apparently had something like that in mind for our little *chabanashi*.

"Niwano-san wants to thank you. He does not think they would have come this far without you."

"I am glad Shūji feels that I can help him."

Tanaka-san nodded and took another sip of tea. "The Henro Michi affects him very much now. He thanks you for this. He thanks Kōbō

Daishi for meeting you. He hopes we will complete the pilgrimage together."

I remembered once saying to Shūji, after he told me he was worried that Jun wanted to quit: "No excuses, no complaints. Just walk. That's all a man can do." I wasn't speaking particularly seriously, but Shūji took it that way, writing the phrase in his notebook. I hadn't given it any thought since then. Now, though, I asked myself, was it a worthy motto for a pilgrim? The English word "pilgrim" comes from the Latin phrase *per agrum*, or "through the fields." To the Romans, to be a pilgrim was to be an alien or stranger, to leave family and community and wander into the unknown. In the unknown, of course, you can't be sure of what will happen. The only thing you can learn to control as a pilgrim is how you respond. It struck me that perhaps Shūji was worried that he'd crossed some kind of line the night he'd confessed his fears, that I'd been offended or put off by his admissions and might no longer want to continue the pilgrimage with him and Jun. Was I, in his eyes, some kind of good luck charm, a talismanic assurance that he and Jun would complete their walk?

"I am happy to walk with Shūji. We will finish all together, ne? Dōgyō ninin." "Pilgrims together."

Tanaka-san smiled. "That is good. Shūji will be pleased." He paused for a moment and then said, "In Japan we have another name for the Shikoku pilgrimage: Shikoku *byōin*, Shikoku hospital. Shikoku heals those who follow Kōbō Daishi."

We finished our tea talk and went to meet Shūji and Jun in his new shoes. As we walked the ten kilometers to Taisanji, Temple Fifty-Two, and then on to the Uematsu *minshuku* where we spent the night, I kept thinking about the idea of the Henro Michi as a place of healing. What I wanted to know was: what is the illness for which the pilgrimage is the cure?

6

Enchantments

Roadside Jizō
smiling in a field—
village of young leaves.
—SHŪJI NIWANO

Tanaka-san taught me how to pray properly as we stood between the pillars at the entrance to Emmyōji, Temple Fifty-Three. Inside the temple, facing out toward us, was the gilded and cloth-draped statue of Amida Nyorai, the temple's *honzon*, or deity. I tried to ignore the feeling that I looked foolish as Tanaka-san showed me how to make the *gasshō*, or prayer mudra, with my hands positioned palm to palm and my head bowed.[1] Then I tried to imitate him as he chanted the Heart Sutra.

After five weeks on the Henro Michi, I was attempting to be more diligent as a pilgrim. Shūji's tormented confession a few days earlier had me thinking that our pilgrimage together had taken on a darker hue, a more somber significance. Like it or not, I'd been made a witness to a family drama whose outcome I couldn't predict or alter, much less direct. In some obscure inchoate way, I'd started to think that if chanting the Heart Sutra can open the heart to the wisdom of the Buddha, as tradition claims, then maybe it would help me to be a better witness.

So began my sixth week on the Shikoku pilgrimage, offering early morning prayers at the Temple of Circular Illumination, in the town of Wake, to deities I didn't believe in, chanting a prayer whose efficacy I doubted, and uttering words I didn't understand. Or so I'd told Tanaka-san the night before at dinner in the Uematsu *minshuku*.

"It does not matter," Tanaka-san had said, explaining that many Japanese don't know the meaning of the words either, or regard themselves as devout Buddhists. "To learn the Hannya Shingyō is to learn with your heart. You understand with your heart." The Heart Sutra, he explained, is the embodiment of the Buddha in sound. To recite the words, even in ignorance of their meaning, is to kindle the presence of the divine within yourself. Faith comes with practice.

I wasn't very good at praying, it seemed. Even as I tried to follow Tanaka-san, my mind drifted elsewhere. I was aware of the morning sun falling through gaps in the cedar trees surrounding the temple courtyard, dappling the damp gravel pathways in shifting patterns of shadow and light. I peeked at the watch on my left wrist when the sleeve of my pilgrim vest fell back to my elbow: it was nearly 8 a.m. I noticed how tanned my forearm had become after the weeks of walking. I enjoyed the warmth of the sun on my head and shoulders and the cool morning air on my face as I stared at Amida Nyorai, wondering if he, too, preferred the sun and the wind to all the supplications that came his way.

After we finished our *henro* rituals, we trundled along to the temple office to get a sleepy priest to stamp our *nōkyōchō*. Then we sat on a bench against a wall and enjoyed the early morning peace and quiet of the temple compound. We had to wait for Shūji and Jun. Jun was having a harder time getting moving in the mornings, and he and his father were late leaving the Uematsu *minshuku*.

I didn't mind. It was pleasant to sit in the cool shade of the wall, nursing a can of hot Georgia Café au Lait and inhaling the smell of the overhanging azaleas as we waited for our companions. I watched a priest in burgundy robes rake the bare earth around the bell tower. A man in a blue business suit walked across the courtyard to the main temple, setting his briefcase at the foot of the steps before climbing to strike the *waniguchi* bell three times before praying. Tanaka-san had explained to me that each ring of the bell represents a wish to rid yourself of one of the 108 deadly desires that plague human beings. I wondered which desires bothered this businessman. The sonorous bong seemed to echo for a long time within the walls of the compound. I could just make out the indistinct sound of the man's voice. Strangely, though, I seemed to hear in my head his chanting of the Hannya Shingyō, low and almost inaudible, despite the distance between us.

Tanaka-san was equally content to wait. His right foot had been bothering him for the past couple of days, causing him to limp. He shrugged off my inquiry with a grin, saying, "Kōbō Daishi is punishing me for drinking too much *shōchū*."

After Shūji arrived with Jun in tow—Jun still looking half-asleep—we followed the coastal road between Matsuyama and Imabari. We had lunch by the sea at Kazahayanosato Fuwari Beach, sitting against the driftwood logs, watching freighters and tankers and ferries as they churned along the Inland Sea between the islands of Shikoku and Honshu, and enjoying the cool wind off the emerald water.

It was much the same for the next few days. Along this stretch of the Henro Michi, the pilgrim path pretty much follows the northern coastline of Shikoku, cutting through suburban areas and across flat stretches of farmland and rice fields. Many of the temples were close together, separated by only a few kilometers, which meant that we would visit several in one day. I remember the walking as a cluster of images: the children's shrine at Emmeiji, Temple Fifty-Four, stuffed with toys and candy and bottles of juice at the feet of the Buddha statue; a packed field of *haka*, or family graves, and the war memorial outside Imabari; old men playing *shōgi*, Japanese chess, in a park; the green spread of the Imabari valley and the Inland Sea, blue and bright below us as we climbed to Senyūji, Temple Fifty-Eight; an elderly woman on her knees at Hōjuji, Temple Sixty-Two, weeping as she rocked back and forth in front of the statue of Kōbō Daishi. I wondered what sorrow caused such tears.

The other thing I remember from those days is Shūji becoming quieter and more somber. Weeks earlier he'd told me that he'd been born and raised in Imabari. He'd met his wife, Ikuko, there, and it was where Jun was born. Walking through Imabari on our way to Nankōbō, Temple Fifty-Five, we detoured off the pilgrim route to follow Shūji through the streets. He showed us the school he attended as a boy. We lingered in front of the high school where he met Ikuko after her classes. We wandered the nearby streets, the neighborhood where he'd spent his boyhood. We found the apartment, a wooden three-story building, where he and Ikuko once lived. Shūji pointed to a second-floor room with a window overlooking the intersection.

"That is where we lived after we got married," he said, staring up at the window. "Some days I wish we did not leave."

As we walked along a broad avenue and passed a Shinto shrine, Shūji spoke to Jun and then explained to me what he'd said. "I reminded Jun that this was the temple where we came for his"—Shūji paused, not knowing the English word—"hatsu miyamairi."

Following Shinto traditions, many Japanese parents take newborn children to the neighborhood shrine to introduce them to the presiding *kami* guarding the community. The *hatsu miyamairi*, or First Shrine Visit, is in some ways comparable to a Christian baptism in the sense that the infant becomes a member of the shrine. For boys, the visit occurs on the thirty-second day after birth, and for girls, on the thirty-third day. Similar visits—*shichigosan*, as they are called—occur when children are three, five, and seven years old in order to maintain the future protection of the *kami*. These visits are special occasions. Girls dress in a bright kimono, and boys wear the traditional *hakama*, a sort of split skirt with separate legs.[2]

We had our *bentō* lunch in a small park near the Shinto shrine. I asked Shūji why he left Imabari.

"There were no jobs on Shikoku when I was young," he replied. "Everybody went to Osaka or Tokyo."

Shūji was sixty-three, which meant he would have been a young boy in the aftermath of the Second World War. Like many Japanese cities, Imabari had been heavily bombed. Many of the city's shrines and temples went up in flames. Did Shūji have childhood memories of the war years?

"I still remember the fires," he said. "Many buildings were bombed and everything burned." He paused and looked up at the vermilion torii gate that stood at the entrance to the shrine. "Even this shrine had to be rebuilt."

After lunch, Shūji went to pray at the shrine, leaving the rest of us to our own devices. Jun smoked his cigarettes. I asked Tanaka-san why Japanese would be "baptized" at a Shinto shrine but then undertake a pilgrimage to Buddhist temples.

"Japanese people are born Shinto and die Buddhist," he explained.

"What is the difference whether you pray at a temple or a Shinto shrine? Your prayers are heard wherever you are."

Tanaka-san's remarks reinforced what I'd read about Japanese religious sensibilities—that they aren't like those in the West. Indeed it was only after Christian missionaries arrived in Japan in the sixteenth century that the Japanese came up with a word, *shūkyō*, for religion. *Shū* means "sect" and *kyō* means "doctrine." But both words, and the concept to which they refer, are contrary to the fluid attitude that Japanese take toward matters of the spirit. They don't believe you need to adhere exclusively to one "faith" or another. You can follow both Shinto and Buddhism if you so wish. Unlike Christianity, Judaism, and Islam, monotheistic religions with one omnipotent deity, Shinto and Buddhism are pantheistic and polytheistic. For the Japanese, there are many buddhas to worship and many *kami* whose help is available. Unlike churches, synagogues, or mosques, Shinto shrines and Buddhist temples can be the earthly abode of several deities.[3]

I'd also read that few Japanese—and certainly none I'd met—describe themselves as followers of Shinto, worshipping rocks and mountains and trees as the embodiment of guardian spirits. Nevertheless, parents continue to perform the *hatsu miyamairi* and other memorial rites for ancestral spirits, and the crowds visiting the shrines and temples grow each year. Much of this activity, scholars say, reflects a kind of nostalgic aestheticism rather than any claims of belief. People often partake of these traditions not because they believe in their underlying spiritual references but because the ceremonies foster a sense of social identity in an increasingly fragmented world.[4]

Perhaps so. But as I listened to Tanaka-san and Shūji and watched other pilgrims at the temples, it occurred to me that a Shinto sensibility and spirituality still bubbled below the surface in the Land of the Gods. Not surprisingly, Tanaka-san showed me where to find it.

***

We'd booked rooms for that night at the Miyako Ryokan in Imabari, and after our end-of-the-day baths we donned our *yukata* and our outdoor slippers and went searching for dinner. As usual, I had difficulty walking in the too-small slippers, as they kept falling off, and my too-small *yukata* was always threatening to flap open.

We paused outside several restaurants. Most of them had in their window displays plastic models of the food they offered: sushi, *ton-katsu, donburi*, soba, *shabu-shabu*. My stomach growled just looking at them. I waited impatiently for Tanaka-san and Shūji to stop their great debate as to which one was worthy of our patronage. Eventually, after much nodding and bowing, they finally agreed on a *koryōri-ya*, a small restaurant that specializes in a "small-dish" menu.

The Nisiya restaurant occupies a room on the second floor of a building near the Imabari train station. It has half a dozen tables, a gleaming zinc-topped bar, polished wood walls, and a wraparound picture window overlooking the street. There were only six other diners in the place when we arrived: a middle-aged couple and a foursome, two men and two women. The women were stylish and pretty, and I liked how they covered their mouths with their hands when they laughed. Inexplicably, the stereo played my favorite American jazz—Chet Baker, John Coltrane, and Ben Webster. It was dining satori as far as I was concerned.

The meal also proved enlightening, thanks to Jun and Tanaka-san. The waiter, a young man in black pants and a gleaming white shirt, set a tray of sauces in white porcelain bowls on the table. Jun explained the contents: one bowl was filled with a greenish sauce made of salt and tea leaves, the name of which I didn't catch; another contained sour vinegar called *ponzu*; and a third bowl held a garlic sauce known as *ninniku*. There was also a brass cup containing chopped zucchini and cabbage and slivers of raw onion bathed in a tangy sauce.

The food came on a series of brass platters. When we finished one, another arrived. Jun supplied me with the Japanese words for the different items on each platter: morsels of fresh raw *ika*, squid; *tako*, octopus; and *mūru-gai*, mussels. Then there was sliced lotus root stuffed with minced meat, deep-fried chunks of pork, and spears of asparagus. A third tray offered batter-fried shrimp; slices of shiitake mushrooms; and skewered chicken and *unagi*, eel. We nursed the meal with bottles of cold Kirin beer—but not before I got a lesson in Japanese spirituality.

I was struggling to pick up a piece of octopus when Tanaka-san leaned across the table and tapped my hand with his chopsticks.

"Chotto matte," he said. "Wait a minute."

It was a startling gesture from such a gentle man. I paused with my *hashi* hovering above the stubborn morsel. "Nan desu ka?" "What?" I asked, setting my chopsticks down on the little porcelain chopstick holder, the *hashi-oki*, next to my plate. I thought perhaps I'd shown bad manners, forgetting to wipe my hands with the hot damp cloth that Japanese restaurants provide for customers. Or maybe I'd forgotten to offer the ritual thank you that Japanese utter before each meal. So I bowed and said, "Dewa, itadakimasu." "I humbly receive."

Tanaka-san waved his chopsticks. "No, no," he said, "look at the food. Japanese people eat first with their eyes."

I'd noticed that he and Shūji, and sometimes Jun, paused for a brief moment to gaze at their food before eating. I'd assumed that they were offering a silent prayer. But Tanaka-san was articulating something I'd read about in my research but apparently not absorbed: the Japanese practice of not beginning to eat your food as soon as it's set before you. Instead, you take a moment to appreciate the food visually before you appreciate its taste. This spiritually aesthetic—or aesthetically spiritual?—practice of briefly pausing to take pleasure in and appreciate even the ordinary activity of eating is an essential part of Japanese culture.[5]

Another core concept is the principle of purity. This notion, while rooted in religion, has passed from shrine to society. For example, the Japanese insistence on meticulous ablutions reflects Shinto's emphasis on cleanliness and having everything in its proper place. But the idea of purity was also at work in the Nisiya restaurant. Japanese cuisine demonstrates a poetic regard for the products of nature from land and sea.[6]

"Look at how everything is arranged on the plate," Tanaka-san explained. "You place the food on the plate to please the eye. This is very Japanese."

I tried to absorb Tanaka-san's lesson, tried to *see* the food in front of my eyes. And for a moment I came close: the four morsels of eel side by side on a small, rectangular ceramic plate, the darker hue of the seafood enhanced by the white background of the plate. The white slices of lotus root formed an upside-down crescent on a circular blue plate. They reminded me of the fronds of a bamboo tree silhouetted against the sky. The gleaming surface of the red lacquered tray made the dark green of the asparagus spears more vivid. I thought of the forests I'd walked through over the last month and a half.

I looked up at Tanaka-san and Shūji. "Wakarimasu," I said. "I see."

My companions smiled. "We make you Japanese someday," said Shūji.

"Tabemashō," said Tanaka-san. "Let's eat."

After Tanaka-san's lesson I began to see things just a bit differently. Whatever I looked at with conscious intention—trees and temples, sea and sky—stood out in sharp distinction from the surrounding background. Ordinary things—a child's tricycle in a driveway, three oranges in a roadside shrine, the wind rippling on the water in a rice field, green spring wheat—shimmered with an aura of significance.

But it wasn't only my sense of sight that became more acute. In sound, smell, and texture—the crunch of gravel, the whiff of a barnyard, the smoothness of a bamboo stalk—my senses buzzed like wires humming with electricity. I felt as though I'd reached a kind of psychic plateau that left me feeling both deeply contented and, at the same time, strangely excited. Everything was clear and intense yet also peaceful and quiet.[7]

The next day's walk was an example of this new sensibility. In the morning, we traipsed beyond the suburbs of Imabari, praying at the small temples of Taisanji and Eifukuji, Temples Fifty-Six and Fifty-Seven, in Koizumi and Tamagawa. At about 11 a.m. we stopped at a Lawson convenience store to buy food, thinking we would have lunch at Senyūji, Temple Fifty-Eight. In addition to the usual bottles of water and Pocari Sweat, I bought a *bentō* box.

It took about an hour to climb to the temple. The hike was a feast for the senses: the scent of cherry trees along a suburban street; rhododendrons nodding in a garden behind a wall; a gargoyle grinning on the corner of a tiled roof; a caterpillar crawling across the road; a pair of hawks playing in the sky; the refracted sparkle of water drops on the filaments of a cobweb attached to a trailside shrine; the hot diesel smell of a passing farm tractor—I took it all in like a parched man given a bottle of water.

The path to the temple climbed through a narrow gorge with moss-covered walls looming overhead. A canopy of cedar trees turned the sun green. Every few feet shrines were set into alcoves in the rock face. A stream tumbled down on the right, splashing and gurgling. The air was cool, damp, and fragrant. The climb was also steep, especially for the last half-kilometer. By the time I reached the temple gate, I was panting and soaked in sweat, and my legs screamed for mercy. I collapsed on a bench beneath some old maple trees in the small courtyard. Only after I caught my breath did I do my *henro* ablutions and perform the proper rituals. Then I returned to the bench beneath the white-draped statue of Kannon to enjoy my *bentō* lunch and to admire the view of Imabari in the valley below and the gleaming spread of the Inland Sea.

It was Tanaka-san's lesson, of course, that made me pause before picking up the chopsticks. A *bentō* box has compartments for different morsels of food—everything from rice and vegetables to sashimi and tempura. I'd been buying and consuming them for weeks, but this was the first time I really looked at one. Mine had four compartments. One contained rolls of rice wrapped with bands of dried seaweed. Another held slices of sashimi—*maguro* and *shimesaba*, tuna and mackerel—along with a green dab of wasabi, the hot Japanese equivalent of horseradish. A third was reserved for vegetable tempura. Finally, there was a fourth section for *takenoko* and a piece of *tamago*, bamboo shoots and sweetened omelet, and a couple of slices of *kamaboko*, a fish-paste roll.

I tried to eat with my eyes, tried to see the scenery of my lunch. For a moment, I think I had it. For a few seconds I was looking down on a Japanese landscape from a great height: the white rice from the valley fields, the raw fish from the sea, the slices of bamboo from the mountain slopes. But then the vision blinked out like a lighted room suddenly darkened by the flick of a switch. Still, I continued to eat slowly, savoring the flavors—the melt-in-your-mouth *maguro*, the crunch of the bamboo shoots, the sweet sashimi that complemented the sour vinegar taste of the rice—hoping the light might go back on again.

Western psychologists label such experiences as direct perception—that is, moments when the normally self-referential, constantly chattering ego is quiescent and doesn't immediately try to judge, second-guess, or analyze its actions. For a brief moment there is no distance, no gap, between the experience and the awareness of the experience. The Japanese are also familiar with the psychology of these moments of intense awareness, and they call it *yoin*.

The word *yoin* refers to a reverberation or resonance, such as that made by a struck bell. But it is also used to describe, however inadequately, moments of deep feeling that are experienced without reflection. A silent smile between husband and wife, the unstated recognition between lovers reunited after a long absence, a parent's wordless caress of a sleeping child—such situations embody *yoin*. But *yoin* is also evident in situations where the ordinary turns extraordinary—where, as it seems, you are on the threshold of some degree of transcendence, modest or otherwise.[8]

I like to think that my *bentō* epiphany was a moment of *yoin*. In those brief seconds, I saw Japan in the way that Tanaka-san wanted me to see it. I don't mean that I acquired some deep insight into the Japanese soul. It was simply that I momentarily perceived something meaningful that I hadn't previously grasped. I suddenly felt my two months in Japan resonate in me like, well, the reverberations of a struck bell.

As I sat in the shade of Kannon, it struck me that Bashō's poems reflect this quality of *yoin*, their initial articulation as close to a spontaneous expression of a moment's epiphany as you can get with words. I remembered one of my favorite haiku: "Along the roadside, / blossoming wild roses / in my horse's mouth."[9] In my head I saw Bashō resting on the edge of some road, watching his horse forage, and suddenly seeing the animal pulling up a mouthful of wild roses and finding this a revelation of the extraordinariness of the ordinary. Such moments seldom last more than a few seconds. But I think this is what both Bashō and I experienced: a second or two when the gap between the perception of the object and the awareness of the experience disappeared, and we knew the essence of that thing.[10]

***

The remainder of the day had a similar quality. The world hummed and thrummed with significance. I saw omens and portents, meaning and metaphor, everywhere. Tanaka-san's sore ankle, for example: he'd been favoring his right leg for several days now, limping as he pulled the trolley holding his backpack. So far, though, he'd coped with the pain. But the climb to Temple Fifty-Eight was too much. I was clearing up the remnants of my lunch, looking around for a garbage can, when he hobbled toward me, grimacing with each step. He sat beside me and hiked up his pants leg. His right ankle was red and swollen and bulged over the top of his boot. He'd loosened the laces to relieve the pressure, but now the whole boot bulged.

"Can you take it off?" I asked, remembering my own blister problems from a month ago.

Tanaka-san shook his head. "I don't know. I haven't tried. I don't think I can walk anymore today."

Shūji and Jun came up to us. "I am going to take a bus or a taxi to the next temple," Tanaka-san said. "My leg is bad." He suggested that the three of us go on to Temple Fifty-Nine, Kokubunji, about seven kilometers away. He would get a taxi and meet us later at the hotel where we had rooms for the night. Shūji and Jun left, but I decided to stick with Tanaka-san, at least until Temple Fifty-Nine. I could see he was worried. I offered to split the cab fare.

While we'd been having our lunch, two tour buses had arrived. The courtyard was crowded with bus pilgrims. After performing their *henro* rituals, they milled around the main hall, ready to depart.

"Maybe they will give us a lift," Tanaka-san said.

He got to his feet and limped across the courtyard to find the group leader. I followed, shouldering my pack and pulling Tanaka-san's trolley. My companion spoke to a white-haired man dressed in white pilgrim robes, a group leader, *sendatsu*, by the name of Kenji Imanishi. Unlike Tanaka-san's and mine, Imanishi-san's *hakui* was spotlessly clean. Tanaka-san told me that he'd explained about his ankle and that the bus pilgrims were glad to take him, but they weren't sure they had any extra space for me. I said that was fine, I could walk.

In the end I didn't have to. Imanishi-san spoke to the driver of the second bus, which did have a spare seat, and a pilgrim on the first bus took that seat so that I could ride with Tanaka-san.

"Settai," said the pilgrim, bowing as he transferred to the other bus.

I bowed to the rows of elderly Japanese when I stepped onto the bus. Some forty or fifty men and women stared at me. Someone uttered "gaijin da"—"it's a foreigner"—loud enough for me to hear.

Just before boarding the bus, anticipating how I should behave, I'd quickly looked up in my research notebook one of my stock Japanese phrases: "Dōzo yoroshiku. Goshinsetsu ni arigatō gozaimasu," I said. "I am glad to meet you. Thank you sincerely for your kindness."

They must have understood me, however awful my pronunciation. There was a burst of laughter, and the bus pilgrims applauded the foreigner's attempt at politeness.

I repeated the performance half an hour later, thanking the group and Imanishi-san when we stepped off the bus at Kokubunji after a short drive through a maze of rice paddies and vegetable farms. One of the pilgrims insisted that Tanaka-san and I pose for pictures with him and his wife. Then everybody's camera came out. There were handshakes and bows all around. I had to sign several *osamefuda*. When we finally left the temple minutes later—Tanaka-san to catch a cab and me to walk on alone—I noticed a dozen or so members of the bus group squatting in a line on a low wall in the temple parking lot eating their lunch. In their clean white robes and conical hats, they looked like big mushrooms on a log. Somebody must have said something because they all stood in unison and bowed as I passed. Maybe it was the heat of the day or the soporific lassitude I felt after the bus ride, but for a moment I thought I was seeing a row of white-draped statues stepping forward to greet me. Maybe I was; I returned the bow.

The Hotel Tachibana-Bekkan was about five or six kilometers from Temple Fifty-Nine, part of a complex of resort hotels off Highway 156 near the town of Kokubu. After the noise and diesel smell of the road, the hotel was an oasis of greenery and serenity. I had to hike about a kilometer off the highway into a park-like setting, following a loop of road past posh-looking glass-and-stone buildings—other hotels, I presumed—until I found the Hotel Tachibana at the end of a cul-de-sac. After weeks of modest *ryokan* and *minshuku*, it was positively luxurious.

The hotel was set back in the trees on a plateau overlooking the Inland Sea. I had a splendid room. The tatami were clean and the futon freshly laundered. A thermos of hot water and a lacquered tea caddy occupied a low polished table in the middle of the room. A fresh *yukata*, starched and pressed, lay on the table. The room also had its own *o-furo*. There was a small alcove-like sitting area off the main room, with two wicker chairs on either side of another low table. A wide picture window looked across a lawn toward a beach that fronted the blue sea. A stand of cedar trees shaded part of the lawn. Behind the cedars was a gray stone shrine surrounded by gravel paths leading down to the waterfront. Not bad for 6,600 yen a night, or about $66.

Naturally, I found the beer machine just down the hall. After I got the hot water running in the bath, I bought two cans of Asahi beer. I took one into the bath with me. I saved the other can for sitting in my dry *yukata* in the alcove, with my tired legs propped on the table, and watching the passing ships. The long shadows of the cedar trees had stretched across the lawn and the sea was growing dark when there was a knock at my door.

"Dōzo," I called out. "Come in."

Tanaka-san, dressed in his *yukata*, limped into the room, his right ankle badly swollen. He declined the offer of a beer, so I made him a cup of tea. Shūji and Jun had just arrived, he said, and they were going to have their baths before joining us for supper. Tanaka-san had arrived at the hotel several hours early. He'd been sleeping, hoping to give his foot some rest. If it wasn't any better in the morning, he would find a pharmacy or a doctor and then take a train to Komatsu while the rest of us walked. He was worried that if his foot didn't improve, he wouldn't be able to make the climb to Temple Sixty, one of the hardest climbs on the pilgrimage route.

When Tanaka-san mentioned wanting to find a drugstore, I suddenly remembered the anti-inflammatory pills my doctor back home, Dr. Roger Wray, had prescribed for me in case I needed them. I rummaged through my pack and found the bottle buried in a side pocket. "These might help you with the swelling," I said, explaining their purpose. I suggested he take one now and another before bed.

We had supper in the hotel's cavernous dining room. We were the only diners. The cook seemed overjoyed to have something to do. He came to our table twice to make sure we liked the food. The waiter, too, was eager to please, although somewhat startled at my repeated requests for cups of coffee. When we left, I made sure to bow to him and express my gratitude for his service. "Gochisosama." Of course I also left a big tip.

After the others went to their rooms, I bought a small bottle of sake from the machine and parked myself on one of the black leather couches in front of the picture window. I replayed the day's walk in my head, caught up on my notes, and watched the lights of the ships float past in the darkness.

The pills did the trick. The swelling on Tanaka-san's ankle had subsided considerably by morning. The pain, too, had diminished. He was effusive in his gratitude.

"You have saved my walk. You are Kōbō Daishi."

"My doctor, he is Kōbō Daishi," I said, suggesting another pill after breakfast. On a pilgrimage, such serendipity constitutes a miracle of sorts.

Better or not, Tanaka-san nonetheless wanted a doctor to check his foot. He decided to take the train to Komatsu and walk the remaining short distance to Temple Sixty-One, Kōonji, which by the route we followed actually came before Yokomineji, Temple Sixty. I was tempted to go with him. We planned to visit three nondescript temples that day— Kōonji, Hōjuji, and Kichijōji, Temples Sixty-One, Sixty-Two, and Sixty-Three—since they were in close proximity to each other. All told we would be walking twenty kilometers along a busy highway through suburbs and industrial areas—not exactly a scenic or spiritually uplifting trek.

On the other hand, the sun was shining and the sky was clear, and unlike Tanaka-san, I had no justifiable excuse for not walking. In the end, we—Shūji, Jun, and I—left the hotel at 7:30 a.m. to follow Highway 196, leaving Tanaka-san to catch a taxi to the train station.

Kōonji, the Temple of the Incense Garden, has to be the ugliest pilgrimage temple on Shikoku. This is not because it's old and run-down but because it's new and modern. The *hondō* is a huge Western-style building that wouldn't look out of place in a North American city. The small, white-painted *daishidō* has a lovely statue of Kōbō Daishi. But the main hall reminded me of a government office or a university building. Its saving grace is the stunning second-floor hall with its theater-like seating in front of a huge golden Buddha. That was impressive. But I still preferred the plain temples, Hōjuji and Kichijōji, Temples Sixty-Two and Sixty-Three, with their tree-shrouded, raked-gravel courtyards and their weatherworn, slightly tattered-looking halls.

These two older temples were only a few kilometers from Kōonji, so we visited them before calling it a day and finding the Business Hotel Daichi in Komatsu. We had rooms there for two nights, since we would be coming back to it the next day after our hike to Yokomineji. Tanaka-san was waiting for us at the hotel. His foot, he said, was much better after a day of rest and more of my pills.

That night after supper, Tanaka-san, Shūji, and I found a *nawa-noren*. It was barely bigger than the kitchen in my house, with a long bench for sitting in front of a stained and cigarette-burned counter. Behind the bar a set of sagging shelves held rows of sake, beer, and *shōchū*. The air was thick with smoke. Half a dozen men with their ties loosened sat around a low table, laughing and yelling and banging the table as they knocked back their beers. We sat on the bench. Tanaka-san spoke to the bar owner, a short, round-faced woman with a missing left incisor. She grabbed a brown keg of *shōchū* from the shelf, filled a *tokkuri*, and set the slender bottle and three mismatched cups on the countertop. I remembered my manners and let my companions fill my cup while I filled theirs.

We didn't talk much that night—not that it would have been easy with all the noise. I inquired after Tanaka-san's ankle. How was he feeling?

"Much better, dōmo," he replied. Tanaka-san had seen a doctor and had an ingrown and infected nail on his big toe removed. He was taking pills to treat the infection and the inflammation. He thought he would be able to walk in the morning.

Shūji said he was relieved that Tanaka-san was still able to walk and that with only twenty-five temples to go—after tomorrow's long climb to Temple Sixty—we might be able to complete the pilgrimage together.

"Kampai," we said, toasting that thought.

Otherwise, we sat quietly, keeping an eye on each other's cups, watching the other patrons getting drunk and loquacious, and thinking our own thoughts. I liked that about the Japanese: the ability to sit quietly without feeling compelled to natter. Unlike most North Americans, the Japanese aren't afraid of silence, including their own, and they regard it as the unsaid part of a conversation between companions who are comfortable with each other. If there is no need to talk, there is no embarrassment in silent togetherness.

Sipping my *shōchū*, I went over the events from the past week in my head, trying to figure out whether my sense of their extraordinariness was merely the result of endorphin overload or the product of what the psychologist Carl Jung called synchronicity. After four cups of *shōchū* I was tilting toward synchronicity—the idea that, as Jung argued, there can be an equivalence of psychic and physical processes; meaningful relationships can exist between psychic and physical events that have no apparent causal connection. The world is ripe with meaningful coincidence, and the meaning of those moments is occasionally discoverable in the subterranean chambers of the mind. The trick is to learn ways to tap those regions, and walking was one of those ways, or so it seemed to me.[11]

Synchronicity certainly provided a tempting concept to apply to the string of serendipitous situations and beneficial coincidences that had given my Henro Michi such resonance. I thought of the Toyota metallurgist who got me my new walking shoes, the nurse who'd given me a foot salve, and the Buddhist nun who gave me a ride that allowed me to keep walking with Shūji and Jun. Then there was Tanaka-san: meeting him had unquestionably made the pilgrimage more meaningful—especially for Shūji, I thought, remembering his soul-wrenching confession of anger and despair about Jun. Was it all meaningless coincidence?

Weaving our way back to the hotel, I saw the dark bulk of the mountain we would be climbing in the morning, silhouetted against the evening sky above the roofline of the buildings. The only way to reach Yokomineji is on foot. There's no transportation all the way to the temple, and the climb, according to my guidebook, is "a perilous, unpaved path that makes you fear for your life."[12]

✳✳✳

The next afternoon I descended the rock-strewn slope, dropping deeper into the dark cedar forest of Mount Yokomine. The trail looked the same as all the other mountain paths that I'd been taking in the hope of finding one that would lead me back to the valley town of Komatsu. I had to admit I was lost.

Earlier that day, the four of us had made the long climb together to Yokomineji. I had to agree with my guidebook that, at 709 meters above sea level, Temple Sixty was "the single most difficult temple to reach." The climb had been a lung-aching thigh-burner, and if I'd had to climb the mountain in the early days of my pilgrimage I probably wouldn't have made it, or would have taken an inordinate amount of time to do so. But after nearly seven weeks of walking, I was in much better shape physically. I was huffing and puffing after the four-hour climb, but it took only a few minutes' rest for my breathing and my heart rate to return to normal. I was pleased that I felt ready to keep going.

Yokomineji itself had been worth the climb. Hidden in the forest, the 1,300-year-old temple, with its gray and weatherworn halls, possesses a haunting sense of isolation and timelessness. When we had finished our rituals, we sat in the courtyard among the rhododendrons and azaleas and ate lunch, enjoying the cool quiet and the distant view of the surrounding mountains. I liked the swept courtyard, the hard-packed ground showing the scratch marks of the twig brooms still used by the temple priests, and the curving lines of raked gravel swirling around the large boulders in the rock garden. I imagined the generations of priests who'd spent the last millennium maintaining a modicum of order and beauty in their small world.

After lunch, Shūji had said he had something he wanted to show Tanaka-san and me. "A special place," he said. Tanaka-san begged off. The morning's climb hadn't done his ankle any good. He was going to head back to our hotel in Komatsu. I wasn't enamored of the idea of more climbing, either, but I owed Shūji the courtesy of interest. So I followed him and Jun up a narrow path above the temple to a small plateau in a forest clearing. On one side of the plateau, set in a copse of trees, was a stone grotto containing apron-wrapped statues of Buddha and Jizō. The wax of guttered candles, vases of flowers, and a scattering of oranges rested on the rock shelves beside the statues. Beyond the grotto, the ground sloped across the plateau to the edge of a cliff overlooking a cedar-thick valley. Near the edge of the precipice stood a Shinto torii gate.

Torii are a common sight in Japan. The gates are composed of two pillars topped by curving crossbeams. They are usually made of wood and painted a brilliant vermilion.[13] You find torii in front of Shinto shrines or at the ends of tree-lined lanes. The gate tells visitors they are entering the dwelling of *kami*, of spirits. To walk through a torii is to enter sacred space. I liked their elegant lines and graceful simplicity, but they always gave me a lonely feeling, as though they were sentinels of a lost cause, guardians of a treasure that nobody remembered having lost.

Approaching the torii on Mount Yokomine, Shūji and I had stopped on one side of the gate, dropped our packs, and bowed before walking between the pillars. Across the valley was the gray mass of Mount Ishi-zuchi, the highest mountain in western Japan, at 1,982 meters. While Jun scrounged through his pack for cigarettes, Shūji walked to the edge of the cliff to stare in silence at the mountain. I followed him. We squatted on the ground.

"When I was young, Jun's age, I climbed Ishizuchi," he said, gestur-ing at the mountain.

"Alone?" I asked.

"Hai, by myself. It took me three days. I camped."

"Before you were married?"

"Hai."

"Never again?"

Shūji shook his head. He lapsed into silence as he sat cross-legged with his palms on his knees and his back straight, staring at the moun-tain and glancing occasionally at Jun, who had stretched out on the ground nearby for a nap. Shūji looked up at me, but for a moment I had the feeling he wasn't seeing me at all. There was a startled, almost frightened look in his eyes. He had seemed to wrench himself away from whatever inner vista he'd been staring at to focus on me. I thought he was about to say something, but he shook his head, stood and bowed, and walked away. I watched as he went to the grotto and stood before the statues, with his head bowed and his hands held palm to palm at his breast. I recognized the prayer mudra known as *gasshō*. It's often used when seeking the Buddha's forgiveness. I thought back to the evening of Shūji's confession after we'd visited Temple Forty-Four. I wondered what he'd seen, looking across the inner landscape of his memory, and why he needed forgiveness. It occurred to me that Shūji was a very lonely man despite his companions. I wished that I could speak better Japanese, that I could do more to help my friend.

When Shūji finished his prayers, he woke up Jun and we walked back to Yokomineji. That's when I dawdled, letting Shūji and Jun get ahead of me. I wanted to walk alone through the cathedral-like silence of the forest. About two kilometers below the temple, I turned off the asphalt road to follow a path that I thought would lead me back to Komatsu by a less-traveled route. But I didn't pay attention to where I was going and ended up somewhere on the side of the mountain, wandering through a criss-cross maze of logging trails and farmers' tracks.

An hour later I was sitting on a half-rotten log at the edge of a trail, studying my map to figure out where I was. I looked at my watch: 1:44 p.m. I had plenty of daylight left, lots of time to get off the mountain before nightfall. Not to worry.

The map showed two pilgrim trails leading from Komatsu to Yokomineji but not the logging trails or the farmers' tracks. I retraced on the map my last hour's walk, locating the fork in the trail that I'd taken after leaving the road. I figured I had two choices: retrace my steps back to that fork and return to the highway, or go on. The prospect of climbing the mountain again had no appeal. I decided to stick with whatever trail I was on, figuring that sooner or later it would reach the valley floor where, presumably, I'd find either the pilgrim route or a road back to Komatsu.

On the basis of such vague reasoning, I ended up having some of the most memorable hours of my entire pilgrimage. I might have been lost in the geographic sense, but I was also lost to the senses. After nearly seven weeks of walking, I perceived the world in a different way. Psychologically, my sense of time had shifted as the pace of walking literally forced my mind to slow down. The landscape of cedar forest and distant vistas, the downpour of sun and rain, the shower of birdsong and prayer—instead of work, traffic, bills, television, and radio—had cast a spell of enchantment. I now attended to more important things: sunlight in the trees, flowers in a ditch, birds in the bush.

So it was on this day, too. I was absorbed by mountain air pungent with damp cedar; trails edged with blue wisteria, azaleas in pink, yellow, and red, along with purple iris; slabs of sunlight falling through gaps in the trees; the shuffling sound of my feet on leaf-strewn paths; nightingales singing *hō-hokekyo, hō-hokekyo*. And then there was the enchantment of the inner voyage. I seemed to float above myself, watching as my body did the hard work of climbing up a slope or scrambling over rocks while my mind wandered on its own. Images from the past weeks replayed in my head: the green glow of a sunlit river; black-bellied clouds far out to sea; a parade of low-lying clouds floating through a mountain valley; a village street silent except for the rain gurgling in the gutters.

My mind was a pilgrim mind now. There were even moments in the silence of the forest when I was willing to believe, as Buddhist tradition claims, that I was never alone, that Bashō and Jizō and Kōbō Daishi were my constant companions, walking nearby but just beyond my field of vision.

As it turned out, it was Jizō, the bald-headed deity who keeps an eye on children, the souls of the dead, and, as it seemed, inattentive travelers, who restored me to the proper path. I'd been following a farmer's trail that consisted of two rutted tracks and a line of grass running down the center. High grass and bush edged the trail, and a wall of trees loomed overhead. I didn't know where I was, only that I was heading north and would presumably reach civilization sooner or later. Rounding a corner, I came to an intersection with three trails leading off in different directions. I squatted in the middle of the crossroads, looking up one path and then another. I had no idea which one to follow. Then, out of the corner of my eye, I caught a flash of color. There, at the edge of a track, poking above the grass and drooping weeds like a child playing peek-a-boo, was a small statue of my pilgrim hero, Jizō. Bless his tiny red toque.

Always follow the Jizō, I told myself. Where there is one Jizō, there will be more. I wanted to prance down the trail, singing, "Jizō loves me, this I know, because the Buddha tells me so." I straightened Jizō's toque and splashed him with generous dollops of water from my bottle. Two hundred meters down the track, I came to another Jizō and another intersection. This one turned onto a two-lane asphalt road with a beautiful yellow stripe down the middle. I splashed more water on Jizō by way of thanks.

But the little deity wasn't done with me yet. The road dropped steeply around a sharp turn. Trotting down the hill, I saw below me on the right side of the road, through a gap in the treetops, the roof of a temple set in a narrow gorge. I could hear a waterfall. At the bottom of the hill I found a small gravel parking lot and a pathway that disappeared into a grove of cedars. I looked at my watch. It was nearly 3:30 p.m. I hesitated to stop, uncertain how far I was from Komatsu. But instinct—Jizō demanding his due?—told me not to pass this temple without offering a prayer. It doesn't pay to ignore the gods, especially when they've been good to you. I crunched across the gravel and through another tunnel of trees and found one of the strangest and loveliest places on the Henro Michi, a place that, as it turned out, provided me with one of my most meaningful pilgrimage experiences.

***

The Kōōnji *okunoin*, as I later learned, is a *bangai*, an unnumbered temple that isn't counted among the eighty-eight temples that make up the formal Shikoku pilgrimage circuit, although it is officially attached to Kōonji, Temple Sixty-One. *Okunoin* means "inner sanctuary," and, in the case of this *bangai*, Buddhist ascetics use it to perform some form of *suigyō*, a meditative technique that involves standing under waterfalls, immersing yourself in icy water, or dousing yourself with buckets of freezing water as a form of spiritual discipline. The discipline, which has various names in Japanese and has a long tradition, reflects the belief that rigorous physical exertion is a means to greater spiritual awareness. The essential idea is to push the body to its limits in order to break down the barriers of reason and logic and interrupt the incessant chatter of everyday consciousness. The idea, as I'd read, is "to achieve the 'dropping off of body and mind.'"[14]

I had no such expectations as I followed the footpath toward the *shōrō* and rang the bell to announce my presence. Next to the bell tower was a wooden building. The door was unlocked, and I peeked inside. Rows of benches were set against the walls and ran the length of the building on each side. Plastic flip-flops were lined up in neat formation on the slat floor in front of the benches. It looked like a gym teacher's dream of a high school locker room, only much cleaner and better smelling.

Beyond the tower was a small courtyard. High cliffs enclosed the compound. A gurgling creek ran through the courtyard on the right. Benches, statuary, incense urns, and candleholders were set against the sheer rock face on the left. At the far end of the courtyard was a waterfall guarded by three statues, green with age. Two were set in alcoves on each side of the waterfall, and the third, larger one stood on a cairn of rock at the top of the falls.

The place was empty and silent save for the cascade of water falling into a pool. The cedars on the cliffs formed a canopy overhead, filtering the sunlight to give the courtyard a green glow. Shafts of late afternoon sun fell in a sharp slant through gaps in the trees to create pools of light on the ground. Mist rose above the creek, floating in the cool air like a batch of newly minted souls. I wondered if I'd stumbled into a secret retreat where *kami* and bodhisattvas took their breaks after tending to all those beseeching humans.

I sat on a bench against the cliff face to listen to the waterfall and to absorb the peacefulness. The sound of the water was hypnotic. After a while I strolled across the courtyard to the pool to study the statues. I recognized the one at the top of the waterfall as Fudō Myōō, the fierce-faced protector of the Buddhist faith. Below him, beside the pool, were his child servants, Kongara and Seitaka. A line of stepping-stones stretched across the pool from the edge of the courtyard to a flat rock shelf under the waterfall directly beneath Fudō Myōō.

According to legend, Fudō Myōō appeared to a ninth-century priest named So-o, a Grand Patriarch of the Tendai sect of Buddhism, as he stood under a waterfall. The shock inspired the priest to establish Tendai Buddhism's main temple on Mount Hiei, near Kyoto, and to begin an ascetic discipline known as *kaihōgyō*—the practice of circling the mountain—in which practitioners try to transform themselves into the living embodiment of Fudō Myōō. The discipline of *kaihōgyō* symbolizes the monk's willingness to withdraw from the community of the living and to recast himself as a wanderer in the land of the dead. After years of initiation, a would-be Tendai monk is required to complete the *hyaku-nichi*, a practice in which monks walk forty kilometers a day for one hundred consecutive days, repeatedly circling Mount Hiei. They sleep maybe two hours a day and eat little more than a couple of rice balls and a bowl of soup. With only straw sandals on their feet even in winter, the monks walk the mountain's rough trails, enduring blisters, frostbite, and fever. The point is to die to this world and become a living embodiment of the divine.[15]

The hundred-day practice is nonetheless basic training. There are more rigorous seven-hundred-day and thousand-day practices. Not everyone makes it. Mount Hiei's trails are dotted with the grave markers of monks who died during their training. Those who do make it, however, apparently acquire amazing perceptual powers. I'd read about

Gyosho Uehara, a senior monk at Mount Hiei Temple—and one of only fifty or so monks who have successfully completed the thousand-day *kaihōgyō* in the last four centuries—who claimed that some monks could hear the sound of ash falling off incense sticks.[16]

Standing in the courtyard at the Kōōnji *okunoin*, staring at Fudō Myōō, I envied those Tendai priests their self-discipline. What kind of mental strength did it take to go beyond physical limits? Compared to them I was a spiritual dilettante. Beyond the walking, I hadn't imposed many austerities on myself. If pilgrimage involves self-discipline and functions as a symbolic act of death, I'd chosen to party. I'd taken advantage of vending machines and convenience stores to indulge in bottles of Pocari Sweat and cans of Georgia Café au Lait. I'd gorged on sashimi and udon. I loved my end-of-the-day *o-furo* and fresh-smelling *yukata*, not to mention the beer and *shōchū*. True, so did everyone else, but that's hardly an excuse. Was I on a religious pilgrimage or a gastronomic holiday? Isn't a pilgrim supposed to die a little?

My self-induced—self-indulgent?—guilt might explain what I did next. Hustling to the bathhouse, I stripped off my shoes and clothes, stuffed my watch in a pocket, donned a pair of the too-small blue flip-flops, and toddled back across the courtyard clad in a small white towel. I stepped gingerly on the stone path across the pool, trying not to lose the flip-flops in the water. I slipped only once, but Kōbō Daishi—my walking stick, that is—saved me from an embarrassing plunge.

There's probably a technique for stepping into an ice-cold waterfall, but I didn't know what it was. As I stepped forward on the flat rock under the water, I could hear Dr. Wray back home saying, "You idiot, you'll give yourself a heart attack."

There was no heart seizure, but I certainly got a shock. The icy water drilling into the top of my head and shoulders not only stripped the towel away but also ripped the breath out of my lungs. I lasted all of a nanosecond before I leapt out, gasping and shrieking. Of course I couldn't accept such humiliation. I gritted my teeth and plunged under the waterfall again. This time I tried chanting the Heart Sutra, getting in as many "gyate, gyate, hara gyate" as I could before stepping out, shaking and shuddering. I tried a third time, stretching out the chants for as long as possible, clenching my teeth and willing my body to stillness. This time I stayed in the icy shower chanting away until my shoulders and head felt numb. I stepped away when I could no longer catch my breath and everything started to go dark before my eyes.

Fudō Myōō didn't reward my meager effort at asceticism with his presence. The only witness to my effort at spiritual discipline was a jeering nightingale. I made my way back across the courtyard to the bathhouse, towel in hand, wincing at the sharp gravel on my bare feet after my flip-flops had flown off and into the pool. There was no way I was going to retrieve them. I was shivering and shaking like a wind-blown scarecrow on a winter field. I used three towels to scrub myself dry and restore my circulation before I dressed. I folded the wet towels and hung them on a rack to dry and then left two 1,000-yen notes to pay for my trespassing and for losing the flip-flops.

I felt lightheaded and unsteady as I walked back across the courtyard. At the same time, I was exhilarated. I sat on a bench near the candle stand again, waiting for the wooziness and the occasional shiver to pass. In terms of spiritual conditioning, I was seriously out of shape.

I checked my watch. It was just after 5:30 p.m. The sky had turned overcast. Without the sun filtering through the treetops, the courtyard took on a twilight luminescence, as if the light were rising from the earth instead of falling from the sky. The maples and cedars on the cliffs lost their distinctiveness in the absence of light, blurring into a solid gray-green canopy. Yet I remained, waiting and listening to the waterfall and the faint stir of the trees. As I waited, the sound of the waterfall seemed to fade into the background. And slowly, through some alchemy of solitude, silence, and the day's exertions, stillness settled on me. The world fell away, and the memory of an all-but-forgotten incident from my childhood took over my mind: the day I fell off a playground swing and knocked myself out. The image surfaced like an iceberg emerging from the water.

I was eight or nine years old again, at a playground in northwest Calgary, with a neighborhood girl, Carol Papworth. We were standing on separate swings, pumping with our legs to see how high we could go. Carol's blonde hair flew like a flag. The swing's metal links screeched and groaned as we sailed back and forth. The rush of wind pulled at my clothes as the swing plunged downward. I bent my legs to push myself higher. As the swing reached its apogee, I felt a mix of fear and thrill as I leaned back, legs stiff and straight, arms rigid and pulling on the metal links, to enjoy the fall backwards and the momentary weightlessness. But that day, either my grip wasn't strong enough or my foot slipped on the seat, and I fell.

I have no memory of hitting the ground. So I can only assume that I lost consciousness for a few moments, because the next thing I remember was looking up at Carol bending over me, her eyes wide and scared. It was odd, though, because I wasn't seeing her from the perspective of where I lay on the ground. Simultaneously I was looking down on the scene as if I were floating above it. I heard the metal-on-metal squeak of the swaying swings, sensed the grit of sand in my hands and the ground against my back, and felt my chest clawing for air. But I also saw myself, from above, lying on the earth. In that bifurcation I knew a moment of sheer terror: the separation of the boy on the ground from the boy overhead.

My psychic split lasted a couple of seconds at most. But staring at Fudō Myōō, I again felt that childhood sense of dislocation—as if, like a kite lost to an unexpected tug of wind, I might drift away, never to return. I could remember the relief that flooded me when the floating boy and the boy on the ground slammed together again like a pair of clapped hands. I was back in my body, whooping for air. I experienced nothing so intense at this *okunoin*, but for a moment, with my eyes locked on the deity gazing back at me, I was close to that bifurcated boy and felt the strangeness of my existence, aware that my connection to the world was tenuous and temporary.

Japanese Zen practitioners describe the point in meditation when a practitioner can experience hallucinations, resurgent memories, or other unusual mental phenomena—anything from talking statues and marching Buddhas to ghostly apparitions and feelings of disembodiment—as *makyō*. According to Zen teachings, the experience of *makyō* indicates the emergence of the mind's subconscious elements. *Makyō* is not enlightenment, but it's generally a good sign because it suggests that the hard effort of *zazen*, or sitting meditation, has finally broken the mind of its obsession with logical argument and instrumental reason. But *makyō* can also produce psychosis—Zen madness—if a master teacher doesn't properly direct it.[17]

Had nearly two months of walking up and down mountains, reciting the sutra, and occasionally sitting *zazen* in my room at night driven me around the bend? My periodic chats with Jizō or bathing with Fudō Myōō might suggest a suspension of normal behavior. On the other hand, I couldn't deny the tide of peacefulness that had washed over me in recent days, the sense that I had received balm for the soul. The restoration of an all-but-forgotten childhood experience was another enchantment. But then, as I thought about it, it seemed to me that my entire pilgrimage had taken on an aura of enchantment. When I began it, I'd assumed it would be an adventure in cultural exoticism. That was no longer the case. A combination of time, geography, and circumstance had produced a much different journey along with experiences I couldn't have imagined at the beginning.

It seemed to me at that moment that if the real purpose of my pilgrimage, however inchoately acknowledged, had been to cross some liminal threshold within myself, then this *okunoin* had fulfilled it. Jizō had guided me there, and Fudō Myōō had given me a hint of what it meant to *be* in this place. In the morning, I would leave Komatsu with my companions to begin my next to last week on the trail. But at that moment, in the twilight darkness of the temple courtyard, it seemed to me my pilgrimage had reached a kind of completion.

I would be proved wrong, of course, as later events would show. The Henro Michi still had other things in store for me and for my companions. Still, as I gazed around the temple, I felt as though I'd returned to the world after a long absence. I didn't hear ash falling, but there was the rustle of leaves on an overhanging branch, the grate of gravel beneath my shoes, and the slow thudding metronome of my heart. The boy was home.

I stood up to leave. I dropped a 1,000-yen coin—about $10—in the offertory bin. I lit as many candle stubs and remnant incense sticks as I could find in the temple urns, and I imagined them burning long after I was gone. I shouldered my pack and grabbed my walking stick. At the courtyard entrance I turned for a last look. Fudō Myōō cracked a farewell smile, a final enchantment of *makyō*.

7

Blossoms

Mountain cherry blossoms
the mountain becomes
slightly pink.
—SHŪJI NIWANO

I wandered among Buddhas. There were hundreds of them: life-size figures lining the maze of paths around Unpenji, clustering in groups in the corners of the courtyard, lurking half-hidden in the forest, standing in phalanxes near the pagodas and prayer shrines, and peering out from a copse of mist-shrouded cedar trees. There was something spooky about the massed ranks of statuary, large and small. At 1,000 meters above sea level, Temple Sixty-Six is the highest temple on the circuit, offering a mountaintop view in all directions toward three of Shikoku's four prefectures: Tokushima, Ehime, and Kagawa. The Temple of the Hovering Clouds, however, is best known for its vast garden of statues representing the myriad manifestations, good and bad, of the human psyche. The figures of five hundred *rakan* dominate the collection. These are disciples of Buddha who achieved enlightenment through their meditative and spiritual efforts. According to tradition, if you study the *rakan* closely you will find your own true face. And so I wandered among them searching for mine.

We'd reached Unpenji on a misty morning about a week before completing the Henro Michi. We'd performed our pilgrim rituals, gotten our pilgrim books stamped, and then found a spot under the eaves of the temple to eat lunch out of the spattering rain. Afterward, while my companions rested—it had been a hard climb to the temple—I strolled around the statuary. It was both hypnotic and unsettling. I saw joy and laughter, care and compassion, serenity and wisdom, on the stone faces. But there were other expressions, too—faces you encounter in the dark alleys of the unconscious: lips curled in a snarl of hate or a twist of contempt, eyes wide with murderous rage or narrowed with suicidal despair, mouths stretched in a rictus of horror or of fear. I was, I realized, wandering through a gallery of human psychology in stone. I found myself wondering at my ease in recognizing the dark and disturbed faces. Walking along a narrow path lined on each side with life-size sculptures expressing the gamut of human emotions, I imagined all that psychic energy cracking free of the stone in an orgy of slaughter. It wasn't a vision I would have normally associated with pilgrimage, but then the path to Buddhahood is not necessarily pleasant.

I was grateful to Shūji for showing me another side of Unpenji's sculptural legacy. When I returned to the temple courtyard, he pointed out a small stone monument commemorating the visit of the poet Taneda Santōka in 1939. Santōka died in 1940 at the age of fifty-seven after a tragedy-filled life. When he was eleven, his mother committed suicide by jumping down a well. At the age of forty-three, after a failed marriage and a botched suicide attempt—he jumped in front of an approaching train that managed to stop just in time—he entered a Sōtō Zen monastery and was eventually ordained as a monk. Santōka spent the rest of his life wandering around Japan as a mendicant, keeping a diary of his travels, and writing haiku that are now much admired. His poems have been described as capturing shards of experience, singular moments of attention so sharp and poignant that the banal becomes profound and the insignificant extraordinary. I was familiar with Santōka's poetry, but I had no idea he'd been a Shikoku pilgrim. I thanked Shūji for showing me the monument, pleased at the serendipity of encountering a favorite poet in such a place.

"You will have to write haiku for your visit, too," I said to Shūji. I'd often seen him writing poems in his journal and once expressed the wish to read them. He'd smiled shyly and said, "I am only amateur."

Gazing around the compound at the gray-tile roofs, shiny from the morning rain, the mist clinging to the tops of trees on the slopes behind the temple, I imagined the poet standing all those decades ago where I was standing now. I wondered if he had any intuition that he would live only a few months more. I glanced at Shūji. He was staring intently at the monument. Some lines from one of Santōka's poems came to mind: "Each day we meet / both demons and buddhas."[1] It seemed an appropriate sentiment for the time and the place.

After Temple Sixty-Six, the remaining twenty-two temples of the Henro Michi come in clusters. On some days we visited three, four, or even more temples. Inevitably they began to look the same. This shifted the psychology of the pilgrimage. Not only did it seem to speed up as we counted down several temples each day, but we started to focus on reaching the end. I didn't like this shift. I felt that the pilgrim-mindedness I'd acquired during the long weeks of walking was slipping away.

There were also small annoyances to plague us. The days of sunshine surrendered to on-and-off cloudbursts. Tanaka-san's right ankle gave him trouble again. Shūji had more difficulties with Jun, either getting him moving in the morning or keeping him walking during the day. I sometimes walked with Jun, cajoling him with the mantra of "no excuses, no complaints, just keep walking." I made him give me more language lessons. It worked for a few kilometers, but then he would want a break. I worried that Jun's "condition" was dragging Shūji down. I told Tanaka-san I was concerned that Shūji might quit so close to the end because of Jun.

"That would be bad karma," he said.

Tanaka-san's use of the phrase startled me, making me wonder if Shūji might have more at stake than just the satisfaction of completing the pilgrimage. Karma is a Sanskrit word used in Buddhism to refer to a person's fate as it has accumulated through successive reincarnations. The Japanese word for karma is *innen*, but the Japanese use the Sanskrit word interchangeably. Karma reflects the notion that every action has consequences, redounding to the person most associated with the behavior.[2] Worse, according to the scholars I'd read, it is possible for karma to span generations unless expiated by rituals such as prayer, acts of purification, and pilgrimage. The lifelong task facing an individual is *karuma ō kiru*, or to "cut [one's] karma."[3]

I began to think that Shūji's pilgrimage meant something at such a deep level that even he wasn't fully aware of an attempt to cut his karmic cord. Maybe he was trying to exorcise whatever bad karma he and his family had inherited in the hope of changing his fate and Jun's.

I wanted to dismiss the notion as nonsensical. We inherit DNA from our parents but not their spiritual misdeeds. Mental illness is the product of chemical imbalances in the brain or of socially induced psychological trauma; it's not the product of spiritual neglect, irritated ancestors, or beyond-the-grave guilt.

But it hardly mattered what I thought or believed. What did Shūji believe? Had Shūji's pilgrimage awakened him to his karmic burden? I thought that maybe Shūji needed help in cutting his karma. Behind my shield of Western rationalism, I might dismiss the idea as superstition. But even if it were superstition, what would be the harm in pretending otherwise? My inability to understand the Hannya Shingyō didn't prevent me from trying to recite it with Shūji and Tanaka-san. There was no reason not to adopt the same attitude toward a concept like karma if it helped Shūji.

When we left Unpenji, heading down the mountain to Daikōji, Temple Sixty-Seven, I made a point of walking with Jun. "Come on Jun," I said, "time for you to be my teacher again." Maybe it helped. Jun walked without complaint as we visited four temples that day, following a path along the Saita River and then cutting across a plain of rice fields, vegetable farms, and quiet back roads to Iyadaniji, Temple Seventy-One.

Over the next two days we visited ten temples. The days, and the temples, blurred one into the other. But there were always a few images that stayed with me: the shopkeeper sweeping the damp ground in front of his souvenir stand early in the morning at Kannonji, Temple Sixty-Nine; Norijuki Watanabe, the owner of an udon shop in Takase who insisted that our lunch was *settai*; an evening spent soaking in the hot spring pool at Fureai Park Mino; the hundreds of weatherworn rock carvings that decorate the cliff face along the stone stairway to Iyadaniji—according to tradition, if you look carefully enough among the 1,500 images carved into the rock wall, you can see the faces of those you loved who are now dead; and finally the peace and quiet of the gurgling rock pool beneath the trees at Kōyamaji, Temple Seventy-Four. They all claimed a place in my memory temple.

After Kōyamaji, the birthplace of Kōbō Daishi was a shock. Zentsūji, Temple Seventy-Five, is huge, the largest temple on Shikoku, with two sprawling building complexes connected by a wide walkway. Food stalls, ice-cream stands, flower kiosks, gift shops, and souvenir stores crowd each side of the tree-lined walk. Stands of oak and maple shade the statues and shrines as well as the rock gardens and carp ponds. Kōbō Daishi's father, Yoshimichi Saeki, the local ruler, donated the temple to his son. Sand from holy sites in India provided the foundation for the building project, which took six years to complete. Beneath the *hondō* is a hundred-meter-long tunnel, the walls lined with eighty-eight Buddha carvings. A small square in the tunnel marks the spot where Kōbō Daishi was born. Walking through the tunnel, I couldn't help but imagine the millions of pilgrims who'd come here for more than a millennium in search of the divine. I liked the idea that I was now one of them.

After Zentsūji, Tanaka-san said that his foot was hurting him again. He decided to take a taxi to Konzōji and Dōryūji, Temples Seventy-Six and Seventy-Seven, and then go on to the Plaza Hotel in Marugame, where we'd planned to spend the night.

We all should have taken the taxi. Maybe things would have turned out differently. But I was committed to walking, and Shūji agreed. Jun reluctantly went along. We walked to the temples easily enough, following the pilgrim path through farm fields and industrial parks. By the time we got to Temple Seventy-Seven, it was late afternoon and we were tired and footsore, although we still had another four or five kilometers to go to reach our hotel. Jun, in particular, was dragging, stopping frequently for cigarette breaks, which is probably why Shūji and I got too far ahead of him and weren't aware of anything being wrong until a police car pulled up beside us.

I had a moment of panic, thinking something had happened to my family back home. But then I saw Jun in the backseat. The police officers, two hefty men in dark suits, got out of the car and approached Shūji. I didn't understand the exchange, of course, but Shūji seemed to shrink visibly as he talked to the police. His shoulders slumped, and weariness pulled at his long face. He leaned in the window to talk to Jun. When he stepped away he said something to the police and then to me.

"Sumimasen, Sibley-san." "I am sorry. Please, you go to the hotel. Jun has made some trouble. I must go to the *keisatsusho*."

I recognized the word for police station. Shūji was embarrassed and ashamed. That was plain to see. But most of all I saw his sadness, as though he realized that his hopes for the pilgrimage had come to nothing.

I'd checked into the Plaza Hotel, had my bath, and was sprawled on the futon reading Bashō and sipping a beer when Shūji and Tanaka-san knocked on my door. Shūji had a cut above his left eye and a scrape on his right cheek. Shūji, Tanaka-san said, wanted to apologize. He also wanted my advice. I insisted on treating Shūji's cuts with iodine and bandages from my kit before we talked. I could guess what had happened. Treating Shūji gave me a chance to tamp my anger.

With Tanaka-san translating, Shūji explained that Jun had walked into a convenience store when the two of us were out of sight, grabbed some snacks, and walked out shouting *settai*. The store clerk didn't agree and phoned the police. Shūji had spent the past few hours apologizing to the clerk, paying for the snacks, and explaining his son's "condition" to the police. When they got to the hotel, Jun wanted to find a restaurant. Shūji said they would eat in their room. Jun started shouting, hit Shūji, and ran out. Jun apologized when he returned, but Shūji phoned his wife, Ikuko. She thought they should abandon the pilgrimage and come home.

"Shūji would like your view on this matter," Tanaka-san said.

What advice could I give? My first impulse was to belt Jun. I was even tempted to suggest that Shūji charge him with assault. But I remembered the night we celebrated having reached the halfway point on the pilgrimage and how Shūji, in a moment of candor or out of some desperate need to share his burden, confessed his darkest thoughts. At the time I'd thought, why ask me? I asked myself the same question again as I finished putting a bandage on Shūji's forehead. It wasn't any of my business. I didn't need this aggravation. I had ten temples to go. I could finish the pilgrimage on my own or maybe with Tanaka-san. I didn't want to be involved in some family tragedy. But somehow I was already involved. Even if I was tempted to, I couldn't abandon Shūji.

But facing Shūji, I had no solutions, no cure, nothing to cut the cord. I knew only that he had to complete the pilgrimage. Walking was the only response. "You must keep walking," I said. "You will be unhappy if you don't finish after having gone so far. And Jun needs to finish, too.

Maybe it can still help him," I said, even though I no longer believed that. Tanaka-san translated, and Shūji nodded as if in agreement.

"But Jun must apologize to you, in front of all of us," I said.

I wasn't sure I believed that, either. I'd grown used to Jun's acts of contrition, how he would apologize for some impulsive act but then do something similar the next day. Jun, I sometimes thought, used his "condition" to avoid taking responsibility for himself. But then maybe I was too harsh in my judgment. When I returned home, I described Jun's behavior to a psychiatrist I know, especially his impulsiveness and his apparent inability to learn from his mistakes. The psychiatrist speculated that Jun's "condition" might be more biological than cultural. Jun may have been suffering from a form of psychosis as a result of inadequate brain development.

Perhaps. For some reason, though, Jun seemed to respond to my cajoling. He often looked to me for approval before acting. Both Shūji and Tanaka-san remarked on Jun's apparent willingness to do as I urged. Maybe that's why I thought my advice wasn't unreasonable: both Shūji and Jun had to complete the pilgrimage for their own sakes. To quit so close to the end would undermine whatever they had accomplished, or—and the thought came unbidden—erase any karmic credit they might have gained on the journey.

Tanaka-san and Shūji talked among themselves. Then Tanaka-san said, "I have told Shūji I think you are right. I said he is close to the end and it would be a disappointment for him not to finish. I said we would help him with Jun."

"Will Jun apologize to his father?"

"He already has," Tanaka-san said.

"Jun needs to apologize to us, too, because"—I paused, recalling what I'd read about the Japanese concept of *wa*, or the harmony of the group—"Jun has disturbed our harmony." The concept is rooted in the Confucian morality that Japan inherited from China 1,400 years ago. *Wa* privileges good relations with others over notions of individual self-assertion. It's not that the Japanese deny individuality; rather, they recognize that individuality depends on relationships. Without others, there is no self. *Wa* is the glue that gives Japanese society its sense of cohesion.

Tanaka-san went down the hall to get Jun. When they returned, I offered him a beer. Jun sat on the tatami looking abashed, almost fearful. Did he genuinely regret his behavior? Or did he merely regret getting caught? I was flummoxed: why was I, a gaijin, pretending to offer advice on the domestic problems of a Japanese family? I had no insight into the Japanese mind, much less that of a disturbed young man. I just wanted to be a pilgrim, enjoy the scenery, and indulge in a few minor epiphanies. Instead, I was pretending to wisdom I didn't possess. I wasn't that good at maintaining harmony in my own life. Nevertheless, by some twist of fate—karma?—I was sharing a pilgrimage with three people who thought I could help.

No doubt Kōbō Daishi would have offered wise counsel. The best I could do was tell Jun that Tanaka-san and I couldn't walk with him if he didn't apologize to his father and to us. I think Jun got most of it in English, but Tanaka-san translated anyway. There was a startled look on his face and the shine of fear in his eyes. I had the feeling that no adult had ever threatened him with the consequences of his actions. He protested that he'd already apologized to his father.

"Not good enough," I said. "We are all pilgrims together. You have to apologize to all of us."

Jun asked for another beer. I shook my head. We waited. Finally, looking at the floor, Jun apologized to Tanaka-san and me.

"Your father, too," I said. "He is your father and you must honor him."

Jun didn't stand to bow, but he looked at Shūji, bent his head, and said, "Sumimasen, otōsan." "I am sorry, father."

Was he sincere? I don't know. During the next few days, he walked without complaint. He took my cajoling and prodding with a grin. There was a curb on his impulsiveness. He even joined his father a few times in offering the temple prayers. It made the last days of our pilgrimage more enjoyable than they otherwise might have been.

***

It took us five more days to complete the Henro Michi, and they were good days. From Marugame we traipsed through the suburbs of Sakaide to Temples Seventy-Eight and Seventy-Nine, Gōshōji and Tennōji, before turning into the mountains. From Kokubunji to Ichinomiyaji, Temples Eighty to Eighty-Three, the *henro* trail climbed through mountains and then descended to a coastal plain and the city of Takamatsu. Jun was, as always, late to get moving in the mornings, but he remained on his best behavior.

The weather was sunny and warm. I slept and ate well. And when I wasn't sleeping or eating, I walked, just walked, disappearing into the rhythm of footfalls and the steady tapping of my walking stick. My body walked while my mind wandered, enveloped in the mysticism of the ordinary.[4] There was no transcendent insight, no breathtaking ecstasy, no eruption of the ineffable. Instead, those final days on the pilgrim road provided me with sheer delight in the mundane—the sunlight on a rain-wet highway, the song of a nightingale in a forest, the lunch-time companionship of turtles on a nearby log.

We trooped through Takamatsu, following Highway 172 to the city center. Ritsurin Park offered a brief reprieve from the assault of roaring trucks, belching buses, and blaring music that poured out of the shops and stores. The seventy-five-hectare park is nearly four hundred years old. With its half-dozen ponds, tiny lakes, curving paths, ancient trees, tea pavilions, and rock arrangements, it is one of Japan's best-known strolling gardens. Tanaka-san had seen it before, and neither Shūji nor Jun was interested. But I wasn't going to pass up the opportunity to stroll through one of Japan's most famous gardens. It was like stepping into one of those nineteenth-century woodcuts by Hiroshige in which tiny characters wander through a sublime landscape.

I treated the park as if it were a miniature pilgrimage, a kind of reward to myself for having come as far as I had on the Henro Michi. It was also pleasant to be alone. I spent a couple of hours walking around the park, following paths edged by bamboo fences across the hump-backed bridges that connected the delicate islands. I strolled through groves of trees—pine, maple, chestnut, cherry—and past mounds of moss-covered stones donated by shoguns and princes. I admired the crane-tortoise pine—so called because it is supposed to look like a crane spreading its wings on the back of a tortoise. The tree has the most beautiful shape of all the pines in the park, or so the sign in front said. Everything was in good order and well maintained: the fences straight and upright, the paths free of litter, the grounds cleared of dead leaves and twigs.

After making several circuits of the park, pausing to admire a display of bonsai outside the park museum, I had lunch in the Kikugetsu-tei Pavilion, a feudal-era teahouse overlooking the South Lake. A pretty girl in a brightly patterned kimono served tea and sweets. Sitting cross-legged on the tatami, sipping *o-cha* and nibbling my *wagashi*, an assortment of sweets, I watched the ducks softly quacking on the lake and imagined myself as a feudal *daimyō* surveying his domains.

I left Ritsurin Park feeling restored. This was just as well, since it took me another two hours to walk to a hotel, the Wakasa, in Yashima, a suburb on the northern edge of Takamatsu, where Shūji had booked our rooms for the night. The two-story hotel was in a weed-filled courtyard behind a peeling whitewashed cement wall just off the street that we would take the next morning to climb to Yashimaji, Temple Eighty-Four. Sadly, the interior was equally run-down: the tatami needed changing, it was so dry and brittle, and light bulbs were missing or burned out. On the other hand, each room had its own *o-furo*.

Tanaka-san explained that an elderly woman ran the place. Her husband had died several years earlier, and she was unable to manage the upkeep herself. She tried, though. When I arrived, she hustled out of a dim back room to greet me with a chirpy "irashaimase," "welcome, please come in." Then she escorted me upstairs to my room, where she insisted on filling the *o-furo* with hot steaming water while I put on the too-small *yukata*. Just as I was lowering myself into the tub, she came into the room bearing a towel and a tea tray. She left me to pour my own tea, but she had a grin on her face as she bowed herself out.

The *okami-san* was there in the morning, too. She escorted us to the gate and bowed as Tanaka-san and I walked up the street, leaving Shūji and Jun to follow. Tanaka-san told me that she'd never had a gaijin as a guest. He said she'd been impressed with my manners.

Yashimaji sprawls across a mountaintop plateau overlooking the Inland Sea. On a clear day you can see the main Japanese island of Honshu. My favorite object, though, was a particular cherry tree near the temple gate. It was one of seven cherry trees planted in 1665 by Kasho Hanzaemon Matsudaira, a Takamatsu nobleman, as consolation in his old age. Six of the trees eventually died. But one gnarled, moss-covered specimen remains. Just before he died, according to a plaque near the tree, Kasho wrote a poem:

> When the cherry trees are in full bloom
> And someone passes and asks their name,
> Tell them they are Kasho's cherry trees.

Not a bad memorial, I thought, hoping Kasho's spirit would be pleased that I'd paused to remember him.

Tanaka-san didn't want to strain his ankle more than necessary, especially since the next day—which would be our last—was going to be particularly hard. He decided to take the cable car—or ropeway, as the Japanese call it—down the mountain to the hotel where we'd reserved rooms.

I waited in the temple compound for Shūji and Jun, but when they didn't show up I walked on my own to Yakuriji, Temple Eighty-Five. The route to the temple led down Mount Yashima to Highway 150. The road ran alongside a canal. It took three hours to hike the eight kilometers to the temple. I would have done it faster, but I kept having to shelter from the rain showers that came in short-lived but heavy bursts. I was lucky, though, because just before each deluge I found shelter. One time it was a convenience store, where I bought a freshly baked ham bun and a pint of chocolate milk for a late breakfast, which I ate standing under the shop eaves near the door. The clerk kept smiling and bowing whenever I looked in the window.

Another time I sheltered in the entrance of a stonemason's shop, surrounded by dozens of statues of Buddha, Jizō, and Kannon, along with turtles and stone pagodas, as the rain pounded the roof and road. The statues were lined up in such a way that they seemed to be staring at me. I had the oddest feeling that they were urging me to stand still until I, too, turned into a statue. I left when the rain stopped, but not before placing an orange at the feet of a dark-stained Jizō. I wasn't sure if I was saying thanks or sending my regrets at having to decline the invitation.

Perhaps the offering earned me my next reward. I was hustling along Highway 146, hoping to make it to Temple Eighty-Five before the next dump of rain. Judging by the low, black-bellied clouds, it was going to hit any minute. I didn't think I would make it. I still had two kilometers to go when the first fat drops splatted on the pavement. This time, though, I was in the open with no shelter nearby. I resigned myself to getting soaked. But then, rounding a curve in the road, I saw the pylons for a cable car system running up the side of the mountain. And just ahead was the ropeway office. I ran as fast as I could, ducking under the platform roof just as the sky cracked open. Praise Jizō, I made it.

Waiting on the platform for the next cable car, I watched the rain come down in opaque sheets and inhaled the sweet cedar smell of the surrounding forest. I reminded myself to make an extra donation at the *hondō* after my rituals. Somebody, or something, was watching over me, keeping me dry that day despite the weather.

After Yakuriji, I hiked south in sunshine and cool breezes on Highway 145 toward Shidoji. The pavement steamed in the sun. Wind shook the trees, sprinkling me with remnants of the rain I had earlier avoided. I had a *bentō* lunch at a reservoir just before the intersection of Highway 11, sharing a log with five sunbathing turtles. I caught myself laughing at the pleasure of turtles as luncheon companions. By way of thanks, I left them balls of rice.

I reached Temple Eighty-Six shortly after 4 p.m. Shallow puddles pocked the grounds. The wooden walls of the *hondō* and the *daishidō* were dark with age, their roofs showing the gaps of missing tiles. Weeds grew in the eaves. I liked it, particularly the rock-and-sand garden that dated to the fifteenth century. After I got my *nōkyōchō* stamped, I sat on a bench in the shade of a copse of maples, sipping Pocari Sweat and watching two children chase pigeons. It seemed a perfect way to end the day's walk. Pleasingly enough, though, there were a couple of other perfect moments before the day was out. That night I stayed at the loveliest *ryokan* of any I'd seen, and my friends and I enjoyed a meal to remember.

***

The pride on the face of Yasuyoshi Yamamoto, the owner and operator of the *ryokan*, was evident as he surveyed his garden. "I make the fence all myself," he said, a broad smile stretching across his round face as he led me down the garden path. "No nails. Only rope. Tradition is best."

At Yamamoto-san's urging, I crouched to peer at the intricate rope lacing and complex knotting that bound the hundreds of crosshatched bamboo slats. I made appreciative noises. "Totemo utsukushii." "Very

beautiful." And it was: the pale yellow fence marked off the small garden in perfectly straight and level lines.

But then I was enamored with the whole garden that filled the
courtyard at the Ishiya Ryokan in Sanuki, where we stayed on our next
to last night on the Henro Michi. I'd just finished my pre-dinner bath
in the o-furo and was back in my room to slip on the freshly laundered
yukata to go outside. Somewhere in this establishment was a cold beer,
and I meant to find it. I slid open one of the room's shōji panels. There
on the other side of the narrow veranda was a small-scale park of
sculpted trees, curved pathways, and moss-covered stones. I was looking at a miniature Ritsurin Park within the confines of the inner compound of the ryokan. After I found a can of Kirin beer, I headed back
toward my room and sat on a stone in the garden.

That's where Yamamoto-san found me. From the surprised look on
his face, I got the impression that he'd never had a guest, much less a
foreigner, sitting on a rock in his garden and drinking a beer. I stood
and bowed, hoping I was not being ill-mannered. I made a sweeping
gesture with my hand and said, "heiwa teki na niwa." I meant to say
that his garden was peaceful, but I think it came out as a stilted "garden
peaceful."

Yamamoto-san seemed to understand because he bowed, thanked
me for the compliment, and proceeded to give me the guided tour of
his ten-meter by five-meter garden. I didn't understand anything he
said, but I went along, uttering "utsukushii" and "sugereta," "beautiful"
and "excellent." Then, when I thought the tour was over, Yamamoto-
san had me wait in the garden, gesturing with his hands for me to stay
where I was while he ran inside. He returned with his wife, Takaka,
and a camera. I posed in the garden with her—an act she accepted with
stunned acquiescence—while he clicked away. After that, there was
more bowing and smiling and thanking until, finally, I was alone with
my beer in the garden, which was all I wanted in the first place.

Soon afterward it was time to join my companions for yūshoku, or
supper. Tanaka-san had arrived before me, and Shūji and Jun showed
up an hour or so after I did. The garden's perfection carried over in
Takaka Yamamoto's kitchen. Our meal was exquisite: melt-in-your
mouth sashimi, chicken yakitori, and himono, or grilled mackerel, so

tender that the flesh lifted off the bone with a light pull of the chop-sticks. It was also a cheerful meal. Jun was laughing and chatty, again teasing me about looking like the French movie actor Jean Reno. Tanaka-san told stories about working in China. And Shūji was quietly ebul-lient, pleased—and relieved—that he was one day away from finishing a pilgrimage that he'd wanted to make since he was Jun's age.

After Jun went to bed, we ordered a large bottle of beer and sat around the table while Yamamoto-san and his wife cleared away the dishes. It struck me how extraordinarily blessed I had been in having Shūji and Tanaka-san as companions on my pilgrimage.

It seems they felt the same way. With Tanaka-san translating, Shūji said he'd phoned his wife and told her they would be completing the pilgrimage tomorrow. She was happy for them and wanted him to thank me for having been so helpful with Jun. "My wife is most grateful for you being a good friend to Jun."

I accepted the gratitude, although I didn't think I deserved it, con-sidering how angry I often felt toward Jun. But then Shūji sprang an-other surprise.

"My wife asks if you would honor our family by staying at our home when you come to Tokyo. This is Tanaka-san's wish, too," he said.

My pre-pilgrimage research had indicated that Japanese rarely in-vite foreigners to their homes, especially when they have known each other for only a short time. This reluctance isn't because the Japanese feel superior. Rather, they fear that foreigners will find their homes substandard. I assumed the sentiment was a hangover from the post-war years when Japan struggled to rebuild its shattered economy. I rec-ognized that I'd received a singular honor; the invitation was an expres-sion of their regard.

"I would be most honored to stay at your homes," I said, bowing to both men. I was never sure if I was responding with the proper politeness, but I'd also learned that the Japanese would forgive slip-ups in etiquette by a gaijin if they felt the effort was sincere. Since both my companions were grinning—and Tanaka-san was filling my glass again—I assumed I'd acquitted myself with reasonable decorum.

Our party broke up a few minutes later, and I returned to my room, not forgetting to thank the Yamamotos in proper Japanese fashion for the meal. "Goshisosama deshita." "I have been treated well."

It was dark by then, though there was enough light from the rooms surrounding the courtyard that I could see the stones and trees in the garden. I sat on the edge of the veranda outside my room, staring at the dark shapes and listening to the cicadas. I remembered a line from Søren Kierkegaard, the nineteenth-century Danish philosopher: "It is the accidental and insignificant things in life which are significant."[5] Buddhism takes a similar position: the most profound spiritual experience is to comprehend fully the immensity of the everyday. This notion—and the paradoxical task it implies—is captured in the Zen Buddhist aphorism, "When you sweep the floor, just sweep; when you eat, just eat; when you walk, just walk." Sitting on the veranda, entranced by the garden, I felt as close as I had ever been to recognizing the reality of that exhortation, to understanding that spiritual experience entails perceiving the extraordinary in the ordinary. But then I reminded myself that Buddhism also teaches the concept of samsara: the impermanence of all things, the fact that everything changes.

I went to bed to the chorus of cicadas, wondering what tomorrow would bring.

***

Each of us ended up walking alone on our last day on the Henro Michi. We left the *ryokan* together just after 7 a.m., but we were soon strung out along the road as we settled into our individual rhythms of walking. It was perfect walking weather, cool and overcast.

The hike to Nagaoji, Temple Eighty-Seven, was boring. The path paralleled Highway 3 for the first five kilometers, and there wasn't much to see except passing cars and trucks. I stopped at a convenience store to buy my usual *bentō* lunch and my requisite can of Georgia Café au Lait. I sat on the curb outside the store to enjoy the sunshine, watch the commuters, and sip my first coffee of the day.

I had more coffee at a small café attached to the stamp office at Temple Eighty-Seven, which I reached about 9 a.m. I wasn't impressed with the temple. The *hondō*, an ordinary two-story hall, and the small *daishidō* were crammed together on one side of a wide compound of hard-packed sand. For some reason the temple had a statue of the Daishi carrying a clock. I guess being the next to last temple of the circuit means you don't have to try harder.

The longer hike—eighteen kilometers—to Ōkuboji, Temple Eighty-

Eight, was much better, if also much harder. Five kilometers beyond the town of Nagao, just before the Maeyama Dam, the pilgrim path turned off the road and ran along the edge of a reservoir below the dam until it entered the cedar forests of Mount Nyōtai. I strolled through the woods. Sunlight splashed through gaps in the trees, falling on the leaf-padded paths like cheerfully flung splotches of paint. The shaded earth exuded a rich pungency. A gurgling creek lined by thickets of bamboo accompanied me at the edge of the trail. I was careful to duck under the rain-jeweled cobwebs that spanned narrower portions of the path. An occasional butterfly looped around my head.

I stopped for lunch at a dilapidated trailside shrine surrounded by several cherry trees. I set my *bentō* box on a wobbly wooden table, patchy with moss and speckled with the pink petals of the blossoms. I was hungry, but I ate with my eyes for a few moments before digging in. I noticed that I had dining companions again. A line of ants trooped across the tabletop. I was in a generous mood and shredded pieces of my rice ball, laying out kernels for them.

Then another luncheon guest arrived. A lizard, black with silver stripes, poked its head over the edge of the tabletop. I remained still as it crept forward on the table. The creature must have seen me, but it didn't seem to be afraid as it waggled up the length of the table, its silvery head swaying back and forth and its tail flicking. I reached out slowly with one of the chopsticks and pushed a piece of rice ball across the table. The lizard took it. I poked another piece forward. My companion ate that one, too, swallowing it in a gulp. He seemed to be looking straight at me.

Staring at him, I remembered another lizard encountered years ago, a green one that I'd plucked from a fountain on the Camino de Santiago. I knew it was ridiculous to connect the lizard in front of me on a mountainside picnic table in Japan to the one I encountered in Spain, but I felt the hair rise on the back of my neck. One lizard reminds me of another. No big deal. Or was it more synchronicity? Maybe I was lunching with some species-jumping *kami*, the lizard being one of the spirits that tradition says occupy the mountains and forests of Japan. After two months in Shikoku's haunting landscape, I could appreciate why the ancient Japanese believed the world was enchanted by spirits.

And so I indulged in my speculation, happy to share my lunch with a new companion.

I don't know how long I sat there before I became aware of how quiet it was. I didn't even hear birds. I looked up through the trees at the sky. There was no breeze, nothing to rustle the leaves or sway the treetops. I looked back down. The lizard was still there. And a thought rose unbidden in my mind: "Let time stop now. Let this moment last. This is reality: this table, this food, this creature, this silent forest—everything else is unreal." A strange sense of heaviness came over me, as though I was supposed to remain at that moss-flecked table forever, immobile, while plants grew up around me, entwining me in their roots and branches until I became part of the forest. I had a vision of myself metamorphosing into a moss-covered trail marker, planted in this place like an oversized Jizō, greeting passing pilgrims across the ages.

Then the wind came up and blew through the trees, and blossoms from the cherry trees rained down; another moment of *yoin* wafted away on a breeze. I looked up as the petals fell around me, and when I looked down again I saw the lizard streak across the table, jump to the forest floor, and disappear into the foliage. Plucking blossoms from my hair, I started to laugh, remembering that the lizard I'd encountered in Spain did the same thing after I'd rescued it from the fountain. For a moment, I felt immensely happy, like a child given a surprise Christmas gift.

On impulse, I pulled a notebook from my waist pouch and wrote my first poem in more than thirty years, scribbling down the words to a haiku as they flared in my head:

> Wind shakes blossoms
> from Nyōtai's cherry trees—
> Spring snow for *henro*.

It wasn't Bashō-quality, but I thought the use of "spring" and "snow" as the requisite seasonal words provided a nice juxtaposition that captured my modest epiphany.

I put away the notebook and cleared the table. I didn't want to leave, but I had three hours of walking ahead of me to reach Ōkuboji, the Temple of Completion. I left the remains of my *onigiri* at the foot of the shrine's Jizō statue, thanking him for the poem. If the deity didn't want the rice ball, it was there for my lizard friend.

The deities, however, weren't going to let me simply stroll to my last temple. The rest of the walk to Ōkuboji was much harder, and the path grew steeper and steeper until I was practically climbing on my hands and knees. In hindsight, I think I took a wrong turn somewhere on the path because at one point, I had to climb a cliff that was near-perpendicular in some places as the trail went from an elevation of 490 meters to 740 meters in less than a kilometer. I'd never done any rock climbing, but that day I learned why it's not a good idea to carry a heavy pack when you do. The weight wanted to pull me backward. I had visions of myself plunging to the rocks below. I paused to strap my walking stick to my pack, fearful that I might drop it otherwise. I was careful to make sure I had a strong grip on the rocks and my feet were firmly planted as I pulled myself up Mount Nyōtai.

It took a long and aching hour to clamber up the last part of the cliff. I was soon cursing the ancient Buddhist priests who built temples on mountaintops. At the same time, though, I was pleased with myself, knowing I wouldn't have been able to make the same climb two months earlier. My soul might not be in such great shape, but my body wasn't doing too badly. Still, by the time I heaved myself over the final ledge and crawled onto a plateau, I was sweat-soaked and trembling.

I rested on my hands and knees for a few minutes, staring at the grass and waiting for the spots floating in front of my eyes to disappear. I undid the straps and buckles of my pack and let it slide to the ground. Then I slid to the ground, too, flopping on my back to catch my breath. A larger-than-life statue of Kōbō Daishi loomed above me, silhouetted against the bright sky. I silently thanked him for my deliverance. Then two other silhouettes appeared next to the statue—Shūji and Jun. They laughed at me lying on the ground like some oversized turtle. I grinned and gave them the V-for-victory sign. It turned out that they, too, had mistakenly followed the same path I had, reaching the plateau about half an hour earlier. They saw me climbing and decided to wait in case I got into trouble.

I was glad they did. It seemed only proper that the three of us walk the last half-kilometer of the pilgrimage together. It was a knee-jarring, thigh-aching descent to the Temple of Completion. I was ahead of my companions this time, and as I rounded the last curve in the pilgrim path, the rooftops of the prayer halls suddenly appeared below me, and I heard the gong of the temple bell. I stopped, listening to the echoes, flooded by the memory of ringing the *shōrō* bell myself after completing my first hard climb to Shōsanji, Temple Twelve. It felt as though that had happened a long time ago, and to another person.

A few minutes later, at 3:07 p.m.—fifty-four days after beginning my pilgrimage—I emerged from the forest to follow a flagstone walkway past a line of Kōbō Daishi statues and into the temple courtyard.

Ōkuboji, founded in 717, sits in a green hollow on Mount Nyōtai. The temple halls are set in a line against the mountainside, their swooping gray roofs giving them the appearance of being an extension of the mountain. The trees around the courtyard are thick with *o-mikuji*, the knotted pieces of paper containing wishes for good fortune that pilgrims tie to the branches. The trees looked snow-covered. And everywhere there were statues of my favorite deity, Jizō.

Tanaka-san was sitting on a bench next to a statue. He wasn't wearing his conical pilgrim's hat, and it struck me that he looked like Jizō with glasses. He'd reached the temple an hour earlier.

I performed my last pilgrim rituals with extra diligence. I scrubbed my hands at the cistern. I rang the bell in the tower to announce my presence to the gods. I lit candles and incense at the *hondō* and the *daishidō*. I chanted the Hannya Shingyō as best I could. I dropped extra donations in the offertory bins. And then I went to the temple office to get the final stamp in my *nōkyōchō*. Outside again, I flipped through the brocade-covered stamp book, skimming the calligraphic symbols for the eighty-eight temples of Shikoku, oddly stunned that I'd collected all of them. How had I done that? I could remember when all the pages were blank.

According to tradition, pilgrims leave their walking sticks—the symbol of Kōbō Daishi—at the temple for burning in a special ceremony. But I'd grown attached to my scarred stick. It was shorter by a couple of inches than when I'd acquired it, but it had become part of me, an extension of my arm, a brace for my legs, a prod for snakes, a companion. I decided that Kōbō Daishi might like to come home with me.

When Shūji and Jun finished their rituals, we posed for pictures with each other and then walked down the road to the Yasokubo *min-shuku*, where we had rooms. I think we all felt a sense of anticlimax—Is that all there is?—but we still celebrated the completion of our journey with a cheerful meal.

Later, climbing the stairs to our rooms, I asked Shūji how he felt. He nodded solemnly, "I am most happy." I was happy for him, and re- lieved. Maybe things would be all right.

The pilgrimage may have been over, but the pilgrim habit of ris- ing early remained. I was up and dressed by 6 a.m. But then I didn't know what to do. Breakfast wasn't for another hour. I felt disoriented. I decided to go to the temple. The morning was crisp, and my breath hovered in the air. I found a vending machine, bought a can of coffee, and took it into the temple courtyard.

Priests in their blue work clothes were sweeping the courtyard, their twig brooms leaving looping scratch-patterns in the damp ground. I sat on a bench, the pale sun warm on my face and legs. Birdsong drifted from the forested cliffs above the temples. Water dripped from the cis- tern, loud in the stillness of the morning. I sipped my coffee slowly, savoring the sweet, creamy taste.

I lingered after the coffee was finished. So long as I stayed at the temple, I was inside the magic circle of the Henro Michi. I knew that once I left, the enchantment would begin to fade. My mind flipped through images of the last eight weeks: trails through bamboo for- ests, mountain vistas, quiet temples, bibbed statues. I remembered the waterfall at the Kōōnji *okunoin* and knew I would often return in mem- ory to the place where I had briefly disappeared. I thought of other pil- grims, corporeal or otherwise: the nurse and the nun, the banker and the engineer; the poet who had been a constant, if ghostly, compan- ion. And what about Jizō? Hadn't the squat little deity been a faithful guide? I would no longer be looking for his red-capped figure around the next bend, no longer sharing my lunch with turtles and lizards.

A *henro* staggered down the walkway into the courtyard. He stopped to lean on his walking stick—just as I had the previous day— and surveyed the temple grounds. I assumed he'd slept out on the mountain overnight. He noticed me and bowed. I returned the bow and watched as he performed the rituals. When he went into the tem- ple office, I walked to the *daishidō* for a final prayer to thank Kōbō Daishi for his gifts. Then I returned to the hotel for a last breakfast with my fellow pilgrims.

We caught the 9:15 a.m. bus to Nagao. In thirty minutes we covered a distance that had taken seven hours the day before. In Nagao, we took a commuter train to Takamatsu, where we said our goodbyes in the cavernous lobby of the main railway station. Tanaka-san was taking the Shinkansen train to Tokyo, while Shūji and Jun were returning to Imabari to spend a few days with Jun's grandmother. I still had more than a week before I was due to fly home, and I'd planned on a return visit to Mount Kōyasan and then visits to Kyoto and Hiroshima. I was to contact my friends when I returned to Tokyo. The train at 12:47 p.m. took me to Tokushima City, where I checked into a Western-style room at the Clement Hotel. It was strange to sleep in a bed again.

The next morning I took a commuter train to the village of Bando, on the outskirts of Tokushima, and walked the two kilometers from the train station to Ryōzenji, Temple One, where I'd registered at the temple office as a walking *henro* at the beginning of my pilgrimage. According to some purists, my pilgrimage wouldn't be complete until I reported back to Ryōzenji and showed the priests the eighty-eight temple stamps in my *nōkyōchō*. So that's what I did, and I received another Temple One stamp for my effort. I also found my name in the register where I'd written it nearly two months before. I tried to remember what I felt like then. I scrawled my name and the date beside my old signature. Maybe it was my imagination, but the handwriting seemed different.

Then I caught a train back to Tokushima, my Shikoku pilgrimage behind me. Except that it wasn't. And considering what happened later, it never would be.

⁂

I spent my remaining time in Japan pretending I was still a pilgrim. I followed tradition and visited Mount Kōyasan. It was too beautiful not to want to see it again. Set in the mountains south of Osaka, the temples and monasteries there—dozens of them—are immaculate. The necropolis that surrounds Kōbō Daishi's mausoleum, with more than 200,000 graves, was impressive. The Buddhist saint, who died in 835, is considered to be in a state of perpetual meditation, waiting for the end of the middle time when Miroku, the Buddha who comes after

Gautama Buddha's successor, arrives to achieve full enlightenment and teach the pure dharma, the way of righteousness. Standing in front of the saint's crypt, I couldn't help but think that if his spirit were anywhere, it was hoofing it up some mountainside on Shikoku.

The temples and gardens in Hiroshima and Kyoto were also splendid. But when I tried to recite the Hannya Shingyō at Ryōanji, the famous Zen Buddhist temple in Kyoto, the endlessly repeated announcements on the loudspeakers destroyed any pretense of the temple as a place of spiritual repose. In Hiroshima, I devoted an afternoon to touring the atomic bomb horrors in the Peace Memorial Museum before fleeing to Shukkeien Garden with its twisting trails, miniature mountains, tiny rice fields, and carp-filled ponds where I could at least imagine that I was still on the pilgrim road.

Tokyo assaulted my senses with all its noise and bright lights. I found a quiet hotel near Ueno Park, where I spent a day walking. Two days before I was due to fly home, I visited Shūji and his wife, Ikuko, and then the next day, Tanaka-san and his wife, Kazuko, bringing small gifts as Japanese custom requires.

At Shūji's, I walked around the area near his home with him, Jun, and his younger son, Makoto, an autistic young man who insisted on holding my hand. Ikuko-san prepared a salmon dinner. Afterward, Shūji and I sat on the tatami in the living room with a bottle of *shōchū*. I noticed he'd already placed pictures of our pilgrim family on the mantle in the household shrine. Shūji kept glancing at Ikuko as she bustled around the kitchen. She kept smiling at us.

"I thank you, Robāto," Shūji said, after we'd pretty much drained the bottle. He had tears in his eyes. "Ikuko-san, she tells me Makoto was smiling today for the first time in a month. I thank you for this."

Tanaka-san told me the next day, while I was staying with him and his wife, that things had been tense in Shūji's household after Ikuko learned that Jun had attacked his father on the pilgrimage. She attributed to me Jun's willingness to complete the pilgrimage. And they regarded my willingness to visit their home despite the family's situation as a good omen for the future.

I spent my last day in Japan with Tanaka-san and Kazuko-san. It was a fun day. They took me to Hakone National Park, where we rode the Tozan Railway up Mount Sounzan to see the steaming volcanic vents and to admire Mount Fuji in the distance. Then back at their home, after another meal of everything I had come to enjoy in Japanese cuisine, Tanaka-san and I spent the evening talking over the bottle of Scotch I had given him—mostly about Shūji and Jun.

But I also reminded him that when we first met, he told me he was walking the Henro Michi to fill "an emptiness in his heart."

"Is your heart filled now?"

Tanaka-san looked at me in his Jizō-like way. His eyes dropped to the half-filled glass in his hand, then he looked at me again, extending the glass. I knew my Japanese etiquette, so I picked up the bottle and topped up the glass. Then we laughed.

In the morning, Tanaka-san took me to the local station where I boarded a train to Narita Airport. To my surprise, Shūji and Jun showed up to say goodbye. It got rather emotional. I think Shūji was genuinely sorry to see me go, and even a bit afraid. I said something about wanting to walk the Henro Michi again.

"You must remain *henro* in your heart," he said.

It is common at the end of a pilgrimage to feel a sense of letdown. You lose the daily rhythms as you make the transition back to your normal life. Having grown used to walking eight hours a day, you find the sudden cessation of movement a shock to your body. This shift in physiological circumstances produces psychological consequences: depression and restlessness. This is why I was grateful, once I was back home at the end of May, to hear from Shūji and Tanaka-san. Judging from our e-mail exchanges, they too had post-pilgrimage blues.

Three months after I got home, a letter and a package of photographs arrived from Shūji. "Thank you for your kindness and encouragement in Shikoku. Now I am on another *henro* with my family." Another letter came in September: Shūji said he was ill, but not doing too badly. "I miss our time as *henro*. I hope to go to Shikoku again."

I also heard from Tanaka-san. He was taking English lessons: "I have started to refresh my English conversation because I felt insufficient through our talks during the Shikoku walk. I hope to be improved when I meet you next time." He and his wife were planning a trip to Europe.

Then, in late November, I received another package from Shūji. It was a set of thirty-three haiku that he'd written during our pilgrimage.

There was also a letter. "In March we left Tokushima while the cherry blossoms were in bloom and embarked on the Shikoku pilgrimage. In May, when the fresh leaves began to appear on the cherry blossom trees, we finished the pilgrimage at last, thanks to the encouragement of the bush warblers, the stone Jizō statues, and the kindness of our companions."

When I had the poems translated, I was surprised to see how similar our emotional experiences of our respective pilgrimages were, how we both responded in much the same way to the same things. Judging by the imagery in his haiku, Shūji had been paying attention; he was present in the moment, having his own epiphanies. I smiled to read his poems. I recognized many of the places and moments that had affected him. His last poem, written after we reached Temple Eighty-Eight, made me laugh. I visualized the dining room where we'd had our final pilgrimage meal:

> The beer tastes good
> after completing the hike
> to Ōkuboji Temple.

And for a moment, remembering, I was back with my companions on the pilgrim trail.

In December, I received another letter. It was from a niece of Shūji's, Rie, who lived outside Japan and spoke English. "I am not sure where to begin," she wrote. "My mother told me that we got a phone call from one of our relatives to notify us that Uncle Shūji had killed Jun and then taken his own life."

Somehow, I wasn't shocked. Sorrowful, yes. Sickened, yes. The tragedy seemed to bring Shūji's pilgrimage into focus for me. I could finally see what had been there all the time, but I'd been too blind to recognize, too absorbed in my own pilgrimage to admit. Or so I tried to rationalize. In Buddhist tradition, a pilgrimage can be an act of expiation before death, an attempt to cleanse yourself in the hope of being reborn without all the bad karma of previous lives.

I wrote to Shūji's niece, expressing my sorrow and offering condolences to Ikuko-san. I asked for more details. Rie responded. Apparently, a few months after the pilgrimage, Jun became increasingly violent, attacking both Makoto and his mother. Shūji had to use sleeping pills at night to get Jun to sleep. One night, while Ikuko-san was away from the house, Shūji drugged Jun into a stupor and then smothered him. Then he hanged himself, leaving a message for Ikuko-san: "I am grateful for having married such a good woman. I cherish every moment. I am sorry for being such a bad father."

Another letter came from Rie, letting me know that Ikuko had placed Makoto in an institution while she went to stay with her mother on Shikoku. "Ikuko-san wanted me to tell you that she and her family are grateful to have had the chance to meet you. She said that Jun respected you a lot and his behavior changed somewhat after he came back from the *henro*. Ikuko-san spoke of how Jun always thought of you and the things you taught him. He would think about you whenever he felt like lashing out in order to stop himself."

Obviously, I told myself, I didn't teach him well enough. I kept wondering if there was something I could have done—some extra effort I could have made to reach Jun, some magical mantra that might have prevented the horror. I tried to imagine how Shūji must have felt—caught in an ever-tightening vise with no prospect of release, fearful at leaving his wife and younger son alone with his older son, anxious in a house that was always tense, and anticipating violence.

Just before Christmas, I got a letter from Tanaka-san. "Shūji-san is gone. I cannot believe that." Neither could I. But reading the letter, I knew I wanted to do something to help Shūji, and Jun, to ease their karmic burden. It was a mad idea, probably pointless, and utterly contrary to my rationalist skepticism. But what did that matter? They were my friends, and I needed to bear witness to that friendship.

Epilogue

It had rained in the night, and I stepped carefully as the winding path descended through a copse of dripping cedars. Rounding a curve in the trail, I spotted the red bench half-hidden in a cavern of sumac on the edge of a cliff overlooking the Strait of Juan de Fuca. I sat for a few minutes to absorb the view of the sun-sparkled water and the long stretch of the coastline of Washington state's Olympic peninsula across the strait. I tried to recall the last time I'd been here—was it really three decades ago?—before I continued along the twisting trail until I emerged from the woods onto a cliff edge overlooking the crescent beach. I scrambled down the rocky path to the sand. The tide was out, and as I walked toward the shelter of the rocks on the far side of the beach, I looked back to see my boot prints following me in the sand.

Nothing had changed at Point-No-Point. The rocky outcrops at the top of the beach, all smooth and rounded and marbled black, crouched at the base of the cliff like smooth-shouldered beasts huddled with their backs to the sea. The fissured cliff soared overhead, containing the beach in a curving embrace. Salt rime dried on exposed stones. Tidal pools swirled with their secret worlds. Feather-like cirrus clouds stretched across the blue sky. But what struck me most powerfully was the smell of the sea—stranded kelp, seaweed, wet sand, cedar. It was the same sea smell that I'd encountered for the first time in my life when I'd arrived in Victoria, BC, to attend the university there. The hauntingly familiar smells surged through the subterranean caverns of my memory like an incoming tide. I could feel the buried treasures shifting.

I found a place among the rocks and out of the wind. Leaning against them, I looked out at the water and squinted against the broken fragments of the sun. A ship was in the strait. I followed it as it moved slowly westward toward the Pacific Ocean. I lifted my face to the sun, absorbing its warmth.

It was the end of January. I'd taken a few days off work to fly to Victoria. It was as close as I could get to Japan. I roamed the University of Victoria campus, following the ghost of my younger self through the corridors, lecture rooms, and library carrels. I looked up addresses where I'd once lived, conjuring the rooms and apartments I'd occupied. I stalked the streets and the beaches and coves that had once been my favorite retreats. Everything was both familiar and strange.

I'd spent one day walking myself into exhaustion, hiking from my downtown hotel, the Cherry Bank on Burdett Avenue, to Cadboro Bay, following Beach Drive and trying to keep the ocean in sight. It was the best I could do to replicate the coastline of Shikoku, not to mention the blister I acquired after several hours of walking.

The day before I flew home, I drove out to Point-No-Point, near the town of Sooke, north of Victoria. I thought of how, only a few months earlier, I'd been with Shūji at Katsurahama Beach, where I'd had a vision of my youthful discovery of Point-No-Point. It was oddly disorienting to recall those few moments on a Japanese beach where I'd felt displaced by my remembrance of this Canadian one. But then it seemed strange to have reached an age when I have memories of memories, when there is more behind me than ahead. A nonsensical thought flitted across my mind: where do our memories go when we die?

As I crouched among the rocks, images of Shikoku washed over me. I thought about Shūji, wondering if his pilgrimage had been a preparation for death, a final attempt to cut the karmic cord. Buddhists, I'd read, believe that until we gain enlightenment, we're stuck in a cycle of transmigration, revolving through various worlds and spiritual realms. Our fate in the next life, whether we're reborn as human or animal or end up in hell, depends on our behavior in this life. When we die, our souls exist for a time in a state between death and the new life to come. This suspended state lasts for seven weeks, during which time the deities judge the soul to determine the realm where it will be reborn. Family and friends are supposed to hold memorial services during this period, beseeching the deities who help the dead to intervene on behalf of the deceased.[1]

Shūji and Jun died in mid-December. Now at the end of January, it was almost seven weeks later. Maybe, I thought, it was time for them to be reborn.

That's what I'd come here to help with: their rebirth. I left the shelter of the rocks and walked down the beach to the shoreline, where I recited the Heart Sutra and read some of Shūji's haiku. Then I bowed my head and prayed that the gods, if any existed, would give my friends a better fate in the next life. I could only hope they heard me over the pounding sea.

Notes

I. BELLS

1. Reader, "Dead to the World," 108.
2. Ibid., 125.
3. Reader, *Religion in Contemporary Japan*, 92.
4. Tennant et al., *Awa Henro*, 29.
5. Reader, *Making Pilgrimages*, 27–28.
6. Ibid., 197–98. Reader cites complaints from a variety of Japanese pilgrims about the asphalt roads that they are forced to walk along because of a lack of forest paths. Similarly, numerous long dark mountain tunnels—"exhaust gas hell," as one pilgrim puts it—mark these roads that the pilgrims use.
7. Nobutaka, "From Religious Conformity to Innovation," 24.
8. See Morinis, *Sacred Journeys*, 17.
9. See Weiss, "Echoes of Incense," chapter 1, n.p. He writes: "There is a standard routine for *henro* at the temples; wash hands, rinse mouth, bow, pray, sing, light incense, ring bells." But, as he notes, the core of a pilgrim's temple performance is the Heart Sutra, which is chanted at both the main hall and the small hall devoted to Kōbō Daishi. I would like to acknowledge my debt to Weiss. I found his account immensely valuable in researching and planning my journey. The eighteen-part series is available at www.davidmoreton.com/echoes.
10. Let me here thank David Moreton, a Canadian scholar who lives on Shikoku and teaches there. He was generous with his time and advice in the earlier days of my pilgrimage, including booking several accommodations. Moreton has written a number of articles on the Henro Michi, including, as coauthor with Tatsuro Muro, a historical guidebook, *A Journey of the Soul: The Shikoku Pilgrimage and Its 88 Temples.*
11. The Japanese fashion is to place a person's surname in front of their given name: Niwano Shūji, Sayama Goki, Murakoshi Takashi, for example. Since I'm writing for an English-speaking audience, however, I thought it less awkward to follow the Western tradition and reverse the order, placing the given name ahead of the surname.
12. The travel writer Chris Rowthorn points out that a foreigner who tries a few sentences in Japanese is likely "to receive regular dollops of praise." See Rowthorn et

al., *Lonely Planet Japan,* 7th edition (Melbourne: Lonely Planet Publications, 2000), 90.

13. See Tennant et al., *Awa Henro,* 29–32.

14. Statler, *Japanese Pilgrimage,* 26. Oliver Statler, an American scholar and one-time bureaucrat with the United States Army during the American postwar occupation of Japan, walked the Shikoku route several times in the late 1960s and 1970s and even settled on Shikoku for a number of years to study the Henro Michi. His book is one of the loveliest pilgrimage travelogues I've read. It greatly influenced my own pilgrimage, both in my anticipation of what I might experience and in my subsequent reflection on that experience. I have drawn on Statler for much of the history of the Shikoku pilgrimage.

15. Ibid.

16. See Reader, "Dead to the World," 111–12, and "Pilgrimage as Cult," 271. He refers in the first essay to the Shikoku pilgrimage as "a voyage in the symbolic realms of death" and, in the second essay, says that in donning *henro* garb the pilgrim symbolically signals that he or she is "dead to the mundane world." I have relied on Reader's extensive knowledge of the Shikoku pilgrimage for much of my background material, and I readily acknowledge my debt to his scholarship.

17. See Reader, "Dead to the World," 112–13. He writes: "A common belief, that has developed over the centuries out of accumulated pilgrimage lore, is that the pilgrim's completed book acts as a form of spiritual passport that enables the possessor to enter the Buddhist Pure Land, after death."

18. Reader, *Making Pilgrimages,* 57–58.

19. Statler, *Japanese Pilgrimage,* 44.

20. Ibid., 46–47. Statler provides a more detailed account of the temple's founding myth.

21. Reader, *Religion in Contemporary Japan,* 112–13.

22. Statler, *Japanese Pilgrimage,* 48.

23. See Weiss, "Echoes of Incense," chapter 11, n.p.

24. Richie, *The Inland Sea,* 17.

25. I refer readers to *The Way of the Stars: Journeys on the Camino de Santiago* (Charlottesville: University of Virginia Press, 2012).

2. COMPANIONS

1. Reader, *Making Pilgrimages,* 192.

2. It seems that my experience is quite common. "Those on foot tend to spend less time and to perform fewer rituals of worship at the sites than do those on organized tours," says Reader, citing a priest who argued that the bus pilgrims are "closer to the heart of the pilgrimage because they actually engaged in extended prayer and acts of devotion" at the temples, while walking pilgrims used the temples as "points of reference on a long walk." Ibid., 189.

3. Again, Reader suggests that such memories are typical for a walker. Recalling

one of his own walking pilgrimages, he writes: "The memories that abide are primarily of paths, roads and the places in between." He concludes his comparison of bus and walking pilgrims this way: "For those traveling by bus there is a growing sense of expectancy as they travel between or approach sites; this is what they have come to visit, and hence when they arrive at the sites, there is generally an excited readiness to pray, chant sutras, and engage with the location. Those on foot, however, often find that the noise and chaos of temple courtyards contrasts disturbingly with the quiet they have experienced between sites, and hence they may be keen to hurry on rather than tarry at the sites." Ibid., 190.

4. I have taken the story of Emon Saburō from Statler's *Japanese Pilgrimage*, 55–56, in addition to Reader's *Making Pilgrimages*, 60–61, and "Dead to the World," 118. Statler says the story is the "primary legend" of the Shikoku pilgrimage in that it underscores the pilgrimage's central concept: "the *henro* travels always with the Daishi, for it is implied that Kōbō Daishi guided Emon Saburō all through his grueling quest."

But one thing troubles me about the legend: why did Saburō's children have to die when it was the father's actions that offended the Daishi? Their deaths left him grief-stricken and set him on the road to salvation. But the children, who presumably had nothing to do with their father's behavior, paid the price for his redemption. That's a rather steep requirement for the father's recognition of the Daishi.

5. The red silhouette markers were initially installed by Tateki Miyazaki, a retired man from Matsuyama. He apparently got lost one time when he was walking the Henro Michi and decided to spend his retirement marking the trail to help others. He erected some two thousand markers along the *henro* trail. He also published a guide-book that Japanese-speaking pilgrims regard as the "Henro bible." Miyazaki-san went missing in late November 2010. Searchers found his body in early December along a trail north of Matsuyama City. It seems he'd been clearing brush when he died. I am indebted to one of the anonymous readers of my manuscript for the University of Virginia Press for drawing my attention to Miyazaki-san's death and reminding me of his contribution to the Shikoku pilgrimage. I gladly honor the man who did so much for Shikoku pilgrims, including gaijin *henro* like me.

6. Again, I refer the reader to the account of my first pilgrimage, *The Way of the Stars*.

7. Quoted in John Berger, *Selected Essays*, 188.

8. I have largely drawn my brief biography of Kōbō Daishi and the history of Buddhism in Japan from these sources: Statler, *Japanese Pilgrimage*; Nicoloff, *Sacred Kōyasan*; Kitagawa, *On Understanding Japanese Religion*; and Reader, "Dead to the World," *Making Pilgrimages*, "Pilgrimage as Cult," and *Religion in Contemporary Japan*. Readicker-Henderson's *The Traveler's Guide to Japanese Pilgrimages* was also helpful.

9. See Nicoloff, *Sacred Kōyasan*, 201–38. Nicoloff's book is a scholarly labor of love, the only English-language study of the Mount Kōyasan monastery and temple complex of which I'm aware.

10. Readicker-Henderson, *Traveler's Guide*, 125.

11. It's interesting to note that some scientists estimate that the sun has about another five billion years left. Long before that, however, it will turn into a red giant and engulf all the planets close to it, including Earth and Mars.

12. Reader, "Dead to the World," 114–15.

13. Reader, *Making Pilgrimages*, 115–16.

14. Blisters are the bane of any pilgrim trek and understandably so. As Reader puts it, citing the experience of some Japanese walkers: "Feet are, naturally, the most common source of pain, with Satō Takako, for example, speaking of how her feet hurt and how she was wracked by pain and fear and often burst into tears as a result. Satō Ken, quite early in his pilgrimage, complains of sore feet, while [Nobuo] Harada recounts difficult hikes up hillsides, the struggles of battling against the elements, and, in physical terms, the problem of blisters and sore feet" (ibid., 209).

15. Readicker-Henderson, *Traveler's Guide*, 153.

16. Quoted in Tennant et al., *Awa Henro*, 111–12.

17. Reader, *Making Pilgrimages*, 202–6.

3. BLESSINGS

1. Reader, *Making Pilgrimages*, 57–59.

2. Statler, *Japanese Pilgrimage*, 65.

3. Reader, *Making Pilgrimages*, 228–29, 253–54.

4. Statler, *Japanese Pilgrimage*, 191–92. He refers to pilgrims taking on "a trace of the Daishi's aura." In terms of his own experience, he writes: "As a man with hair gray enough to imply some wisdom; as a stranger—there is a mystery in that word, the mystery of a person unknown unexpectedly appearing from a world unknown—and doubly a stranger, a foreigner; and above all as a *henro*, I am being asked to minister to a sick girl." He also relates examples of pilgrims being seen as "potential miracle workers and healers" through their being empowered by Kōbō Daishi. See also Reader, *Making Pilgrimages*, 62.

5. Statler, *Japanese Pilgrimage*, 191–92. He writes: "I have no religious power, I tell this woman. I am wearing a *henro* robe but I have no religious power. I have no ability to diagnose an illness or to cure it." As he later put it, "I failed and the failure still weighs on me."

6. See Reader, *Religion in Contemporary Japan*, 10–13.

7. Reader writes that pilgrimages also serve "as a mode of escape from modernity and from the pressures of urban life." "Dead to the World," 125.

8. See Tennant et al., *Awa Henro*, 117–20.

9. It is worthwhile to address this phenomenon in some detail. For example, Reader writes that for many pilgrims "their pilgrimages and relationship with Kōbō Daishi are highlighted by smaller, less dramatic events that are pregnant with meaning for them alone." Indeed, pilgrims sometimes regard seemingly happenstance events or situations as "miracles and as personal messages from Kōbō Daishi. . . . The miracles experienced by Shikoku pilgrims come about because of the pilgrim's relationship with Kōbō Daishi, who acts as a mediating agent bringing the world of the holy closer

to the human domain." "Pilgrimage as Cult," 278–80. The anthropologist Alan Morinis, commenting on this psychic state, observes that certain pilgrim experiences "loom significant" for those who undergo them. See *Sacred Journeys*, 17.

10. Bashō, *Narrow Road to the Interior*, 14.

11. I probably owe this line of thought to Jennifer Westwood's book *Sacred Journeys: The Illustrated Guide to Pilgrimages around the World*, which I read before my Henro Michi. Westwood writes: "The things Bashō thought worthy of contemplation on his journey included sights that any ordinary tourist might have wanted to see." He trekked "the narrow road to the deep north as he traveled through his life on Earth—seeking a vision of eternity in the everyday" (58–60).

12. See Reader, *Making Pilgrimages*, 28. He writes: "While the image of the pilgrimage may have undergone a transformation in modern times, there also remains much continuity from the past in terms of the motivations of the pilgrims, with the wish to find new meanings, to search for their roots, to escape, change, or remake their world, or to get away from, or seek solutions to, misfortunes and such unhappy events impelling pilgrims both in pre-modern and contemporary times."

13. Ryu Murakami, "Japan's Lost Generation," *Asia Times*, May 5, 2000. He writes that Japanese youth "could not afford to be socially withdrawn if their parents were not affluent enough to provide them a home, meals and extras that have come to be thought of as basics—audio and video equipment, software, mobile phones, computers." http://www.cnn.com/ASIANOW/time/magazine/2000/0501/japan.essay murakami.html.

14. Statler, *Japanese Pilgrimage*, 66–68. He also quotes Kōbō Daishi as saying: "Gradually I came to hate worldly success and wealth and longed for the mist-hung woods. When I saw the lives of noble people with their fine, light clothes, fat horses, carts as fast as flowing water, the transience of it, like lightning or illusion, made me sigh. Everything I saw urged me to enter the priesthood. No one could stop me, just as no one could chain the wind" (67).

15. Ibid., 68.

4. SPIRITS

1. There is a plaque on the beach inscribed with this poem.

2. See Frank Gibney, *Japan: The Fragile Superpower*, 3rd revised edition (New York: Tuttle Publishing, 1996).

3. Reader points out that one of the main complaints pilgrims have about the Henro Michi is how much of the route requires walking along often narrow highways and through tunnels. For example, he cites one Japanese *henro* who was upset that "there are few places where the pilgrim can walk in peace" and who "complains about how painful and unpleasant it is to have to walk so much on asphalt and concrete—again, a concern that surfaces in many pilgrims' accounts." *Making Pilgrimages*, 197.

4. David Turkington, an American who first walked the Henro Michi in 1999, expressed a similar sentiment in his pilgrim journal, which he maintains online at the most comprehensive Shikoku-related website of which I'm aware. "People are cor-

rect when they say that in the end I will remember this with fond memories. I will look back on the struggles and realize that those were minor in comparison to all the good that I have experienced. That the disappointments with the temples and the anger at the highways will be an insignificant piece of the much larger puzzle." www .shikokuhenrotrail.com/shikoku/thoughts1999/thoughts5.html.

5. Bashō, *Narrow Road to the Interior*, 20.

6. Ibid., 12.

7. Ibid., 5, 31.

8. See Sam Hamill's "Translator's Introduction" to Bashō's *Narrow Road to the Interior*, xx, xxxi. Hamill describes Bashō's journey as "a vision quest," a walk into "the geography of the soul."

My thinking on this topic has been informed by three essays: two by Steven D. Carter, "Bashō and the Mastery of Poetic Space in *Oku No Hosomichi*" and "On a Bare Branch," and a third by Thomas Heyd, "Bashō and the Aesthetics of Wandering."

9. Indeed I credit my Camino pilgrimage for inspiring me to write a book on "paying attention" and on the various experiences of "everyday mysticism." See *A Rumour of God: Rekindling Belief in an Age of Disenchantment* (Toronto: Novalis, 2010).

10. See Tennant et al., *Awa Henro*, 32–33. They quote Kōbō Daishi: "This mantra has a marvelous power. When we chant it, our ignorance can be removed, because thousands of truths are contained in each word."

11. I refer readers to David Turkington's excellent website for a commentary on the Heart Sutra.

12. See Statler, *Japanese Pilgrimage*, 143. He remarks: "The contorted rocks seem to beckon; the endless breakers offer surcease."

13. See Maraini, *Japan*, 14. He writes that nature is "the point from which all avenues of thought depart, and to which they finally return."

14. See Alex Kerr, *Dogs and Demons: Tales from the Dark Side of Japan*, 51–76. He writes: "Japan is now full of unnecessary tunnels, roads that go nowhere, lifeless rivers, bridges that nobody crosses, half-empty museums, and theme parks that few care to visit."

15. Maraini, *Japan*, 19. He describes Shinto as "a warm-hearted, positive cult of life."

16. Ibid., 19–22. Maraini quotes a poem from Motoori Norinaga: "All who are called Kami, / You may think, / Are one and the same. / There are some that are birds, / And some, too, that are bugs!"

5. DREAMS

1. Reader, *Making Pilgrimages*, 191. This experience seems to be typical of many pilgrims, at least according to Reader. He refers to a state of *henro boke*—literally, "pilgrimage senility" or, better, "pilgrimage immersion"—in which pilgrims become "absorbed in a world of simplicity in which everything center[s] around just walking, eating and sleeping." It is a state of mind that, according to Reader, is similar to the Buddhist notion of *muga*, or selflessness.

2. See Turner and Turner, *Image and Pilgrimage*, 34, 249–54.

3. I never met any perpetual pilgrims, at least to my knowledge, but apparently so-called drop-out pilgrims have begun to appear on the Henro Michi and have become a source of local complaint. See Reader, *Making Pilgrimages*, 28.

4. I would remind the reader of Alan Morinis's remark that pilgrims often experience various "psychosomatic sensations," and these sensations "are often the most significant aspects of pilgrimage in the view of the participants themselves." See *Sacred Journeys*, 17.

5. It is worth noting, as I've read, that the Japanese recite the Heart Sutra in all kinds of circumstances. Students chant it before an exam. Businessmen invoke it before negotiating a contract.

6. Don Weiss considers this tunnel one of the worst. He writes: "A kilometer long, it lacked sidewalks, and the traffic lanes were very narrow. We walked as far over as we could and flattened ourselves against the wet walls when the big trucks came roaring at us." See "Echoes of Incense," chapter 14, n.p.

7. See Miyata, *A Henro Pilgrimage Guide*, 90–91. The temple's *goeika*, or hymn, is this: "When even a tree and a blade of grass can be enlightened, why not *ashura*, hungry ghosts, animals, men and heavenly bodies?"

8. See Reader, *Religion in Contemporary Japan*, 1–4. According to him, the Japanese are quick to proclaim their lack of religiosity, but at the same time they also display high levels of religious activity and behavior.

9. Ibid., 175–82. Reader refers to *o-mamori* as "charged concretization[s] of power."

10. Ibid., 179–84. See also Reader, "Letters to the Gods," 40–43.

11. Reader, *Religion in Contemporary Japan*, 137–38. He writes: "The entire geography of Japan is laden with markers indicating the presence of the spiritual world." Thus "the whole of Japan is the abode of innumerable *kami*" as well as deities that can "manifest themselves at any time or place," so "each and every place is inherently a potential setting for its [the spiritual world's] realization and manifestation."

12. The quotation comes from Statler, *Japanese Pilgrimage*, 275. See also Tennant's published translation of Takamure's pilgrimage journal, *Shikoku Pilgrimage of Takamure Itsue*, 82–83.

13. I was certainly familiar with this dimension of long-distance pilgrimage, which, as Reader observes, is not unusual. "Walking ... can intensify feelings and leave the pilgrim especially open to raw emotions and feelings. Many pilgrims record how, as they walk and are subsumed by the physical and mental demands of the pilgrimage, they find themselves being brought face to face with painful memories of the past. Often such memories center on issues of death, whose presence is so evident in the symbolic structures of the *henro* and the physical remains in its landscape." See *Making Pilgrimages*, 210.

14. In hindsight, I regard that time in the cemetery as a kind of pilgrimage. I can't think of another time in my adult life when I've been alone with my mother for an extended period. It has remained with me as a rather special memory. In fact, I used it as an anecdote in chapter 2 of *A Rumour of God*.

15. Statler, *Japanese Pilgrimage*, 141, 142.

6. ENCHANTMENTS

1. See Tennant et al., *Awa Henro*, 180. Tennant explains that in esoteric Buddhism, the right hand symbolizes the realm of the Buddha and the left hand symbolizes ordinary creatures in the realm of the mundane. The right hand is pure, while the left is regarded as unclean. "When both hands are put together palm to palm at the breast, it is called *gasshō*," which unites the two realms. This mudra is "the way of paying homage to the Buddha."

2. See Reader, *Religion in Contemporary Japan*, 60–62.

3. I owe this information on Japanese religion to Reader, especially his *Religion in Contemporary Japan*, 6–7, 13–15, 38–40, 55–76.

4. Ibid., 15–17.

5. See Ekuan, *The Aesthetics of the Japanese Lunchbox*, 1–9. He writes: "It is poor manners to start eating the instant you remove the lid of the lunchbox. You must allow your eyes time to peruse and enjoy the food before moving on to gratify your taste buds.... The habit of enjoying things first with the eyes is an integral part of the Japanese lifestyle."

6. Maraini argues that the notion of purity is "one of the principal inner forces of Japanese civilization," and "Japanese cuisine manifests a delicate and poetic respect for the gifts of field, mountain and water as they are presented to man by nature" (*Japan*, 26).

7. I'm not the first, of course, to notice the psychological consequences of long-distance walking. Rebecca Solnit captures the heightened sensibility engendered in walking this way: "Walking allows us to be in our bodies and in the world without being made busy by them. It leaves us free to think without being wholly lost in our thoughts.... The rhythm of walking generates a kind of rhythm of thinking." See *Wanderlust: A History of Walking* (New York: Penguin Books, 2000), 5.

8. On this concept of *yoin*, see Francisco F. Feliciano, *Four Asian Contemporary Composers*, 77–78. Feliciano refers to *yoin* as "a reverberation in the sense of an overtone, resonance," and cites such examples as a young girl bidding goodbye to her family and a son kissing his parents as he leaves for war. On such occasions "words remain unspoken, only the eyes meet and they shy away. Memorable events pass by without words spoken but the parties involved carry an unforgettable memory of the occasion." In this regard, writes Feliciano, "the word *yoin* implies that such experiences ... stimulate the imagination which causes a positive memory to dwell in one's mind." Thus, "a situation in which a degree of transcendent experience is possible is said to contain *yoin*."

I have also found other references to *yoin* as an aesthetic concept used in Japanese literature and visual arts. In literary terms, the concept refers to how poetry can communicate the ineffable. See, in particular, Sandra A. Wawrytko, "The Poetics of Ch'an: Upāyic Poetry and Its Taoist Enrichment," *Chung-Hwa Buddhist Journal* 5 (1992): 341–48.

9. Bashō, *Narrow Road to the Interior*, 31.

10. Epiphanic moments are obviously highly subjective. What is meaningful to one person is insignificant to another. But that doesn't reduce the experience of *yoin*—or direct perception—to solipsistic indulgence. In Bashō's case, the concrete precision of his haiku belies any suggestion that his experience was merely a fantasy projection. His visions were always grounded in the real world. Furthermore, his experiences of *yoin*, like mine, seem to have had much in common with one another, particularly in regard to the ordinariness of the situations and the everyday objects involved. For me on that day at Senyuji, my epiphany came from a small *bentō* box. For Bashō it was the sight of flowers in his horse's mouth.

Others, of course, have had similar experiences. For Van Gogh everything—chairs, shoes, sunflowers, wheat fields—seemed to pierce his consciousness. One of my favorite examples, though, comes from the poet Rupert Brooke. In a letter to his friend Frederic Keeling in the late summer of 1910, he wrote, "Half an hour's roaming about a street or village or railway shows so much beauty that it is impossible to be anything but wild with suppressed exhilaration. . . . In a flicker of sunlight on a blank wall, or a reach of muddy pavement, or smoke from an engine at night there's a sudden significance and importance and inspiration that makes the breath stop with a gulp of certainty and happiness." See *The Letters of Rupert Brooke*, edited by Geoffrey Keynes (London: Faber and Faber, 1968), 259.

11. On this topic, see Robert Aziz, C. G. Jung's *Psychology of Religion and Synchronicity* (Albany: State University of New York Press, 1990), and Roderick Main, *The Rupture of Time: Synchronicity and Jung's Critique of Modern Western Culture* (New York: Brunner-Routledge, 2004).

12. Miyata, *A Henro Pilgrimage Guide*, 112.

13. Reader writes that the color reflects "the sense of brightness and life always associated with Shinto." See *Religion in Contemporary Japan*, 138–39.

14. Ibid., 121. Reader writes: "The action of incessantly pouring icy water over [the body] works to drive or wash out impurities of the mind, removing, or more straightforwardly breaking down, all the barriers, physical and mental, that might prevent the practitioner from achieving higher consciousness and powers."

15. See Robert F. Rhodes, "The Kaihōgyō Practice of Mt. Hiei," 185–202, and Reader, *Religion in Contemporary Japan*, 124–27. See also John Stevens's book, *The Marathon Monks of Mount Hiei*.

16. Rhodes, "The Kaihōgyō Practice of Mt. Hiei," 192, 194, 197. Rhodes says that forty monks have completed the thousand-day discipline since 1571. Reader, ibid., says fifty.

17. See Philip Kapleau, *The Three Pillars of Zen*, 45–47.

7. BLOSSOSMS

1. Santōka, *Mountain Tasting*, 57.

2. Reader points out that some Japanese believe that modern medicine and psychiatry are inadequate because they don't acknowledge that the "root cause" of many psychological maladies "is located in the spiritual realm" and that "problems develop

when one fails to take heed of the spiritual repercussions of one's actions." See *Religion in Contemporary Japan*, 47–48.

3. Ibid., 47–48, 209–10. Reader notes that according to some Buddhist traditions, karmic debts are inherited, and individuals attempt to surmount their "spiritual impediments" by "cutting" their karma through acts of expiation.

4. I've adopted the phrase from James P. Carse, *Breakfast at the Victory: The Mysticism of Ordinary Experience* (New York: Harper Collins, 1995).

5. The line is from Søren Kierkegaard's *Journals and Papers*, edited and translated by Howard V. Hong and Edna H. Hong (Bloomington: Indiana University Press, [1841], 1978), 5:177.

EPILOGUE

1. Reader, *Religion in Contemporary Japan*, 90–91. Reader offers an overview of Buddhist death rites and rituals. I have relied on his account.

Bibliography

Bashō, Matsuo. *Narrow Road to the Interior and Other Writings*. Translated by Sam Hamill. Boston: Shambhala Publications, 2000.

Beasley, W. G. *The Japanese Experience: A Short History of Japan*. London: Weidenfeld and Nicolson, 1999.

Berger, John. *Selected Essays*. Edited by George Dyer. New York: Random House, 2001.

Booth, Alan. *Looking for the Lost: Journeys through a Vanishing Japan*. New York: Kodansha International, 1996.

———. *The Roads to Sata: A 2,000-Mile Walk through Japan*. New York: Kodansha International, 1985.

Buruma, Ian. *Inventing Japan*. New York: Modern Library, 2003.

Carter, Steven D. "Bashō and the Mastery of Poetic Space in *Oku No Hosomichi*." *Journal of the American Oriental Society* 120, no. 2 (April-June 2000): 190–98.

———. "On a Bare Branch: Bashō and the *Haikai* Profession." *Journal of the American Oriental Society* 117, no. 1 (January-March 1997): 57–69.

Ekuan, Kenji. *The Aesthetics of the Japanese Lunchbox*. Cambridge, Mass.: The MIT Press, 2000.

Feliciano, Francisco F. *Four Asian Contemporary Composers: The Influence of the Tradition on Their Works*. Quezon City, Philippines: New Day Publishers, 1983.

Heyd, Thomas. "Bashō and the Aesthetics of Wandering: Recuperating Space, Recognizing Place, and Following the Ways of the Universe." *Philosophy East and West* 53, no. 3 (July 2003): 290–307.

Kapleau, Philip. *The Three Pillars of Zen: Teaching, Practice and Enlightenment*. Revised edition. New York: Anchor, [1965], 1989.

Kasahara, Kazuo, ed. *A History of Japanese Religion*. Translated by Paul McCarthy and Gaynor Sekimori. Tokyo: Kosei Publishing, 2001.

Kerr, Alex. *Dogs and Demons: Tales from the Dark Side of Japan*. New York: Hill and Wang, 2001.

Kitagawa, Joseph M. *On Understanding Japanese Religion*. Princeton: Princeton University Press, 1987.

Maraini, Fosco. *Japan: Patterns of Continuity*. Tokyo: Kodansha, 1971.

Miyata, Bishop Taisen. *A Henro Pilgrimage Guide to the 88 Temples of Shikoku Island.* Revised edition. Los Angeles: Kōyasan Buddhist Temple, [1996], 2004.

Morinis, Alan. *Sacred Journeys: The Anthropology of Pilgrimage.* New York: Greenwood Press, 1992.

Muro, Tatsuro, and Moreton, David C. *A Journey of the Soul: The Shikoku Pilgrimage and Its 88 Temples.* Tokushima, Japan: Education Publishing Center, 2008.

Nicoloff, Philip L. *Sacred Kōyasan: A Pilgrimage to the Mountain Temple of Saint Kōbō Daishi and the Great Sun Buddha.* Albany: State University of New York Press, 2008.

Nobutaka, Inoue. "From Religious Conformity to Innovation: New Ideas of Religious Journey and Holy Places." *Social Compass* 47, no. 1 (2000): 21–32.

Reader, Ian. "Buddhism as a Religion of the Family." In *Religion and Society in Modern Japan: Selected Readings,* edited by Mark R. Mullins, Shimazono Susumu, and Paul L. Swanson, 139–56. Berkeley: Asian Humanities Press, 1993.

———. "Dead to the World: Pilgrims in Shikoku." In *Pilgrimage in Popular Culture,* edited by Ian Reader and Tony Walter, 107–35. Basingstoke: The Macmillan Press, 1993.

———. "Letters to the Gods: The Form and Meaning of *Ema.*" *Japanese Journal of Religious Studies* 18, no. 1 (1991): 23–50.

———. *Making Pilgrimages: Meaning and Practice in Shikoku.* Honolulu: University of Hawaii Press, 2005.

———. "Pilgrimage as Cult: The Shikoku Pilgrimage as a Window on Japanese Religion." In *Religion in Japan: Arrows to Heaven and Earth,* edited by P. F. Kornicki and I. J. McMullen, 267–86. Cambridge: Cambridge University Press, 1996.

———. *Religion in Contemporary Japan.* Honolulu: University of Hawaii Press, 1991.

Reader, Ian, and George J. Tanabe Jr. *Practically Religious: Worldly Benefits and the Common Religion of Japan.* Honolulu: University of Hawaii Press, 1998.

Readicker-Henderson, Ed. *The Traveler's Guide to Japanese Pilgrimages.* New York and Tokyo: Weatherhill, 1995.

Rhodes, Robert F. "The Kaihōgyō Practice of Mt. Hiei." *Japanese Journal of Religious Studies* 14, nos. 2/3 (1987): 185–202.

Richie, Donald. *The Inland Sea.* Berkeley: Stone Bridge Press, [1971], 2002.

Santōka, Taneda. *Mountain Tasting: Zen Haiku.* New York: Weatherhill, 1980.

Statler, Oliver. *Japanese Pilgrimage.* New York: William Morrow and Company, 1983.

Stevens, John. *The Marathon Monks of Mount Hiei.* Boston: Shambhala, 1988.

Suzuki, D. T. *Zen Buddhism: Selected Writings of D. T. Suzuki.* Edited by William Barrett. Garden City, N.Y.: Doubleday, 1968.

Takamure, Itsue. *The 1918 Shikoku Pilgrimage of Takamure Itsue: An English Translation of "Musume Junreiki."* Translated by Susan Tennant. Bowen Island, B.C.: Bowen Publishing, 2010.

Tennant, Susan. "The Liminal Journey of Takamure Itsue: An Account of a Young Woman's Pilgrimage." *Limen: Journal for Theory and Practice of Liminal Phenomena* 1 (2001). http://limen.mi2.hr/limen1–2001/susan_tennant.html.

Tennant, Susan, et al. *Awa Henro: A Bilingual Guidebook for Pilgrims in Tokushima*. Tokushima, Japan: AWA88, 1993.

Turkington, David. "Pilgrimage to the 88 Sacred Places of Shikoku." www.shikoku henrotrail.com.

Turner, Victor and Edith. *Image and Pilgrimage in Christian Culture: Anthropological Perspectives*. New York: Columbia University Press, 1978.

Weiss, Don. "Echoes of Incense: A Pilgrimage in Japan." www.davidmoreton.com/ echoes.

Westwood, Jennifer. *Sacred Journeys: An Illustrated Guide to Pilgrimages around the World*. New York: Henry Holt and Company, 1997.

Index

Other books by Robert C. Sibley

The Way of the Stars: Journeys on the Camino de Santiago

A Rumour of God: Rekindling Belief in an Age of Disenchantment

Northern Spirits: John Watson, George Grant and Charles Taylor—Appropriations of Hegelian Political Thought

www.robertsibley.com